TOWARDS A TRULY COMMON LAW

Europe as a laboratory for legal pluralism

As we move towards a more global legal community, often with accompanying injustice and violence, Mireille Delmas-Marty demonstrates that there is an urgent need to reconstruct the national and international legal landscapes. Legal reasoning can be applied to concepts such as human rights for European citizens in the new world order. In this book the author argues for a rule of law that is common in every sense of the word: accessible to all rather than reserved exclusively for officials, common to the various legal sectors despite increasing specialisation, and common to diverse states. The book will be of interest to all comparative European lawyers, and to social scientists and legal theorists grappling with contemporary issues in legal pluralism and globalisation.

MIREILLE DELMAS-MARTY is a professor at the Université de Paris I (Panthéon-Sorbonne) and a member of the University Institute of France. Her publications include authorship of *Vers un droit commun de l'humanité: entretien avec Philippe Petit* (1996) and *Trois défis pour un droit mondial* (1998), as well as being editor of *Procédures pénales d'Europe* (1995) and *Droit pénal des affaires* (4th edition, 2000).

TOWARDS A TRULY COMMON LAW

Europe as a laboratory for legal pluralism

by

MIREILLE DELMAS-MARTY

Université de Paris I
(Panthéon-Sorbonne)

translated by Naomi Norberg

CAMBRIDGE
UNIVERSITY PRESS

PUBLISHED BY THE PRESS SYNDICATE OF THE UNIVERSITY OF CAMBRIDGE
The Pitt Building, Trumpington Street, Cambridge, United Kingdom

CAMBRIDGE UNIVERSITY PRESS
The Edinburgh Building, Cambridge CB2 2RU, UK
40 West 20th Street, New York, NY 10011-4211, USA
477 Williamstown Road, Port Melbourne, VIC 3207, Australia
Ruiz de Alarcón 13, 28014 Madrid, Spain
Dock House, The Waterfront, Cape Town 8001, South Africa

http://www.cambridge.org

Printed in the United Kingdom at the University Press, Cambridge

Typeface Adobe Minion 10.5/13.5 pt *System* LaTeX 2ε [TB]

A catalogue record for this book is available from the British Library

Library of Congress Cataloguing in Publication data

Delmas-Marty, Mireille.
[Pour un droit commun. English]
Towards a truly common law : Europe as a laboratory for legal pluralism / by
Mireille Delmas-Marty; translated by Naomi Norberg.
p. cm.
Includes bibliographical references and index.
ISBN 0 521 81231 3 (hbk.)
1. Law – International unification. 2. Legal polycentricity. 3. Law – Philosophy.
4. Law – Europe – International unification. I. Title.
K236 .D4513 2002 340′.1 – dc21 2001043695

ISBN 0 521 81231 3 hardback

CONTENTS

PREFACE: TOWARDS A TRULY COMMON LAW

It must seem madness for a French legal scholar to make a plea 'for a common law', insisting on the need in today's world to move towards one that is 'truly common', then risk its translation in the very country of common law.

I hope that this book will be taken not as blasphemy, but as homage to a just concept – so just, in fact, that it has traversed centuries and oceans, even though it is still often poorly received on the European continent, where it is seen as the symbol of non-codified law, considered synonymous with arbitrariness by both the Roman-Germanic mind trained in Roman law and the Cartesian mind that inspired the Napoleonic codes.

The idea of a translation goes back to my stay at Cambridge University in 1998, where I was invited upon the kind suggestion of Professor John Spencer. Those few weeks in an atmosphere devoted to friendship and study were a privileged moment, full of fecund and varied exchanges on both comparative criminal procedure and the European *Corpus juris* project ('introducing penal provisions for the purpose of the financial interests of the European Union'), and particularly in Susan Marks' seminar on the impact of the European Court of Human Rights ('The role of the European judge in the revival of the *jus commune*: meaning and limitations'). Inspired directly by the book *Pour un droit commun*, this latter theme was the decisive occasion to test the usefulness of a confrontation of viewpoints between 'common-law' jurists and jurists of the Roman-Germanic tradition faced with common law's worldwide rise in power. The project was launched with the kind support of Cambridge University Press, and realised thanks to Naomi Norberg, who translated the French betraying neither the spirit nor the letter, and bringing the concision of a language that allows for multiple nuances while avoiding useless chatter.

In rereading the book a few years after its original publication in 1994, I am struck by two things. In this latter part of the year 2001, the move to extend law beyond national frontiers has been amply confirmed by its primary sources (national laws, European law, law with worldwide application). It has also become more specific, between the two poles of the market and human rights, as the phenomenon called economic globalisation has been affirmed and problems have started coming to light. What has become particularly clear, especially since the terrorist attacks of 11 September 2001, is that unilateralism must give way to 'a new multilateralism'.[1]

Confirmation

In just a few years, the movement was confirmed even beyond what I had anticipated, as the following examples will show.

1998: a turning point in the United Kingdom

1998 was a turning point, but was no doubt perceived differently on opposite sides of the Channel. In France, as in most parts of the world, the two House of Lords decisions in the *Pinochet* case (25 November 1998 and 24 March 1999) were hailed as paving the way for international criminal justice. I will not go into a legal analysis here, but the commentators maintained that the Spanish judge (as well as the Belgian and French judges) who requested the former Chilean head of state's extradition, and the English judges who applied the principle of universal competence provided for by the United Nations Convention Against Torture, had 'broken a taboo': that of the impunity of heads of state. Many considered that this audacity on the part of European judges would have a 'boomerang effect', by making it possible for the Chilean Supreme Court to decide to lift General Pinochet's parliamentary immunity (which duly occurred on 10 August 2000). Of course, by showing that national judges are also guardians of international criminal justice, the *Pinochet* case raises issues, such as the risk of divergent interpretations or unacceptable interference, that only the creation of an International Criminal Court can resolve in the long term.

[1] Diane Marie Amann, 'A new international spirit: if the US can cooperate to combat terrorism, it can cooperate to pursue justice', *San Francisco Chronicle*, 12 October 2001.

But for British jurists, the incorporation of international law into domestic law poses even more urgent questions, as 1998 was, above all, the year in which the Human Rights Act was passed. The text, which entered into force in October 2000, enables British judges to apply the European Convention on Human Rights directly. As announced in the government's 1997 White Paper, this text's link with common law lies first in the traditional meaning of the term 'rights brought home'. As Lord Justice Laws stated unequivocally in the 1999 conference organised by Cambridge University: 'This is not Aladdin's lamp for old; it is Robert Browning: "Grow old along with me, the best is yet to be." Our old constitution is given new blood by the Human Rights Act. It strengthens, does not dilute, the common law. And the common lawyers must administer it, according to their ancient methods.'[2] The debate is, above all, national, because the powers thus given to judges raise the question of a new balance between parliament, the executive and judges. Some, like Professor Tony Smith, fear a 'Pyrrhic victory', as a violation of the Convention allows the judges only a 'declaration of incompatibility', and only the government can issue an order, subject to the approval of both houses of parliament. But others express the opposite fear, strongly played up by the media, of thus seeing established 'a pale shadow of one of the worst features of the American constitution, the politicising of the judiciary and the judicialising of politics'.[3] It seems in any case that a new balance should be sought by the judges between 'activism and restraint', to borrow the lord chancellor's phrase.

In this search, it is striking to note that the models envisaged are generally taken from the same family (the United States, Canada and New Zealand) rather than from European neighbours, no doubt considered more foreign. It is true that Europe itself remains a foreign idea for many jurists. Thus, when Lord Justice Auld worries about the interpretation of texts that come from the idea of 'guidance rather than regulation', he is wondering about the appropriate way to apply 'these strange foreign notions called fundamental rights'. For their part, many French jurists consider the European Convention on Human Rights as

[2] Cambridge University, Centre for Public Law, *The Human Rights Act and the criminal justice and regulatory process* (Hart Publishing, 1999).

[3] Dr P. Allot, letter to *The Times*, quoted by Prof. A. T. H. Smith, 'The Human Rights Act 1998, the constitutional context', in the conference cited above (pp. 3–9).

having a typically Anglo-Saxon spirit, as it is rife with expressions, such as 'reasonable' period of time, that are completely foreign to French culture (even though the 1996 reform introduced the term into the French *Code de procédure pénale* with regard to pre-trial custody).

The misunderstanding continues with criminal procedure. In France, British criminal procedure elicits strong reactions. Some lawyers dismiss it with an almost visceral rejection, whether it concerns the absence of civil parties or the specificity of the guilty plea that leads to an unacceptable inequality and constitutes a threat to the presumption of innocence, while others express boundless admiration. These Anglophiles are called Anglomaniacs by their adversaries, especially lawyers who dream of transposing the British system of evidence in its entirety, but who forget that it applies only in the very rare cases where the accused pleads not guilty. As John Spencer makes clear with great finesse, the lack of understanding (be it positive or negative) no doubt stems from a mutual lack of knowledge. We are not comparing the same thing when the 'Rolls Royce of trials' – the trial by jury – that so fascinates French lawyers represents barely a quarter of the criminal judgments rendered, the others being judged according to the ultra-quick procedure of the guilty plea, which the same lawyers do not want to hear about. And British jurists, so critical of French procedure, do not take into account the fact that in the vast majority of cases, the accused would be judged via the guilty plea in the United Kingdom. Clearly, the apprenticeship of a truly common law, at the confluence of diverse European traditions, is yet to be completed and Europe is still, in fact, a laboratory.

Revival of the jus commune *in Europe*

The last few years have been rich in initiatives, both in scholarly works and institutions. Many books are real pleas for the revival of a method and a common vision inspired by the *jus commune* that existed from the Middle Ages to modern times on the European continent.[4] A

[4] See R. Zimmermann, 'Civil code and civil law: the "Europeanisation" of private law within the European Community and the re-emergence of a European legal science', *Columbia Journal of European Law* 63 (1994/5); C. Bar, *The common European law of tort* (Beck, 1998; German edn 1996); H. Kötz, *European contract law* (trans. T. Weir, Clarendon Press, 1997; German edn 1995); and the first book of a forthcoming series of *jus commune* case books for the common law of Europe: W. Van Gerven, J. Lever, P. Larouche, Ch. von Bar and G. Viney, *Cases and texts on national, supranational and international tort law: scope of protection* (Hart, 1998).

very concrete step was the 1995 publication by the famous Lando Commission (named for the Danish professor presiding over it) of its *Principles of European contract law*, conceived of as a sort of 'mosaïc type restatement'[5] consistent with in-depth studies in comparative law. Even in criminal law, symbol of national sovereignty, the idea of a 'European model penal code' was launched in 1996 by Professor Sieber's Memorandum under the supervision of the Council of Europe.[6] At the European Union level, the Convention on Protection of the Financial Interests of the European Union was adopted in 1995, with the aim of harmonising the definitions of fraud, as well as its sanctions and the assignment of criminal liability, but it has not yet entered into force due to insufficient ratification. Another project, called *Corpus juris*, was submitted to the European Commission and the European Parliament in 1996, then published in 1997. More ambitious, because it leans toward a certain unification of substantive criminal law and procedure around a 'European public prosecutor' in order better to fight against infringements on the European Union's financial interests, this widely debated text[7] was completed, and partially amended, by a 'follow-up study',[8] which is currently being published. It is now the subject of a feasibility study in countries that are candidates for entry into the European Union.

Such an effervescence in such a short period (less than ten years) is proof not only of the vigour of scholarship, but also of the high demand on the part of the institutions themselves. It is true that institutional reforms pave the way for a European common law: for the Council of Europe, with the 1998 entry into operation of the European Court of Human Rights in its new formation (which eliminates the filter of the Commission and imposes the jurisdictional path by excluding referral to the Committee of Ministers), and for the European Union, with the Amsterdam Treaty, which was signed in 1997 and entered into force in 1999. The treaty provides new legal bases for harmonising law and

5 See Ch. U. Schmid, '"Bottom-up" harmonisation of European private law: *jus commune* and restatement', in Veijo Heiskanen and Kati Kulovesi (eds.), *Function and future of European law* (University of Helsinki Faculty of Law, 1999), pp. 75ff.

6 See U. Sieber, 'Memorandum on a European Model Penal Code', *European Journal of Law Reform* 1 (1998/9), pp. 445ff.

7 See the House of Lords, Select Committee on the European Communities, prosecuting fraud on the communities' finances – the *Corpus juris*, May 1999.

8 See M. Delmas-Marty and J. Vervaele (eds.), *The implementation of the* Corpus juris *in the member states*, vol. I (Intersentia, 2000).

brings several sensitive areas within the remit of the Community, such as immigration policy and, partially, the protection of financial interests. Adoption of the *Corpus juris*, especially the creation of the 'European public prosecutor', could be envisaged either on the basis of an interstate convention based on the Third Pillar, or more directly as a regulation based on the Community Pillar, but the Nice Treaty, signed in December 2000, did not, in the end, broaden the current legal base for a possible regulation.

European law itself is now faced, however, with the phenomenon of globalisation. The Lando Commission's principles must be brought in line with the Unidroit Principles of International Commercial Contracts[9] and the fight against organised crime cannot be limited to the European space,[10] particularly when it involves a problem that is global by nature, such as 'cyber crime'. The debates in 2000 on the *Yahoo* case[11] show already that European law will not suffice: neither the draft Council of Europe Convention on cyber crime (final draft adopted June 2001), nor the European Union Directive 95/46, which entered into force in 1998 and mandates an 'adequacy standard' for foreign sites, provides a definitive solution. In a peacemaking effort, the European Commission took note of the United States' adoption of an original system called the Safe Harbor Principles (Department of Commerce, 21 June 2000) and officially announced on 27 July 2000, despite the European Parliament's disagreement, that it acknowledged the adequate level of protection in the United States. But there will be no lasting solution in the absence of a truly common law applicable on a global scale.

Two major steps towards a global law

One of two major steps towards a global law is the transformation of the organisations born of the GATT Accords into a permanent structure

[9] See S. Paasilehto, 'Legal cultural obstacles to the harmonisation of European private law', in Heiskanen and Kulovesi (eds.), *Function and future*, pp. 99ff.

[10] See M. Pieth, 'The harmonisation of law against economic crime', *European Journal of Law Reform* 1 (1998/9), p. 527; M. Delmas-Marty and S. Manacorda, 'Corruption: a challenge to the rule of law and democratic society' in P. Bernasconi (ed.), *Responding to corruption* (International Society of Social Defence, 2000), p. 401; *A* Corpus juris *for introducing penal provisions for the purpose of the financial interests of the European Union* (bilingual edition under the direction of M. Delmas-Marty, Economica, 1997); and Delmas-Marty and Vervaele, *Implementation of the* Corpus juris, vol. I.

[11] Order of the referee of the Tribunal de Grande Instance of Paris, 22 May 2000.

(with the creation of the WTO and the Dispute Settlement Body), which prefigures the emergence of a common law of global trade. The other is the signature, in the framework of the United Nations Conference in Rome, of the Convention establishing the future International Criminal Court.

Completing the United Nations' human rights structures, the rise in power of the new WTO structures since their creation in 1994 illustrates the market/human rights bipolarity already seen in the 'European laboratory'. The creation of the DSB, which combines negotiation and decision-making, also heightens the problems of co-ordination with the Community legal order. The Court of Justice of the European Communities (ECJ) is trying to resolve them by admitting the primacy of the WTO but, by refusing direct effect of its rules, it admits a sort of variable geometry lawfulness.[12] We may well ask ourselves if, as an echo of the national margin long admitted for the states' benefit, this is not a Community margin of appreciation contributing to the flexibility of global norms.

As for international criminal justice, in July 1998, a few months before the first House of Lords decision in the *Pinochet* case, it took the form of a new, permanent criminal court. Following on from the ad hoc tribunals created in 1993/4 by two UN Security Council Resolutions for judging the crimes committed in the former Yugoslavia and in Rwanda, the International Criminal Court will in fact be created when sixty states have ratified the Rome Convention. It will be competent to judge the most heinous crimes (genocide, crimes against humanity, war crimes subject to the transitory seven-year clause, and crimes of aggression once defined) touching the entire international community, including those committed by heads of state and provisional governments (Article 27). But we must not forget that several large countries, such as the United States, China and India, which represent close to half the world's population, have refused to sign the Convention. Despite the acceleration of history, we will have to wait many more years for the irreducible human element, which I cite as the primary foundation of a truly common law, to be fully recognised and protected. Even though the United States eventually signed the Rome Convention, it does not seem disposed

[12] See ECJ Case C-149/96, 23 November 1999, *Europe*, January 2000; Court of First Instance Case T-256/97, 27 January 2000, *Europe*, March 2000.

to ratify it, though the terrorist attacks of 11 September will perhaps speed the process. Eminent international law specialists such as Antonio Cassese (former presiding judge of the International Criminal Tribunal for Yugoslavia and professor at the University of Florence) and criminal law specialists such as George Fletcher (professor at Columbia University) believe that the proper response to those attacks is to bring the parties responsible to trial before an ad hoc international criminal court, which could be instituted by a UN Security Council Resolution similar to the 1993–4 Resolutions. In fact, it would suffice to declare the Rome Convention immediately applicable to these attacks: Article 7(1), which defines crimes against humanity, expressly states that the acts must be part of 'a widespread or systematic attack directed against any civilian population, with knowledge of the attack', and Article 7(2) specifies that the attack must be made 'pursuant to or in furtherance of a State or organisational policy to commit such attack'. In other words, even though terrorism is not targeted as such in the statute and was even set aside by the drafters because of the difficulty in distinguishing criminal terrorism from forms of resistance to forced occupation, the form used in New York in September seems to fall within the definition of crimes against humanity.[13] But this solution remains hypothetical. Most likely, the current dispositions will be maintained: according to the Convention's Preamble, the Criminal Court's competence will be only 'complementary' to that of the national jurisdictions. This is indicative of the extent to which the emergence of a common law, far from heralding the disappearance of sovereign states, expresses more this idea of complementarity between the various normative, national, international, regional and global spaces, which makes it, more than ever, necessary to adapt legal reasoning to this increasing complexity. This brings me to the questions my rereading raised.

Questions raised

It seems to me that the problems analysed in 1994 have worsened over time and, whether they are practical (market/human rights contradiction), legal (increasing normative disorder) or political (no global democratic government), it has become impossible to ignore them.

[13] Antonio Cassese, interview in *La Justice pénale internationale*, 4 October 2001.

Market/human rights contradictions

The appearance of the UN/WTO institutional duality has spread the contradictions made clear in 1994 by the European example over the entire planet. One author[14] underlined the dangers of equivocation, amalgamation and even contradictions that would, according to him, oppose the 'globalisation of law', which leads to bringing national legal orders closer to the 'law of globalisation', marked by the appearance of a new legal space that overflows the states. In fact, there is a two-fold risk of contradiction: on the one hand, as to the states' respective places in each process (state impotence would be the first result of economic globalisation, though states are still a necessary relay with regard to human rights); on the other, as to the meaning of a worldwide expansion that cites either the sharing inherent in the very idea of universality, or a market society marked, conversely, by an increase in social inequality. Despite a strong move to catch up with recently industrialised nations, inequalities are increasing not only in wealthy nations, but also in most of the emerging ones: a quarter of humanity lives below the line of extreme poverty, and the spread between the 20 per cent richest and the 20 per cent poorest has more than doubled over the last three decades,[15] which leads one to wonder about economic liberalism's ability to promote general well-being by itself.

The path from contradiction to interdependence has not yet been cut, but signs indicating the conditions for realising a combined market/human rights common law are being posted. As seen throughout the book, the major landmarks are in Europe, be they the efforts of the Strasbourg and Luxembourg Courts to avoid conflicts or, when the conflicts are declared, to find solutions of co-ordination. The draft Charter of Fundamental Rights of the European Union launched in 2000 reflects this effort to conciliate – as long as we do not regress on the contents of the rights protected. In the project's current state, the Charter renounces bipartite division in favour of a construction: based on dignity and the primary freedoms, be they civil and political, or economic; equality,

[14] J. Chevallier, 'Mondialisation du droit et droit de la mondialisation', in Ch. A. Morand (ed.), *Le droit saisi par la mondialisation* (University of Geneva Colloquium, 2000); compare M. Delmas-Marty, *Trois défis pour un droit mondial* (Seuil, 1998).

[15] See the Report on Commerce and Development, United Nations Conference on Commerce and Development (UNCCED), 1998. See also the Report presented at the G8 Summit, July 2000.

which clearly applies in every area; solidarity, which fully integrates social rights; citizenship, which refers to the main political and civil rights; and justice, which refers to procedural rights, valid in every area. The way would thus be clear for enforcing fundamental rights *vis-à-vis* economic agents as well as the states, which reinforces the principle that fundamental rights are indivisible and favours interdependence between the market and human rights. This would be at the risk, however, of a normative disorder resulting from the proliferation of norms and international legal spaces that superpose and entangle themselves, leading to an even greater transfer of power to national and international judges. Hence the need for an 'ordered pluralism', a concept I develop at length in the book.

Disorder, or ordered pluralism?

Beginning with a criticism of the monist conception, still utopian on a global (or even European) scale, and a dualism that does not account for the primacy of the international order and the greater interference in a society that is globalising, I suggested, as of 1994, that we move to a third, pluralist, model. Pluralism allows us to account for both the *vertical* relationship between national and international norms (marked by a normative entanglement with a return to domestic law through borrowing and express references), and the *horizontal* relationship between regional or global international norms, which are non-hierarchically juxtaposed to maintain continuity in the normative chain (for example, between the WTO and the UN or the EU and European Court of Human Rights (ECHR)). But we still must organise this pluralism, the problem being to find a pertinent rule of order, while the norms' hierarchy is weakened (vertical pluralism) or spread out (horizontal pluralism). Here, the margin of appreciation, examined in various examples, remains the primary instrument for building on multiplicity, not only between national and international norms, but also between regional, or even global, norms.

As the examples show, we can use the absence or presence of a margin of appreciation to distinguish unification, which imposes the same rule on everyone, from harmonisation, which is content to gather together around common principles. It makes room for pluralism by laying out a sort of states' right to be different, and replaces classical, binary logic with a logic of gradation that calls on fuzzy sets. In fact, many authors advise granting a national margin of appreciation to British judges applying the new Human Rights Act 1998, as the Luxembourg Court implicitly does in its relations with the WTO. The move from classical to fuzzy logic described in the book thus more than ever becomes necessary – provided we solve the problem of democratic legitimacy, which is very much at issue, especially with regard to the WTO.

Plutocracy or democracy?

Political debate underlies legal debate, and the dangers born of state impotence and the privatisation of law for the benefit of the wealthy openly raises issues of global governance and of the roles of institutions and citizens, and therefore of the agents of globalisation. What we see is state impotence: the master of the territory has lost control of its borders and economic agents, whose networks are now being organised along global strategies, openly traverse and transgress every state's borders. The same is true for controlling the rule of law, which is not adapted to transnational networks (of trade, but also of organised crime and internet communication). The economic actors will end up producing their own rules, naturally adapted to their own interests. In this world of global governance by a cosmopolitan plutocracy sufficiently flexible and mobile to exclude the states, the citizens and the judges, 'cosmopolitan democracy' has yet to be invented.[16] Improving international institutions[17] has become an urgent necessity, and the construction of European institutions, which raises the insightful question of the democratic deficit, has already brought to light a few avenues to explore.

Intended as a work in progress and not a set model, the search for a 'truly common law' constitutes a challenge to legal thinking, which is more conservative than transformational. As practices become global, at the cost of the injustices and violence we are currently experiencing, we must of course preserve the legal accomplishments of the past. But these accomplishments are not enough to respond to the issues now being raised. This book contributes to the search for adequate legal solutions: first, by describing the 'reconstruction of the landscape' seen in examples taken from France and Europe; then by trying to give a few keys for 'building on multiplicity'; and finally, by asking what the

[16] See S. Marks, 'The emerging norm: conceptualising "democractic governance"', *Proceedings of the American Society of International Law* (1997), pp. 372ff.

[17] See D. Archiburgi and D. Held (eds.), *Cosmopolitan democracy* (Polity Press, 1995); Delmas-Marty, *Trois défis pour un droit mondial.*

conditions might be for 'reinventing common law'. Whether it involves the European laboratory or the worldwide game board, the changes seen over the last few years heighten the urgency of such a search, because the answers must be found and implemented while there is still time. Since 11 September, it is clearer than ever that 'Justice and war are incompatible ideas.'[18] War means taking sides, whereas justice must remain impartial and independent. In such a conflict, war can pave the way, but it cannot replace justice. Only an International Criminal Court can offer sufficient guarantees to re-establish peace.

[18] George Fletcher, 'We must choose – justice or war', *The Washington Post*, 6 October 2001.

ABBREVIATIONS

AFNOR	*Association française de normalisation*
Ass.	Assemblée
Bull.	*Bulletin des arrêts de la cour de cassation* (Bulletin of Cour de cassation decisions)
CC	Conseil constitutionnel (Constitutional Council)
CE	Conseil d'Etat (State Council)
CNB	Conseil national des barreaux (French national bar council)
CPP	*Code de procédure pénale* (Code of Criminal Procedure)
CSCE	Conference on Security and Co-operation in Europe
D.	Dalloz compendium
ECHR	European Court of Human Rights
ECJ	European Court of Justice
ECSC	European Coal and Steel Community
EEC	European Economic Community
EHESS	Ecole des hautes études en sciences sociales (School for Advanced Studies in Social Science)
EHRR	*European Human Rights Review*
ERPL	*European Review of Private Law*
Gaz. Pal.	*Gazette du Palais*
HRC	European Human Rights Commission
INSERM	French National Institute of Health and Medical Research
IR	*Information rapides* (Quick references)
JCl	*Jurisclasseur*
JCP	*Juris-Classeur périodique* (or *Semaine juridique*) (French legal periodical)
JO	*Journal officiel de la République Française* (Official Journal of the French Republic)

LGDJ	*Librarie générale de droit et de jurisprudence* (French law and jurisprudence collection)
PUF	Presses Universitaires de France
RAE	*Revue des affaires européennes* (Review of European Affairs)
RFDA	*Revue française de droit administratif* (French Review of Administrative Law)
RSC	*Revue de science criminelle et de droit pénal comparé* (Review of Criminal Science and Comparative Criminal Law)
RUDH	*Revue universelle des droits de l'homme* (Universal Review of Human Rights)

TABLE OF CASES CITED BY JURISDICTION

European Court of Human Rights

European Court of Justice

Introduction

Today's profusion of norms has scrambled our image of legal order and made clear our need for a law that is common, in every sense of the word: accessible to everyone, built from the bottom up as a shared truth, and therefore relative and changing, rather than handed down from on high like gospel, revealed only to official interpreters; common to the various legal sectors, to ensure each system's cohesiveness despite increasingly specialised rules; and common to the different states, in a move toward harmony that will not require them to renounce their cultural and legal identities.

This need is certainly not new. From the twelfth to the sixteenth century, the call in Europe for a *jus commune*, made up of local customs and feudal, Roman, canon and commercial law, accompanied the emergence of national laws. The *common law* of the English royal courts, Roman law and the great continental codifications all stem from this need, and bear witness to the diversity of the legal means for satisfying it.

What is new, perhaps, is that we find ourselves very poor in social organisation. Return of the law or return to the law, it is as if law has become, or is supposed to become, a substitute for religions and ideologies and, as such, the sole founder of its subjects – law to 'institute' people, to 'make them stand upright' as Pierre Legendre said[1] – and the sole bearer of democracy: law as the opposite of totalitarianism. Hence the two-fold danger of reinforcing professional monopolies, and thereby moving further away from non-jurists, and of 'over-ideologising' law, the rule of law and human rights, along with over-ideologising the economy and the market.[2]

[1] *Filiation, fondement généalogique de la psychoanalyse* (with Alexandra Papageorgiou-Legendre) (Fayard, 1990), p. 194.

[2] E. McKay, *Economic analysis of law* (Themis, 2000); M. Delmas-Marty, 'Commerce mondial et protection des droits de l'homme', in J.-F. Flauss et al. (eds.), *World trade and the protection*

But we must set human rights apart, because these rights have always come from the bottom. Taken from states rather than given by them, they stand, as the case may be, in opposition to official law. The big change – the other historical change – is that they have become legally 'enforceable' against the states. Born as declarations of principles, and thus subject to the goodwill of the states, human rights suddenly became, after the shock of World War II, true legal principles according to which a law may be censured or state action condemned.

The initial effect was, in fact, to blur the image a bit more. This is because legal thinking adapts poorly to a plurality of norms, especially when the norms are (a) imprecise, as are most of the principles inscribed in the French *Déclaration des droits de l'homme* of 1789 and applied today as rules of law by the French Conseil constitutionnel or (b) weakly hierarchical, like the principles of the European Convention on Human Rights, for which the Strasbourg Court grants a 'national margin of appreciation' or, worse, (c) non-hierarchical yet simultaneously applicable, without either system having priority in a conflict, as we will see when norms coming from European Community and Union treaties meet up with the European Convention on Human Rights adopted by the Council of Europe. This imprecision of norms revives the old fear of a government of judges, which would be merely arbitrariness under another name, while the lack or weakening of hierarchy seriously disturbs the representation and functioning of a legal order conceived of as unified and hierarchical, unified because hierarchical (because the content of the inferior norms must comply with the prescriptions of the superior norm, unity of the system is guaranteed).

But the idea of granting human rights the role of a 'law of laws' is growing. The expression indicates both their new place in the theory and practice of legal systems and their new vocation: not just to protest, but also to harmonise the various systems.

Going beyond the 'common standard of achievement' proclaimed in the Universal Declaration of 1948 or the 'common language of humanity' evoked by the UN Secretary-General at the World Conference on Human Rights in Vienna, the document adopted at the end of this Conference

of human rights: human rights in the face of global economic exchanges (Bruylant, 2001), pp. 1–17 and J.-F. Flauss, 'Le Droit international des droits de l'homme face à la globalisation economique', in *ibid.*, pp. 217–56.

in June 1993 emphasises that the Universal Declaration now constitutes a 'common model to follow'.

More than the quantitative evolution – from fewer than 60 states in 1948 to 189 in 2000 – it is the change in terminology, from 'common ideal' to 'common model', that shows how far we have come. But this has been at the price of numerous misunderstandings and the danger of giving in to many temptations, beginning with that of a slightly naive universality (in fact strongly denounced in Vienna) that, rather than confronting problems, prefers to deny differences or smooth them over by choosing a 'model' so homogeneous and unified that it strangely resembles the hegemony of one culture over the others.

This is why a long detour seemed necessary to me. First, I size up the transformations that national laws have undergone, by describing the *reconstruction of the landscape* (Part I) where, despite the profusion of norms, or perhaps because of it, the major landmarks seem to have disappeared. But the secret of a common law that respects the plurality of norms is its consideration of legal logics, as the rational formalism of the law presents the danger, like the magical formalism of ancient rites, of favouring 'the symbolic efficacity of each action when, its arbitrariness misunderstood, it is taken for legitimate'.[3]

It is precisely to avoid this 'symbolic violence', founded on logical necessity in order better to hide the arbitrary, that it is absolutely necessary to show how, and under what conditions, combining classical logic with contemporary logics allows us to *build on multiplicity* (Part II) without having to choose between excluding and imposing identity. Only then can one attempt the approach that is this book's *raison d'être* and ambition: using and building on pluralism and the complexity of legal systems to *reinvent common law* (Part III).

[3] P. Bourdieu, 'La Force du droit', *Actes de la recherche en sciences sociales* 64 (1986).

PART I

Reconstructing the landscape

An orderly landscape. That is what we want. We ask the law for a little order, to protect us from disorder.

We ask first that it set limits, trace boundaries – and that it stay within its own boundaries, 'so that the sea isn't without a shore', as Jean-Etienne-Marie Portalis said in his celebrated *Discours préliminaire au projet de Code civil* (1804), wanting to avoid 'regulating everything with laws' and so reassure society in the face of the uncertainties of science. Science, he said, 'left to dispute, offers only a sea without a shore', even if it is also true that by refusing all limits, science (like art) works to overcome disorder through scrutiny.

The law remains remote, however, so we ask it for landmarks to indicate those boundaries not to be crossed, thereby establishing the major, fundamental taboos, such as those that define criminal guilt or civil wrong.

We also ask the law for landmarks to separate the various different kinds of laws, because they express 'different kinds of relationships between people living in the same society' (Portalis again). We ask for landmarks to separate civil laws – laws that bind individuals to one another – from laws governing profit-generating trade, because not everything is 'within lawful trade',[1] and also to separate laws that relate to the administrative and governing authority from those that belong to the sovereign power, which prohibits and punishes transgressions: the administrative and criminal laws that bind the individual to the state. But administration and repression should not be confused.

We ask for landmarks rather than for sources, because we want to be able to delimit the sources of law. The state and, in the Roman-Germanic

[1] P. A. Fenet (ed.), *Naissance du Code Civil* (preface by François Ewald) (Flammarion, 1989), p. 107.

tradition, statute are historically our reference points here in the west where the law, in separating itself from morality and religion, identified itself with the state. In the late eighteenth century, statute – the state source *par excellence* – became, in its majesty, almost the only source and instituted the legal order to which we are now accustomed.

This order is a guiding or directing order, because it also directs our way of thinking about the law: along lines forming a highly visible and explicit map where norms are developed hierarchically and applied linearly in a single direction – from legislator to judge. It is a relief map where the pyramid of norms dominates the landscape, providing visibility and stability to the instituted legal order.

Imagine the surprise of the observer, eyes agog, seeing that the landscape still inscribed in our memories has not disappeared, but its components have dispersed. We can attribute this dispersion to a triple phenomenon: *disappearing landmarks*, *emerging sources* that would relegate state and statute to the rank of accessories, and *lines redrawn* such that the pyramids, as yet incomplete, are surrounded by strange loops that make a mockery of the old principle of hierarchy.

We are thus faced with both impending disorder and the possibility, by moving closer to disorder, of finding there the means to break with 'learned common sense', which Pierre Bourdieu calls 'the Diafoirus effect' because in the name of science, he simply transcribes 'the discourse of common sense'.[2]

The possibility presents itself, then, of breaking with set legal knowledge, without a grasp on this constantly shifting reality that leaves its assigned territories to invent itself in other, infra- or supra-state spaces.

Deconstruction without hope, or reconstruction of a landscape the maps of which we cannot yet read? We are eager to find out.

[2] P. Bourdieu, with Loic J. D. Wacquant, *Réponses* (Seuil, 1992), p. 217. (Diafoirus is the doctor in Molière's *La Malade imaginaire*, who uses complex language to say simple things.)

1

Disappearing landmarks

Using a few examples from the French landscape (which are not intended to be exhaustive), let us take a journey through the highly symbolic – and historically well marked – areas of criminal and civil law.

Landmarks start to disappear when clearly defined legal concepts, such as criminal guilt or civil liability, recede in favour of concepts with much less precise boundaries – dangerousness and solidarity. This is not, as some say, the end of taboos, but the beginning of the 'fantasy of the absence of limits', or at least the weakening of taboos.

But we must not fool ourselves: what is at stake is the contents of the norms, not their existence. Far from realising the libertarian Utopia of which Proudhon dreamed – a peaceful world where 'order freely organised is an order one respects and against which one has no valid reason to rebel'[1] – the weakening of taboos seems to go hand in hand, on the contrary, with an increase in normalisation processes: processes that impose no 'must-be' (legal normativity), but tend more to model behaviours in relation to what is 'normal' – that is, the observable average, 'the is' (social normality).

The transformation is strongly felt in criminal law, where taboos are hidden by the ever more opaque veil of surplus normalisation texts and procedures (neutralisation, adjustment, rehabilitation, socialisation and even regulation) that refer less to guilt than to a vague dangerousness. It can also be seen in civil law, under the pressure of a 'social law' that tends to shape behaviours, independently of any 'must-be', solely through the game of social, and sometimes economic, normality, which tends to replace the principle of liability with a solidarity of unlimited twists and turns.

[1] R. Manevy and P. Diolle, *Sous les plis du drapeau noir, le drame de l'anarchie* (Domat, 1949), p. 13, citing the statement of the anarchists in the Lyon trial; see also Proudhon in D. Guerin, *L'Anarchisme* (Gallimard, 1981).

But the norms' contents are not all that is at stake, because the phenomenon also affects their organisation: the landmarks separating the major areas (or disciplines) of law disappear or are ploughed under. It is when this imprecision in legal disciplines affects the right to punish on the one hand and moral rights (*droits de la personnalité*[2]) on the other that it may become a threat to order.

This is precisely where disappearing landmarks can signify something other than an adjustment of legal techniques that could pass for a simple adaptation to the complexity of the 'post-industrial' world, because it calls into question the law of reason that says that law is not only a means of organising life in society, but of founding society and shaping humanity.

When the outlines of the right to punish become blurred between a highly weakened *légalité pénale* (lawfulness: no punishment without law) and an administrative repression in full swing, or when moral rights, which traditionally protect integrity and make the human body not for sale, start to resemble the law governing goods to the point of taking on pecuniary value, we may well, in fact, lose sight of the law of reason: the very reference point that showed us the way.

From guilt to dangerousness

Officially – all the manuals say so – guilt is at the heart of criminal law: it is because he or she is guilty of transgressing a taboo that the criminal must be punished, and it is the tying of guilt to punishment that gives criminal interdiction its symbolic strength. Taboos thus create order. But this link has been stretched with the development of practices so visibly contradictory that they result more from disorder than from the penal order: a disorder due, perhaps, to the multiple functions assigned to criminal law.

The first such function, at once pedagogical and symbolic, is of a legal–moral type. This 'expressive' function, which first appeared in the early nineteenth century in the codification debates, was still being emphasised in 1988 by Robert Badinter in his commentary on the draft *Code pénal* sent to parliament: 'All societies are built upon certain *values* recognised by the collective consciousness; these values are expressed in

[2] Set of rights (to life and bodily integrity, to honour and reputation, etc.) granted in French law to every person.

taboos; and these taboos in turn give rise to punishments for those unfamiliar with them.'[3] This function has its corresponding guilt/ punishment dyad in the Code, organised according to a double scale of severity: the severity of the punishment, quantifiable by the amount of the fine or the length of imprisonment, for example, must correspond to the severity of the fault (transgression of a taboo).

To this is added the utilitarian, 'repressive' function of protecting society, with which appears, in the 1810 *Code pénal's exposé des motifs*, a second severity scale that ties punishment to the offender's 'state of degradation'. 'Even though the word is not used, a person's dangerousness almost becomes a criterion here for the first time. A criterion that, in the following century, takes an increasingly central position in the appraisal of the penalty.'[4] Thus we slide from a criminal law that is supposed to punish the transgression of a taboo (transgression of the legal normativity) to a criminal law that must protect society by eliminating, separating or normalising those whose state is abnormal: a state of 'degradation', as the writers of the 1810 Code put it, then of 'dangerousness' for the scientifically inspired positivist school, and, finally, of 'social maladjustment' for the social defence humanist tide that called for measures to rehabilitate or reinstate the offender.

Better yet, the idea is dawning today that the function of criminal law should be to correct malfunctions that affect 'situations' more than individuals: such would be the function of criminal law in areas such as the environment, labour relations or economic law, for example. Here again, the goal becomes standardising behaviours by reference to a social or economic normality largely independent of the transgressed legal norm.

From transgression of a must-be to deviation from the social norm (individual state or situation that can involve several persons), the shift in emphasis of the goal should logically have brought with it either the disappearance of 'criminal' law (that is, the right to punish) – disappearance advised, by the way, in perfectly good logic by the abolitionists, who replace offence with 'situation-problem' – or, at the very least, the calling into question of the guilt/punishment dyad in favour of the dangerous-state/safety-measure dyad, as was suggested by the positivist school in the late nineteenth century.

[3] R. Badinter, *Projet de nouveau Code pénal* (Dalloz, 1988), p. 10 (emphasis in original).

[4] P. Lascoumes, P. Lenoël and P. Poncela, *Au nom de l'ordre, une histoire politique du Code pénal* (Hachette, 1989), p. 207.

In fact, nothing of the kind happened, and penal practices developed simultaneously along different lines with the approval of legal scholars.

As Michel Van de Kerchove emphasised, 'We cannot but be surprised by the speed and ease with which the contemporary authors were able to reconcile the points of view and eclecticism between poles apparently so contradictory.'[5] This reconciliation and eclecticism would constitute the entire art of the new social defence movement in its progressive detachment from the more radical positions of social defence, and of the legislature which, after all the reforms, would allow the incorporation of dangerousness into the criminal system's structure without, however, taking guilt out of the equation.

The dangerous state is the basis for certain extra-criminal administrative measures, such as deportation of aliens who constitute 'a threat to the public order', internment of mental patients who 'compromise the public order and the safety of persons', or even, by slipping from the idea of a dangerous state to that of a person in danger, adoption of educational assistance measures 'if the health, safety or morality of a minor is in danger' (*Code civil*, article 375).

But dangerousness is also at the heart of certain criminal reforms, as can be seen in the recent rise in denials of residency permits following passage of the law of 9 September 1986 on terrorism and, with the law of 31 December 1991 and article 131-30 of the new *Code pénal*, consequent banishment from French territory, which includes the right to deport aliens convicted of certain offences.

Moreover, at the intersection of general and specific intent criminal law, there remain ideas such as *attentat* (criminal attempt, usually an attack on state security), which seem to correspond well to the desire to extend repression (*attentat* includes attempt and attempted *attentat* includes the preparatory act) in the face of offences considered more dangerous (poisoning or interference with national interests, for example). Not only does the notion of dangerousness account for the particularity of the legal regime organised around certain offences such as drug trafficking, offences committed in an 'organised group' or, again, terrorism, it is the basis, in such cases, for a different procedural regime (namely, it affects length of custody, search and seizure conditions,

[5] M. Van de Kerchove, 'Culpabilité et dangerosité, réflexions sur la clôture des théories relatives à la criminalité', *Dangerosité et justice pénale* (Masson, 1981), pp. 291ff.

national rather than regional criminal jurisdiction, and criminal court composition).

Such is the first disorder of a criminal law the legitimacy of which is sought where two logically contradictory theories – dangerousness and guilt – converge (namely in surveillance and punishment). Brought to light by Michel Foucault, then by Gilles Deleuze, the disorder results from the fact that:

> prison as visibility of crime is not derived from criminal law as form of expression; it comes from another direction altogether, disciplinary and not legal; and criminal law produces declarations of crime independently of prison, as if it were always needing to say, in a certain way, this *is not* a prison . . . The two forms do not have the same function, the same genesis or genealogy, in the archaeological sense of *Gestaltung*. They do meet, however, even if it is with the help of a bit of sleight of hand.[6]

Another bit of sleight of hand, another factor in the slide toward a social normalisation function, are the consequences attaching to the principle of individualised punishment, incorporated into criminal law progressively since the celebrated work of Raymond Saleilles (1898), and finally appearing in the new *Code penal* (and in the law of 1987 on 'penitentiary public service'). Among these consequences is a whole set of measures that evoke the idea of freedom under judicial, police or medical surveillance: trial probation, freedom under surveillance, conditional release, therapeutic injunction and, more recently, direct and immediate surveillance by electronic bracelet.

Finally, a marginal pragmatic wave has developed. It is pragmatic in the sense that it appears to be founded on the increasing spread between legislative over-criminalisation (between 1985 and 1988, 200 new offences were created in France) and practical under-criminalisation due to the saturation of the criminal justice system. This wave thus favours a system of 'shunts' based on the criminal justice system to try to correct the malfunctions revealed by an offence: admonishment by the police, special arrangements with the prosecutor, summons of a workplace health and safety inspector (*inspection du travail*), injunction of the administration or transactions with its agents. The goal is first to regulate the situation: might not the transgression that motivates the repressive authorities' intervention be just a pretext to use the threat of

[6] G. Deleuze, *Foucault* (Minuit, 1986), p. 69.

penalty to correct the malfunction? Very often, through reference to a set of legal, regulatory and sometimes conventional prescriptions, the idea of transgressing a taboo disappears entirely from these offences, which do not even have their own, definite names. This is why there was nothing to prevent the new *Code pénal* from extending criminal guilt, detached from any real 'subject', to 'moral' persons (companies and partnerships, for example).

The traditional discontinuity of criminal law leaves room for continuous normalisation, where prevention and repression combine in a 'social criminal justice' that tends to model behaviours – those of individuals and those of groups – through ever more detailed and precise prescriptions.

While it is clear that a crime is an act that rends the social fabric – and it is precisely at this point of rupture that guilt and dangerousness meet – the new consequence, which was not foreseen by Emile Durkheim, is that the idea of punishment, as well as the highly attenuated opposition between repressive and compensatory sanctions, is transformed, because social solidarity now demands less that authorities punish than that they prevent. Or even – and this is the last step in the process that could signal the end of criminal law – that they repair.

The idea of collectively compensating victims of offences appeared in France in 1977, relatively late in comparison to the Anglo-Saxon countries, and took on full force with the laws of 1983 for victims of common-law offences and, above all, of 1986 for victims of terrorist acts. Finally, a 1990 law created a new common-law regime largely inspired by the regime specific to terrorism. The victim is now separated from the offender and public or even private solidarity funds are used to compensate him or her, independently of any implication of the offender. With the disappearance of the subsidiarity principle, which limited compensation by local authorities to cases of default by the guilty party, solidarity has priority over guilt, as if the convergence of criminal and civil law were inevitable – ineluctable.

From liability to solidarity

At the heart of the *Code civil* of 1804, the notorious article 1382 sets out the principle of civil 'liability' – the obligation to 'answer for' damages caused to another through one's fault by making reparations. That is, it ties fault, a category of a philosophical and moral order, to its legal sanction, the obligation to repair the damage. The 'tale's structuring function', to transpose Paul Ricoeur's analysis to the law,[7] is so strong here that fault has become inseparable from liability – guilty *and* liable – such that its progressive disappearance is most often interpreted as the decline of liability itself.

Many other factors play a part in this shift from liability to solidarity, however, beginning with the radical change of perspective marking the irresistible rise of the victim. To consider the victim is to make reparation or compensation the primary objective. Fault, which places the perpetrator in the spotlight, progressively effaces itself in favour of accident, which places the victim in the spotlight: reparation loses its function of sanctioning a wrong and takes on value in and of itself as the social consequence of an accident.

The counterpart of what I have called here social progress, accident in fact refers more to society through its objects (traffic accident), techniques (medical accident), machines (workplace accident) or even activities (environmental accident) than to human fault, even if fault continues to reassure us in a certain way because it can be avoided (we think humans are perfectible), while an accident bears the mark of inexorable destiny.

From fault to accident or perpetrator to victim, the passage is almost imperceptible, aided first by the flexibility and plasticity of the concept of fault itself and of its corollaries with regard to liability: imputation or assignment of fault to a specific individual and causality (the tying of fault to damage). It is aided also by 'presumptions of liability' that statute or case law finds in certain situations: of the employer in workplace accidents, of the operator in cases of pollution, and of the driver in traffic accidents (as the person having the vehicle within his or her control). In addition, there is now a 'principle of precaution', which imposes a whole series of preventive measures on any person making a decision that could reasonably be believed to pose a serious threat to the health or safety of present or future generations or the environment.[8]

While the concept of liability does not disappear, it is separated from fault in favour of risk, and the first commentators, such as François

[7] *Soi-même comme un autre* (Seuil, 1990); *Le Juste* (Editions Esprit, 1995).

[8] P. Kourilsky and G. Viney, *Le Principe de précaution, rapport au premier ministre* (Odile Jacob, 1999).

Gény,[9] evoked a 'principle of risk assignment' as the 'primordial' principle from which liability would come: 'Risks and liability represent, in sum, the two reciprocally complementary sides of a general notion necessary to legal life: distribution of damages that affect private interests.'

By the same token, the techniques of reparation are being perfected. We are now seeing the coupling of reparation–sanction with reparation–guarantee in the prodigious development of insurance and public and private compensation funds that enable the socialisation of damages and distribution of risk and, without abolishing chance, make the accidental more bearable by reintroducing humane equity.

The idea of liability without fault thus becomes acceptable. Under a 1968 law, it is established when the perpetrator is the victim of a mental illness that prevents the assignment of fault.

The stage is now set, in the most sensitive sectors, for openly basing the victim's right to be compensated on the idea of collective enforcement – thus breaking away from the liability of the perpetrator. Put differently, even though the word has not yet totally disappeared, the concept of liability (answer to . . . for . . .) has been abandoned in exchange for an openly proclaimed solidarity.

From guilt to dangerousness, from liability to solidarity, an entire way of thinking about law is disturbed because the limit between legal and illegal disappears as the position of fault weakens. With the notion of dangerousness – as with that of accident, risk or guarantee – the judge's decision becomes the work of chance more than lawfulness, and its margin of appreciation is such that the judge's power appears autonomous and, in this sense, discretionary. Certainly, he or she must first look for the criteria of his or her decision in a set of data that the legislature tries to define based on laws that are more and more detailed and prescriptive (labour law and environmental law offer numerous examples). But the decision is based on a balance that cannot be deduced directly and rigorously from the Code. The idea of dangerousness itself, like that of solidarity, is by nature limitless and cannot be understood legally other than by setting a threshold, because risk is never completely suppressed and guarantees are never completely implemented. Compensation as a social defence measure is limited to the threshold of acceptable or

[9] F. Gény, 'Risques et responsabilité', *Revue trimestrielle de droit civil* (1902), p. 817.

reasonable risk, namely whether it is compatible with the economic data of the moment. Especially visible in environmental matters where we speak of 'major' risk, this search for balance demands a complete transformation in legal reasoning. It introduces a graduated scale (more or less compatible) that excludes binary reasoning (conforms or does not conform). This gradation does not, however, preclude fixing a threshold that enables decision-making and a return to a choice that is, in the end, binary: legal or illegal.

If we add that any balance is, by nature, unstable, and that the compatibility threshold thus necessarily changes, we have sized up the current mutation. It is an incomplete mutation, which makes the old liberal concept of law coexist with that of a 'social law' and could foreshadow both a politically ultra-conservative society clutching its corporate interests and a legal decline where the inflation of norms and the disappearance of all objective judgment principles converge. In short, without precise limits inscribed by the legislature into the legal concepts proper to criminal or civil law, statute will no longer suffice to guarantee the objectivity of the law. The disappearance of landmarks would signal, along with the divorce of statute from law, the advent of a 'normative' – or, more likely, 'normalising' – order. Hence the distressing surprise at the idea that 'law could die just as easily of democracy, by democracy, or by blows from statutes'.[10]

This is even more true as this phenomenon is coupled with another that is less perceptible from the outside because it affects the norms' organisation more than their contents: the scrambling of the major areas of law.

I will give, here, just two examples from the right to punish and two examples of moral rights.

The right to punish: from *légalité pénale* to administrative repression

Punishment is in order to establish limits. The chosen site of major fundamental taboos, the essential purpose of criminal law is to found society by restoring, through punishment, the values offended by crime, and to shape human beings by setting limits.

[10] F. Ewald, *L'Etat providence* (Grasset, 1986).

At the heart of the law of reason, then, criminal law separates, or discriminates (same etymology as crime), by instituting the gap between the statute and the subject. This is an instant essential to the criminal proceedings that, thanks to this instituted gap, moves the human subject 'from the register of the act to that of the word'.[11]

Built up through legal reasoning from the 'principle of lawfulness' (no punishment without law), which forbids all reinterpretation by the judge, the law is a matter of limits, for both the judge and the individual.

But suddenly, faced with too many details, criminal law starts to lose its underlying function and becomes a 'criminal bric-a-brac' that the administrators try in vain, if not to make cost-effective, at least to rationalise. The confusion is not a result of this overabundance alone. Competition from administrative law, where recourse to sanctions having a penal character is increasing and becoming commonplace, constitutes a 'criminal true/false' on the fringe of criminal law that scrambles the word of the law even more.

The 'criminal bric-a-brac'

The 'criminal bric-a-brac' is first the consequence of superposing, as described earlier, the concepts of guilt and dangerousness. Supposed simultaneously to punish the former and neutralise or reduce the latter, penalty loses some of its unity and specificity here. Neither fines nor, for the most part, so-called 'alternative' sentences (with the exception of public service work) present any true penal specificity, allying themselves either with civil sanctions (probation coupled with an obligation to repair the damage) or with administrative sanctions (such as professional prohibitions, confiscation, licence revocation or suspension, or plant or establishment closings), or even mediation (deferred sentencing with injunction and ultimately waiver of the penalty). The necessary exclusion of corporal punishments – and more recently of the death penalty – thus tends to make prison the only specifically 'penal' – that is, punitive – sanction.

This does not mean that in generalising the penalty of prison we will have restored the right to punish to its underlying function, not only

[11] P. Legendre, *Le Crime du caporal Lortie* (Fayard, 1989), p. 22.

because prison itself, having broken with its *raison d'être* – to punish the transgression of a taboo – operates more as a place of discipline with a normalising vocation than as a place of penitence; but because the penalty is only part of a process much more complex that also requires a procedure (that is, a production), and is founded on an 'incrimination' (literally, definition of the crime) that separates right from wrong.

Also, the procedure participates just as much as the penalty in the law of reason. It is by the 'necessary theatrics' of the process that the word of the law will be spoken and heard as such, including in the ritual that overshadows it. The managerial approach would end up making us forget – were Pierre Legendre not constantly reminding us – that 'the major taboos are created and spread their effects not only through explicit legal declarations, but above all subject to forms and productions that overshadow the word'.[12]

Here again, there are various signs demonstrating the weakening of penal specificity at different points in the proceedings.

To incriminate is to define a crime, in the broad sense of criminal offence. Thus, it is simultaneously to name and divide – to name a behaviour, which may have been nameless until now, designate it as wrong and, at the same time, to say where right is and divide the social space into licit and illicit sectors. This is in itself a highly symbolic act, theoretically reserved to parliament – an act that parliament should accomplish with prudence and parsimony, after mature reflection: criminal law as *ultima ratio.*

But the reality is something else again, even in common-law countries, which do not have a strong legalist tradition. Almost everywhere, criminal law has been seized with a frenetic criminalisation movement that appears to express the failure of the existing law and the anxiety of some omission – the fear of being caught failing in a duty to incriminate – more than it expresses the desire to construct new references according to a law of reason.

In many cases, however, the need for rules and prohibitions is very real. Whether it is to reduce the risks created by new technologies (computer-based or audiovisual communication or biomedical technologies, for example) or to guarantee the creation of new rights (non-discrimination, respect for the environment), we call upon criminal law.

[12] *Ibid.*, p. 25.

But the response to such calls is not always clear. We must first untangle what belongs only to a 'magical' criminal law: a criminal law the function of which is not institutional but incantatory – a simple legislative exorcism that is not lasting but produces instead, for political purposes, an immediately apparent response to the fears of the moment. We must take into account the inflation, even swelling, of bureaucracy, at first dynamic then sly and more difficult to control, as it develops in legislative offices that are closed to the public. The very existence – and permanence – of such offences is a promise of new laws. Hence the spontaneous proliferation of criminal statutes, further aided by the technique called *renvoi* (referral), which dispenses with reflection and enables incrimination to occur without describing or naming the prohibited act. Criminal law merely sets a penalty and makes a laconic referral to the violation of articles X, Y and Z. As these, in their turn, often refer one after the other to other texts, one can imagine the perplexity of the interpreter, who is supposed to know and tell us which text contains the final definition of the incrimination.

Not only does parliament thus find itself pushed aside – because there are often references to decrees, orders or even international agreements negotiated by the executive power – but the underlying function of penal incrimination is also seriously attacked.

Hidden in a jungle of texts that prescribe the behaviours to be observed in extremely minute detail, the prohibited act, which is never described or named as such, becomes almost incapable of being discovered.[13]

While it is true that such an observation is valid primarily for what is called technical criminal law – namely that which is not found in the *Code pénal* but everywhere else (in about thirty other codes such as public health, labour, tax, urban planning, consumer rights, customs, etc., and innumerable laws regarding companies, the environment and the economy) – it is even more surprising that parliament, responsible for reforming the *Code pénal*, did not start there. Or did not, in any case, tackle head on, at one time or another, the question of these undiscoverable prohibited acts, the transgressions of which are none the less penalised – sometimes heavily.

In fact, the landmarks become less and less perceptible as the competition becomes more aggressive, with disciplinary or administrative punishment invading entire areas of law.

[13] See P. Lascoumes and C. Barberger, *Le Temps passé à la recherche du droit pénal* (Ministry of Justice, 1991).

'Criminal true/false'

True punishments, but a false criminal law, because the administration makes the decision rather than the criminal judge: such is the ambiguous face of administrative repression in full swing. While the French Revolution did not totally break with the hotchpotch of authority that characterised the *ancien régime* and invested the king, the lords and their agents with broad repressive powers, what is new is the scope of administrative sanctions, no doubt the inevitable counterpart of the modern state's increased intervention.

Yet one must distinguish among these sanctions those that serve a disciplinary purpose, a mere consequence of the administrative agents' subordination to a hierarchical authority; those that are the extension of a contractual or quasi-contractual relationship, for example the withdrawal of authorisation inflicted on one who does not respect imposed terms and conditions; and finally, real administrative repression clearly designed to punish those who, outside of any specialised relationship with the administration, do not perform their general legal obligations.

Traditional in fiscal matters, where it goes back uninterrupted to the *ancien régime*, this right to punish extended to many other administrations, primarily in economic and financial matters, or again in the sectors of health, the environment, expression and communication, and circulation and transport. It is a right to 'punish' in fact, because the administrative judge carefully distinguishes these sanctions from other measures, such as preventive measures known as conservatory measures (immobilising a vehicle), police measures (deporting an alien) and compensatory measures (charging fees for delays in fiscal matters). That is, the contents of administrative and criminal sanctions are more often than not identical: fines, confiscation, closure of plants or establishments are, for example, pronounced as often by criminal judges as by the administration. Their meaning, however, is another thing entirely.

The first difference in meaning arises because the interdiction, already weakened in criminal law, is practically invisible in administrative matters, where what is almost always sanctioned is 'non-performance' (that is, omissions defined – with variable precision – in relation to all kinds of obligations imposed by the administration), and not transgressions requiring a positive act and a punishable purposefulness. Even more than in criminal law, the punishment is designed to 'normalise' behaviour: to bring it in line with an average established by the administration, and thus with a purely managerial and changing conception that implies no moral reprobation and proposes no precise delineation of the lines not to be crossed.

This conception also contributes indirectly to the disappearance of criminal landmarks. In practice, in ever more numerous areas, criminal law is not being applied. Instead, administrative sanctions are used, which, aided by a considerably simplified procedure, are much quicker to implement (a hotchpotch of authority is irrefutably a time-saver).

Although it is not well known, administrative procedure carries with it perhaps the most radical transformation implicated in this development of administrative punishments to the detriment of specifically 'criminal' penalties, because it almost entirely does away with the ritual of a trial, which is already weakened in criminal matters. This is, in fact, what differentiates administrative procedure from criminal procedure, despite the extreme heterogeneity of the legal regime applicable to administrative sanctions defined by independent texts for each sector without any common legislative framework. In each sector in fact, the barely formalised exercise of repressive powers is practised in undifferentiated fashion: establishment of the offence, pursuit, inquiry and pronouncement of any sanction are not separated out from one another. In sum, the administration punishes without judging, or at least without there being a judgment in the traditional, ritualised meaning of the word.[14]

Certainly, guarantees have progressively been introduced under the combined influence of the Conseil d'Etat (France's highest administrative jurisdiction), the Conseil constitutionnel (Constitutional Council) and the European courts, but in varying degrees, and incompletely.

Not only is the guarantee incomplete, it is also variable because in many cases, in the absence of any independent administrative authority, it is once again the administration proper, and hence the executive power, that decides the punishment. This is true of the tax authorities, the *préfet* in road traffic matters, sometimes the minister of the environment, and even the minister of the interior, who can decide fines him- or herself – as, for example, fines set down in 1992 to apply the Schengen *acquis* against

[14] See M. Delmas-Marty and C. Teitgen-Colly, *Punir sans juger? De la répression administrative vers un droit administratif pénal* (Economica, 1992).

air carriers that do not respect the rules regarding the conditions under which aliens may enter France. The only guarantee, then, is recourse to a judge: such recourse is always permitted, in theory to an administrative judge but in some cases to a judiciary judge. This is a genuine guarantee, but one that is late on in the procedure: first we punish, then we judge – if the interested party protests.

Under such conditions, where does the right to punish begin? Where is the line drawn between criminal law and administrative law?

A meaningful indication of the difficulty in answering such a question is the suit that was recently brought before the European Commission on Human Rights against the French government, precisely because a new sanction – the withdrawal of points from the notorious '*permis à points*'[15] – was felt by offenders to be a penalty in the true sense of the word. Hence, they claimed the right to a fair trial before an impartial and independent tribunal, invoking a violation of Article 6 of the European Convention on Human Rights. The European Court found that a criminal charge and Article 6 were indeed involved, but did not find a violation.[16] This suit is significant because it was not the principle behind the interdiction that was contested, but the automatic functioning of the mechanism for withdrawing points, imposed directly by the law and considered to be a 'measure' and not a criminal sanction: the offender's act of transgression corresponds merely to another act (of repression), with no true passage 'from the register of the act to that of the word'. This shows that there are cases where only the word, by recalling the existence of limits, puts meaning back into the repressive process.

Moral rights: from unavailability to 'pecuniary' interests

While some biologists believe that biology has little to say about the person, namely about 'that by which an individual of the human species becomes a person, or at least is recognised as such in certain societies',[17] the mystery surrounding the definition of a person remains because the law also says little about it, and only in a fragmentary way.

[15] Driving licence from which points are withdrawn for traffic violations, leading ultimately to suspension or revocation of the licence.

[16] *Malige v. France*, ECHR, 23 September 1998, Reports 1998-VII, Appl. 31534/96.

[17] H. Atlan, 'Personne, espèce, humanité', in F. Gros and G. Huber (eds.), *Vers un anti-destin? Patrimoine génétique et droits de l'humanité* (Odile Jacob, 1992), pp. 52ff.

Take the *Code civil*, for example: rather than the goods discussed in Part II of the Code, people are the subject of the entire first Part. It paints a highly disembodied picture, the main focus of which is *état civil* (civil status), nationality and residence, as well as the ability to enjoy or exercise rights, which varies according to circumstance (the case of minors and adults 'protected by the law' because of mental problems is described in tedious detail). More concrete regarding interpersonal relationships, the Code none the less situates them exclusively within the framework of the family (marriage, divorce, paternity, parental authority). However, there is no general provision targeting 'moral rights', the rights that, consistent with the *Déclaration des droits de l'homme*, confer on every person specific powers that he or she may exercise over others and of which he or she may demand respect.

These rights, whether they express the essence or the attributes of the person, made a late appearance in legislation in a jumbled order.

The attributes of the person – integrity and intimacy – are dispersed in scattered texts. The integrity of the person is primarily guaranteed through the *Code pénal*'s interdictions that protect the body (physical integrity) against blows and wounds or homicide, and moral integrity (honour and privacy) against defamation, insults, criminal attempts and outrage. However, attacks on bodily integrity have progressively been authorised, and even regulated, by various statutes. First, from an exclusively therapeutic perspective, there is the law of 1952 regarding blood donations, complemented by the laws of 1949 regarding donation of the cornea and 1976 on organ removal, even though removal in the two latter cases occurs *post mortem*. Then, in a perspective both therapeutic and scientific, complemented with the law of 1988 on human experimentation and the laws of 1994 on bioethics.

Starting with and by extending integrity of the person, the integrity of literary or artistic creation (*les oeuvres de l'esprit*) is also protected by specific statutes through the so-called 'moral' right of the author. Independently of the author's pecuniary right – which authorises sale of the work – the moral right in fact enables him or her to demand its respect by anyone into whose hands the work falls. This is as if to acknowledge that the work effectively extends the author's personality and that the creator's literary or artistic 'property' is not the same as in property law.

The other attribute of the person – intimacy – is also protected by both the *Code civil* and the *Code pénal*, which punishes certain intrusions into one's private life. Protection began with the home and correspondence, and it is only since 1970 that the contents have also been protected through words or images that express this intimacy. More broadly, data of a personal nature are the subject of a specific protection either when they are given to professionals (trust is protected by making it a misdemeanour to reveal a professional secret), or when they give rise to the constitution of a computer file, no matter what it is used for, whether kept by the police, or for medical or financial purposes (law of 6 January 1978 on information technology and freedom).

From one text to another, from one component to another, the splintering is such that it is extremely difficult, as compared to property law or contract law, to define the legal regime applicable to moral rights. The paradox is that it is precisely where the landmarks should be the most visible – if it is true that the aim of the law is to shape the person – that they are the most scattered (throughout the *Code civil*, the *Code pénal* and various statutes), as if buried. The result is that they separate less and less distinctly what can be 'within lawful trade' and what must remain lawfully 'unavailable' and is not pecuniary (not convertible into money), and thus unavailable for trade. Without clearly established limits between moral rights and property rights, and considering economic pressures (which are always strong), the individual as such could well disappear from the law, traded in spare parts in a gigantic market where everything will be negotiable and convertible into money, bodily integrity and creative works alike (the pecuniary nature of words and images, and thus of certain forms of intimacy, having already been largely acknowledged).

A 'market of bodies'

The phrase is brutal and purposely provocative. The issue was thought to have been resolved with the prohibition of slavery and forced labour, but here it is again, vigorously revived by current biomedical events.

In its various areas, the responses of the law, and French law in particular, are extremely ambiguous. What is clear is the desire to place the human body beyond lawful trade, but even if it is admitted that it is beyond lawful trade, the outline of these notions remains blurred and there exists no legal statute regarding the human body. The laws of 1994 aim to make up for this absence, and solemnly inscribe at the beginning of the *Code civil* that 'the body and its parts cannot be the subject of a pecuniary right'.[18] From this we can deduce that one who offers his or her body for experimentation, for the removal or collection of blood or for other bodily products may receive no remuneration.

Numerous ambiguities remain, however, and the legal limits as to the use of all or part of the human body are still imprecise, particularly since the statute presented was, at the very outset, split into three, highly technical texts emanating from different ministries.

The imprecision stems first from the concept of 'lawful trade' itself – it is broader than act of trade, which necessarily requires a profit, and broader than 'patrimonial', which refers to the possibility of monetary evaluation and thus remuneration. Lawful trade is, above all, the ability to 'dispose of' something. Placing the human body 'beyond lawful trade' means laying down a law of unavailability, that is, of prohibiting all acts of disposition, not only those for consideration (sale or rent), but also those for free (gift, bequest or loan).

This choice seems to have been retained regarding surrogacy on behalf of a third party, because the law introduces a rule of invalidity into the *Code civil* for 'agreements regarding procreation or gestation for the benefit of another'.

In other areas, however, alienability seems perfectly acceptable, even if gratuity or volunteerism preserve, to all appearances, the principle that the body is excluded from trade, provided the word is taken in its most narrow definition of commercial law. In other words, the body is after all within lawful trade (one can dispose of it), but it maintains its non-pecuniary nature (the act of disposition must be for free, such as a donation, bequest or loan) and beyond the scope of commercial law (profit is excluded).

This is the position adopted by the National Ethics Committee under the term (ambiguous though it is) 'principle of non-commercialisation', in the sense of gratuitous or volunteered. This principle is applied, for example, to the practice of surrogate mothers, to removal of embryonic tissue or human foetuses, and to organ or cell donations.

[18] *Code civil*, art. 16.4, para. 3.

The legislature has affirmed the same principle: unremunerated blood donation with the law of 1959, organ donation with the law of 1976, volunteerism of those who consent to be experimented on with the law of 1988. And the laws of 1994 introduce the general principle into the beginning of the *Code civil* that 'the body and its parts cannot be the subject of a pecuniary right' and that 'agreements for consideration concerning the body or its parts are void'.[19] These laws add that 'no remuneration shall be allowed one who offers his or her body for experimentation, removal of its parts, or the collection of blood or other bodily products'.[20] All of these acts of disposition are thus valid, and the body is indeed within lawful trade, especially since the principle of gratuity itself is not absolute. First, the line drawn between prohibited remuneration and compensation, which is still possible, is imprecise by nature (as current prices for experimentation, for example, indicate). Moreover, remember that the statute itself foresees exceptions: 'While affirming the non-pecuniary nature of the body's products, the text reserves the case where the law would dispose of it otherwise.' That is to say, there is nothing to preclude any exceptions the legislature might be tempted to introduce. And once an act of disposition has taken place, even gratuitously, other people may enter into the process of transforming and distributing the body's products.[21]

Finally, the notion of lawful trade refers to the idea of supply and demand, or more precisely here, of a demand that puts pressure on supply,[22] a demand with a therapeutic or quasi-therapeutic purpose ('comfort' medications or the battle against sterility, which is not, properly speaking, an illness), or even a scientific purpose. Publicised sometimes in the extreme, the pressure is so strong that it introduces economic constraints of competition and the market. Proof of this phenomenon is the silence of three draft bills on the status of the human embryo. The question is essential, however, precisely because of the many demands for use in 'planned parenthood', or for therapeutic, scientific and even sometimes purely industrial and commercial purposes (cosmetic manufacturing, for example). This is why the legislature copied the provisions

[19] *Ibid.*, arts. 16.4, para. 3 and 16.5. [20] *Ibid.*, art. 16.6.

[21] M.-A. Hermitte, 'Réflexions d'un juriste sur le rapprochement des mots économie et expérimentation', *Expérimentation biomédicale et droits de l'homme* (PUF, 1988), pp. 111ff.

[22] See B. Edelman, 'La Recherche biomédicale dans l'économie de marché', *Recueil Dalloz* (1991), p. 203, where the author discusses patients as health-care consumers.

of the Conseil d'Etat's draft bill, which permitted, under very strict conditions, the donation of embryos for a third party's planned parenthood or for therapeutic or scientific purposes, but prohibited other uses under threat of criminal sanctions.

It is also true that scientific research in biomedical matters, as well as everything concerning the distribution of products derived from the human body, is subject to European Community (now Union) constraints that naturally favour an economic approach.

Whether we want it or not, there already exists a market for the body and its products, and there is strong resistance to a true legal status that would effectively set 'precise legal limits on the use of all or part of the human body' and codify the human body as an attribute of the person, inviolable and unavailable for trade. But the reality is much more complex and the dividing line between moral rights and property rights remains quite sinuous: unavailable, available but free, pecuniary, search for profit – the splintering of the legal regime is such that it is not possible to pretend that the human body is beyond lawful trade. And it would be even more incorrect to say that creative works escape market constraints.

The market for creative works

The market for creative works is, in fact, of a different nature. Here, the uncertainty does not come from a gradation that leads progressively from absolute unavailability to having a pecuniary nature and even to profit, but from the heterogeneity proper to creative works that arises from splitting the author's acknowledged rights in two: there are rights of a pecuniary or patrimonial nature, estimable in and negotiable for money (this is the concept of monopoly of exploitation, which implies a right to communicate the work to the public and to reproduce the work), and, when the invention is literary or artistic and not only industrial, there are rights of a 'moral' nature that concern both the birth of the work (the right to reveal and the right to claim paternity) and its circulation (the right to take back one's work and to demand respect for its integrity).

It is precisely these rights of a moral nature that mark the inseparable bond between the human being and the author's person. It is a temporary bond, because it lives only a certain number of years after the former's disappearance (seventy years for musical works, fifty for literary works and twenty-five for software), but one by which the work partially escapes market constraints.

It is with regard to these rights of a moral nature that the current trend would remove the landmarks, or, more precisely, move progressively from the system of a moral right to the Anglo-American system of copyright. Under this latter system, the work is detached from the person of its author and takes on complete legal independence: treated as a product, it lives its own legal life and the author cannot oppose the distortion of his or her work unless this right has been expressly reserved in the contract or if he or she succeeds in establishing that the distortion has caused the loss of either the work's value or the author's reputation – and thus market value – with the public being the only judge.[23]

Certainly, French law remains attached to the moral right system, but the dividing line tends to blur between moral rights, which extend the person, and pecuniary rights, which belong to the market. The line is none the less difficult to draw, because we must neatly separate artistic or literary creation from industrial creation.

International texts, which are closer to the system of copyright, make no mention of a moral right and tend to place all rights in the same category, including those designated in France as 'neighbouring' rights.[24] As for Community law, it considers creative works exclusively from an economic angle (they are 'merchandise' within the meaning of the Treaty of Rome, the 'free circulation' of which must be assured).

The market's dynamic itself imposes this removal of landmarks, not only on a national scale, but even more on the European and then international scale. This dynamic, which we have seen is also sensitive to the biomedical sector, collides with another aspect of the internationalisation of law that may very well signal the landscape's reconstruction:

[23] B. Edelman, 'Entre copyright et droit d'auteur, l'intégrité de l'oeuvre de l'esprit', *Recueil Dalloz* (1990), p. 295.

[24] Universal Convention of Vienna, revised in Paris in 1971. See, however, the Directive 93/98 of 29 October 1993 regarding harmonisation of the length of protection of author's and neighbouring rights, which contains certain differences: seventy years after the author's death for literary or artistic works, the same for cinematographic or audiovisual works, fifty years after setting for record producers' rights and after the date of execution for those of performing artists.

the appearance of new taboos – new landmarks – resulting from the emergence of a law of human rights with a supranational aim.[25]

The phenomenon goes hand in hand with the emergence of new sources of law and joins the preceding observation of a weakening of traditional sources: from statute to judge, regarding the concepts of dangerousness and solidarity; from the state to the international community, regarding both the astonishing evolution of the right to punish, and this 'patrimonialisation' of the human person and of what one can still call 'moral rights'.

[25] M. Delmas-Marty, 'Europe du Marché, Europe des droits de l'homme', in Gros and Huber (eds.), *Vers un anti-destin?*, pp. 414ff.

2

Emerging sources

The mystery of the source.[1] An initial investigation allows one to situate it in space and time. Such is the role of the diviner, but he or she does not reveal the source's secret: only the geologist has any idea of the processes that make some spring forth and others dry up.

Diviner and geologist in turn, the jurist tries to situate rules of law according to their connection to a particular space and time (here, I use the phrases 'normative space' and 'normative time') and attempts to understand the processes for generating these rules – as a way of tackling the concept 'of normative order'.[2] The current landscape appears totally confused when compared to the one our collective memory places in the west, in the Roman-Germanic tradition, which is marked reassuringly by unity and stability: normative space is identified with the state, normative time is long term, and the normative order is organised around statute. In this confused landscape, rules of law seem to spring up everywhere, at any time and in every direction: a spatial, temporal and conceptual relativity scrambles all the usual reference points, presenting the modern-day jurist with 'denationalised' normative space, 'destabilised' time and a 'delegalised' order.

[1] From the Latin *fons juris*, the metaphor goes back to Cicero. Traditionally used in law manuals, it is sometimes criticised for its many alternative meanings. Hans Kelsen considers it 'unusable' (Charles Eisenmann (ed. and trans.), *Théorie pure du droit* (Dalloz, 1962), pp. 313–14), and Paul Amselek is suspicious of this vision that is both 'naturalist' (which makes law look like some kind of natural and poetic given) and 'deformed, altered' ('Brèves réflexions sur la notion de sources du droit', *Archives de philosophie du droit* 24 (1982), pp. 252–4). Law is, like Cicero's fountain, both nature and culture, and develops as each shapes the other.

[2] See G. Timsit, *Thèmes et systèmes de droit* (PUF, 1986) pp. 29ff.

'Denationalised' space: state and non-state sources

According to Rudolf von Jhering, to say that the state is 'the sole source of law'[3] is at once to define a certain type of normative order that leaves the creation of norms up to the state and to affirm that all norms belong to a state bounded by a space, to the exclusion of any other normative space.

Even more powerful because it most often remains implicit, such a conception predominates in most law books. It is belied, however, by the questioning, which takes place from several perspectives, of the monopoly of the state. Attacks upon the principal expressions of the state take various forms: the nation state, which expresses the sovereignty of a primarily cultural community made up of overlapping interests and identical aspirations, is attacked by increasingly internationalised sources of law; the centre state, perceived as a form of political organisation, by decentralised sources; and the public sphere state, which results from a differentiation process at once symbolic and actual between the state and civil society, by privatised sources. These attacks sometimes take one form, sometimes all three – the latter being the case in France, where the sources of law are being in varying degrees internationalised, decentralised and privatised all at once.

Internationalisation

Internationalisation is without a doubt the most widespread and deeply disturbing movement in the French legal landscape, marked primarily by the increasing expropriation of European sources of law, mentioned above. Yet one must make it clear from the outset that there is no *one* legal entity called Europe, nor even *one* unique and pre-established vision of Europe. Europe is made up of diverse legal institutions. Each was built according to its own rules and sees itself as an autonomous entity. A primarily economic entity, the European Economic Community (which became the European Community) organises the free circulation of persons and goods with a view toward opening the borders between the fifteen Common Market countries: hence the birth of a 'Community' law arising from the Treaty of Rome and secondary sources, with interpretative unity of this law assured by the European Court of Justice that

[3] *L'Evolution du droit* (Zwech in recht, 1901), French trans. O. de Mecclenaera, p. 215.

sits in Luxembourg. Meanwhile, the Council of Europe, a political co-operation organisation that groups together forty-three member states (with those of central and eastern Europe) in 2001, adopted the European Convention on Human Rights and Fundamental Freedoms in 1950 and created the European Court of Human Rights, which sits in Strasbourg and, when petitioned by a state or individual victim of a violation of the rights recognised by the Convention, reviews the respect of these rights and can grant a victim 'equitable' satisfaction.

I will say but a word about the other structures. Some are broader and encompass non-European states, such as the OECD and the 'common House' that, after conferences in Vienna, Paris, then Copenhagen and Moscow, prepared the transition with the adherence of the central and eastern European states to common principles of law establishing the 'human dimension' as an essential element of security and co-operation in Europe (Conferences of the CSCE in 1989, 1990 and 1991). Others are more narrow, such as the Benelux grouping (three associated countries) or the 'Schengen space', which currently includes fifteen countries.

However, internationalisation of sources of law is evidently not restricted to Europe. Certainly, there are still vast areas of resistance – from the United States to the People's Republic of China – to any form of internationalisation that requires true reciprocal and supranational control rather than the hegemony of one state that imposes its norms on all the others. But regions other than Europe have accepted the idea: here one can cite the American Convention on Human Rights (adopted in 1969 and since ratified by about twenty Latin American states) and the African Charter on Human and People's Rights (ratified by about forty African states), which, despite major differences, are similar to the European Convention on Human Rights.

Beyond these regions, the phenomenon is developing more widely with the appearance of the United Nations' own sources of law. While the Universal Declaration of Human Rights adopted in 1948 has little restrictive legal value, the two 1966 Covenants derived from it, however (the Covenant on Civil and Political Rights and the Covenant on Economic, Social and Cultural Rights), directly bind the states that ratify, and more specifically those (including France) that also ratified the Additional Protocol enabling individuals who believe themselves to be victims of violations to address the Committee on Human Rights in writing. Such communications are examined and can give rise to 'observations' transmitted to the state in question.[4]

Thus, the right to punish is no longer solely a sovereign right. While neither the European Community treaties (primarily the Treaty of Rome, the Single European Act, the Maastricht Treaty on European Union and the Amsterdam Treaty), nor the London statute constituting the Council of Europe, confer criminal competence on the authorities they institute, if one considers in detail the jurisprudence of the European courts, it becomes clear that the right to punish is no longer inscribed solely in the national space, but also in one or another European space. This influence does not stop at the procedural level, but goes to the very essence of the right to punish: to prescribe underlying taboos through penal incrimination. Even in this highly symbolic area, the influence of the two European groups becomes manifest, with regard both to criminalisation (creation of a new crime) and decriminalisation (neutralisation, elimination of an existing crime). The paradox is that the effect of neutralising the national criminal norm with the European norm may be directly taken into account by the tribunals – decriminalisation taking place, therefore, without any intervention on the part of the national legislature – while the opposite effect of incitement to punish (criminalisation) remains dependent on the goodwill of the states because it requires the adoption of new domestic laws.

Criminalisation, the reverse strategy of decriminalisation, also suffers from European influence, though in a more limited fashion. The reasoning is based on the idea that only a penal incrimination can ensure effective respect of either a new Community norm or a right established by the European Convention. This leads to a desire to postulate a crime that the European authorities, however, do not have the direct power to create, as their competence is not equivalent to that of national parliaments on this point. This situation usually changes when it involves protecting European Community financial interests, however. The existence of fraud with relation to sums that constitute a major portion of the Community agricultural budget has forced the Brussels Commission

[4] See M. Delmas-Marty, *Les Grands Systèmes de politique criminelle* (PUF, 1992), pp. 354ff. (European constraints) and 413ff. (international constraints).

to take steps.[5] On the one hand, it can now exercise – and it no longer hesitates to exercise – a 'claim for breach' against a state that does not implement 'effective, proportionate and dissuasive' sanctions against such fraud, which means genuine punishment, be it administrative or criminal. On the other hand, the Commission took the initiative in introducing real administrative sanctions into the regulations enacted for agriculture and fishing. Contested by some states, their validity was finally acknowledged by the Court of Justice in Luxembourg in 1992.

For its part, the European Parliament adopted several resolutions aimed at developing a true European criminal system to repress fraud on Community finances. Incrimination could therefore be guided by a common definition, with a set of sanctions that would be applied by both the Brussels Commission (administrative sanctions) and by national tribunals (criminal sanctions). In the end, harmonisation was imposed in 1995 for both administrative (Regulation of 25 December) and criminal sanctions (Convention of 18 July). If the states consent to apply the former and ratify the latter, the right to punish will be fully inscribed (for criminal fraud) in the European – and therefore supranational – normative space. Even more ambitious, a draft document, '*Corpus Juris* introducing penal provisions for the purpose of the financial interests of the European Union', published in 1997 and amended in 1999, proposed the creation of a European public prosecutor 'applying common rules'.

In the area of moral rights, European influence is more contradictory. First, Community law leans toward internationalising the market, and thus encourages a reduction in overly restrictive national regulation, namely when it places the products of the human body or creative works of an individual beyond lawful trade, or simply outside the commercial systems (see the example of products derived from blood). Secondly, diverse recommendations from the Council of Europe's Parliamentary Assembly are addressed to states with the opposite objective of strengthening regulations that protect human rights.

In particularly sensitive sectors such as the use of human embryos and foetuses, several Recommendations have also been heeded, for example

[5] See M. Delmas-Marty, *Quelle politique pénale pour l'Europe?* (Economica, 1993), Foreward and pp. 121ff.

that of 24 September 1986 regarding 'the use of human embryos and foetuses for diagnostic, therapeutic, scientific, industrial or commercial purposes', and that of 2 February 1989 on 'the use of human embryos and foetuses in scientific research'. Particularly precise, the latter incites the Committee of Ministers of the Council of Europe to 'define a framework of principles from which statutes and national regulations as universal and homogeneous as possible can be developed' and annexes a series of provisions relative to authorising or prohibiting certain research and experimentation practices. Moreover, it incites the states to 'contribute to the framing of a common legal instrument, such as a European convention on biomedicine and human biotechnology, which would be open to non-member states also', and includes an additional Protocol on the prohibition of cloning human beings (12 January 1998). At the same time, there are numerous working groups and expert committees on bioethics under the auspices of both the Council of Europe and the European Community.

It is true that states are not the only ones concerned by the internationalisation of sources of law. Many of the norms in these areas were first defined by local ethics committees that were created spontaneously from diverse institutions such as the INSERM or university hospital centres before 1983, when the creation of the 'national consultative committee for life sciences and health' called the existence of such norms (which were, in fact, established by the law of 1988 on human experimentation) into question. The ethics committees, which have become 'committees for the protection of persons', bear witness to the dynamism of local (and thus decentralised) sources of law.

Decentralisation

There is a gradation of decentralisation depending on whether it is expressed solely in terms of the displacement of sources from the centre to the periphery – decentralisation in favour of territorial authorities that disturbs traditionally centralised states, but which is inscribed in the very logic of federal states – or whether it is accompanied, as with the local ethics committees, by a certain form of 'privatisation' when the local normative space does not fall within the public sphere.

While standards enacted by territorial authorities remain unarguably public law, the analysis is more ambiguous for standards that can be set locally by authorities whose status arises more from the notion of professional ethics and which primarily concern those professions organised into orders (such as lawyers, doctors and architects). Local autonomy is especially marked in France within the profession of barrister – until 1990, the *conseils de l'Ordre* prescribed disciplinary rules (internal regulations) for each Bar on a strictly local level, provided they followed the general legislative framework. In fact, the creation of a national Bar (one of the major innovations of the law of 1990) simply limits, without eliminating, this local autonomy in a few sensitive sectors such as professional training. Provided they are within the legislative framework and appeal to state jurisdictions remains possible, disciplinary rules have kept their mixed aspect (doubly mixed for lawyers): local *and* national, private *and* public.

The analysis is slightly different with regard to the right to punish when dealing either with ethics committees, which are concerned with moral rights, or community councils, which deal with the prevention of delinquency. They were all created spontaneously by professionals and include state representatives and various qualified persons according, however, to a balance imposed by the state.[6] This said, these local councils and committees maintain relations with a national authority (the National Consultative Committee for Ethics and the National Council (and departmental councils) for the Prevention of Delinquency) and they have no directly established normative power. They are brought into the normative process indirectly, however, by being called to give their opinion on general or specific questions concerning research protocols or criminal policies. In this respect, they occupy a discernible place in the movement toward decentralisation, where it coincides with privatising the normative space.

Privatisation

One must distinguish between changes affecting the transmitter of the norm – direct source of law – and its receiver – indirect source. (On the place of the receiver of norms in the process of generating law, see below, 'A "delegalised" order: legislative and non-legislative sources'.)

[6] See the 1983 decree for the Conseil communal de prévention and the 1990 decree, completing the law of 1988, for ethics committees, now known as 'committees for the protection of persons'.

Beyond the ethical norms of professional origin mentioned in relation to decentralisation – to which one must here add disciplinary standards set by company heads for their employees – normalisation has become an area in which private organisations are competent to define technical norms and standards applicable to diverse products. Thus AFNOR (the French standardisation association), set up by a 1941 decree (replaced without really being altered by two 1984 decrees), is responsible for co-ordinating all activities relating to standardisation. It directs inquiries, then publishes approved standards (which can be made obligatory upon simple ministerial decree when, for example, health, safety, environmental protection or consumer defence is concerned) and certifies the compliance of products with these standards by awarding the NF (*Norme française*) label. In addition, AFNOR represents France in European and international standardisation organisations and is responsible for transposing, without modifying, all standards established by European organisations and abrogating national standards that are contrary to European ones (the obligation to transpose exists only at the European level). This means that true normative power (in the broad sense of the term, because it concerns referring to an average – normality – and not a must-be – normativity) is exercised by a private association in which, in fact, representatives of industry and users participate voluntarily alongside the administration, and which accomplishes its mission in close collaboration with standardisation offices: private organisations responsible for developing standards.

While it is true that this privatisation of a large sector of law seems to be the result of the expansion of economic liberalism – as the means to ensure the better guarantee of the conditions of free competition – this explanation remains partial because the approved technical standard can also be used as an instrument of protection, isolating the national market from the world market (Germany and Japan are examples of this), with the result that privatisation of normative sources does not necessarily correspond to a policy of economic liberalism. It can even accompany the development of a 'social law', which favours the principle of solidarity (welfare state). With regard to product standardisation, the cost–benefit analysis effectively introduced not only economic opportunity, but also social equity elements of judgment into legal reasoning. All this is indicative of the extreme complexity of the current transformations in sources of law.

The same can be said for indirect forms of privatisation, namely those that transfer the power to apply the standard to private authorities and at the same time give them an indirect normative power. It is clear that such power is not limited to regulating a market, even when privatisation enables open admission that profit is the motive. Thus, privatising 'sperm banks' would not only have the effect of commercialising a product of the human body, it would also indirectly give power to these banks to define the basic conditions of artificial procreation (for example, whether or not to limit assistance to cases of sterility, or to heterosexual couples only, etc.).

Moral rights are not the only rights at stake. A law of 1991 eliminated, in most cases, the criminal sanction applicable to issuing bad cheques, and the banks themselves exercise the repressive power through the banking prohibition system that existed already but that is now coupled with a 'discharge penalty', the amount of which is set by law and paid to the state treasury. While banking repression thus remains under the supervision of the law, the system appears to be coupled with real private repression, because some banks inflict supplementary and purely private penalties on their customers under conditions they impose according to their own criteria (which presupposes *de facto* economic dependence of clientele, for example when the bank has granted a loan). A bank can thus 'condemn' unscrupulous customers to pay a monthly fine that may, depending on the case, be set for between one and ten years.

Finally, this tendency toward repressive privatisation of social control is further accentuated for the border police by the above-mentioned law of 1992, which was adopted when transposing the Schengen *acquis* into French legislation, and is thus under European influence. Privatisation for repressive purposes is accentuated in the sense that the statute not only permits but requires air and maritime carriers to verify, upon arrival in France, the travel documents and visas of aliens coming from non-European Community countries. Threatened with an administrative fine that can be assessed 'as many times as there are passengers concerned', these companies will inevitably be compelled to define sufficiently broad verification standards to protect themselves from sanctions.

From international sources of law to local or private sources, the spatial, temporal and conceptual relativity affecting the normative space is seen again (the phenomena no doubt being related) when 'normative time' is considered.

'Destabilised' time: permanence and variability of sources

Time is the only true source of law. It is the lesson of prudence and modesty that Jean-Etienne-Marie Portalis gave to all those who would be tempted by legislative will: 'Codes develop over time. We do not, properly speaking, write them.' This was an indirect salute to custom, which favours the long term and is based, precisely, on time. This is not without some ambiguity, because time both builds law through the formation of usage and the accumulation of precedents and destroys it when it eliminates evidence or weakens rules that end up falling into disuse. Hence there is uncertainty surrounding customs written in the past but interpreted in the present, at least as long as the mode of transmission remains oral and the interpreter spontaneously adapts the account to present needs.

It is the writing down of customs that immobilises time in statutes. 'Perpetuity is the wish of statute', proclaimed the preliminary book of the *Code civil* (which was in fact set aside by the *Tribunat* and never promulgated because of its overly broad generalisations).

Let us compare two propositions: 'codes are developed over time', but 'the wish of statute' is none the less perpetuity. To reconcile them, we must accept that this Promethean desire to control time with statutes is a wish only, and as such cannot be realised. This the writers of the *Code civil* knew well: 'How can we curb the action of time? . . . A code, as complete as it may seem, is no sooner finished than a thousand unexpected questions come before the magistrate.'

This will be the case unless the legislature can find formulae that give the statute some chance of having a hold on the future, thereby proving its ability to anticipate. From this angle, the writers of the Code did not do so badly. It is still in force – and full of vigour – close to 200 years after its promulgation. The recipe for success is, again, a lesson in modesty: 'Statutes are not acts of pure power; they are acts of wisdom, justice and reason' – and wisdom, in the early nineteenth century when the revolutionary hurricane was still blowing, was to be 'sparing with legislative innovations'. But the road is narrow. While 'the great art of the legislator is to simplify everything by foreseeing everything', the temptation to veer towards somewhat manipulative legal conservatism is very real: 'Instead of changing statutes, it is almost always more useful to present the citizens with new reasons to like them.'

To avoid the pitfalls between conservatism and revolution, the legislator must learn prudence, but also know, according to Portalis' celebrated formula, that 'the office of statute is to set out, in broad strokes, the general maxims of the law; to establish principles fecund in consequences, and not to descend into the detail of questions that can arise on each subject'.

Such was the liberal conception of law, marked by stability without rigidity – namely, a law that, supported by a written code, sets but does not become rigid. Innovation is therefore not precluded, but balanced, and transitions are orchestrated: a new statute 'disposes only for the future and has no retroactive effect' (*Code civil*, article 2, considered 'counter-revolutionary' by some). Distinguishing between the momentary and the long term, later doctrine and jurisprudence specified that statutes apply immediately to events occurring after they enter into force (marriage or birth), but that ongoing situations must allow for distinguishing between past effects governed by the former statute and future effects, which are the only ones concerned by the new statute. The exception to this is contractual situations, which continue to be governed by the law in force on the day the contract was concluded, so as to respect free will, which is the necessary foundation of contractual obligations.

Stability is further strengthened in criminal law, where retroactive statutes pose even greater risks because they can become instruments of circumstantial repression when punishment becomes politically motivated purification. Included in the *Déclaration des droits de l'homme* of 1789 (which today gives it constitutional force) and in the *Code pénal*, the principle of non-retroactivity is also included in the European Convention on Human Rights and the UN Convention on Civil and Political Rights, and is becoming the pillar of democratic regimes where, according to a well-known adage, 'the law must not strike without warning', the exception being the immediate application of new statutes that are more gentle, presumed by the legislature to be better and by definition more favourable to the accused.

In other areas, it was well after the promulgation of the *Code civil* that some 'public order' laws that called into question a contractual situation were allowed immediate application (in labour law, for example). Later, with a concern for equality – and once the bad memory of the law of *nivôse* (fourth month of the calendar year) in year II (1793), which was declared applicable retroactively to successions open since 19 July 1709, had been forgotten – laws were adopted that were expressly retroactive, such as the law of 1972 validating acknowledgment of children born out of wedlock even for such acts that occurred prior to the law, or that of 1982 allowing paternity to be proved using new methods even for children born prior to the law. The law's desire for stability, and at the same time statute's wish for perpetuity, has weakened little by little while, with the rise of the welfare state, a social conception of law has developed whose primary objective is no longer to protect citizens against the arbitrariness of those in power, but to institute and maintain a balance, which is by its very definition temporary, unstable and changing. By favouring normalisation, which models behaviours, over the taboo, which sets limits, 'social law' sets up a continuous and mobile transformational process that must constantly adapt: 'Statutes are no longer made to last; if social conditions change – a change that the statute is designed to carry out – we must change the law; social law is a law of which each enactment contains the principle of its own reform; an obsolescent law.'[7]

This conception puts law into constant interaction with the social milieu, and current doctrine tries to understand it through new paradigms such as game theory[8] or new theories inspired by biology, such as 'autopoiesis' (a product of the German school),[9] with the goal being to find instruments for regaining stability despite the extreme instability attacking the various sources of law.

Let's not skip any steps. At this point, I am not suggesting any new solutions, but simply describing a landscape undergoing a complete transformation – a shifting image that should account for this instability of sources of law, increased by their multiplication in various normative spaces.

More visible with 'temporary' sources of law, which are, naturally, limited to a predetermined period, this instability also takes on forms more subtle and difficult to perceive with 'changing' sources – those that modify themselves over time, despite being based on an apparently unchanged support.

[7] F. Ewald, *L'Etat-providence* (Grasset, 1986), p. 485.

[8] F. Ost and M. Van de Kerchove, *Le Droit ou les paradoxes du jeu* (PUF, 1992).

[9] G. Teubner, *Le Droit, un système autopoïétique* (PUF, 1993); N. Luhman, 'L'Unité du système juridique', *Archives de philosophie du droit* 31 (1986), pp. 163ff.

Temporary sources

When compared to statute's wish for perpetuity, the term 'temporary law' itself, and more broadly 'temporary source of law', sounds like nonsense. Variability is most often manifested by repeated reforms in sensitive sectors, such as audiovisual communication or the registration process undergone by aliens. However, there are examples that illustrate the idea of a temporary law more directly: cases of emergency, or sometimes of prudence.

Given the urgency of certain situations – during war or an exceptional crisis threatening the state's very survival – temporary laws may be adopted: this principle is even expressly written into the French Constitution (article 16) and the European Convention on Human Rights (Article 15). Such 'exceptional' laws are circumspect in duration, because they most often include waivers of fundamental rights that it is important not to prolong beyond the war or state of emergency that is the pretext for instituting a dictatorial regime. Here, the temporary nature of the exceptional law operates as an essential guarantee of democracy.

The legislative process involved in adopting a trial law is quite another thing. The goal is, conversely, prudence: expressing a doubt, if not about the validity of the law, at least about its advisability. Actually, the most often used technique is 'a test prior to the law', which is slightly different. Frequent in criminal law, where the practice preceded various laws such as those on probation, public-interest work and deferred sentencing with injunction, this technique is used in conjunction with mediation practices that preceded adoption of the initial text in 1993.

A sign of prudence, the test prior to the law has low visibility because the practices are informal and easily abandoned in the case of failure. More visible, and therefore riskier, is the resort to 'trial laws'. The most well-known example is the law on abortion, which liberalised abortion in France, but only for a trial period limited to five years. The law of 1979 ratified the rules set out in 1974, without a time limit. The same is true for the law of 29 July 1994 on bioethics, which will soon be reviewed by parliament. Another trial law, this time international, limited to five years the declaration of acceptance of individual recourse before the European Commission on Human Rights, based on Article 25 of the Convention. This acceptance has been renewed regularly since 1981.

Prudence can also combine with urgency in the adoption of provisional measures either to preserve a threatened situation ('conservation' measures are frequent in administrative law and marked in criminal law by resort to 'temporary' custody, ordered when the evidence might disappear or the accused might flee) or to anticipate the judgment by, for example, according initial damages (a 'provision') to the victim of an accident or offence even before the matter has been judged and liability clearly determined. In either case, the measure may be facilitated by resorting to a quick, so-called 'summary' procedure in which a single judge makes an immediate decision by order. Of wider scope in civil law and extended to administrative and criminal law (but only for the victim's benefit: 'summary provisions'), this originally exceptional procedure is becoming standard, despite the possibility of reversal that characterises this type of decision.

In fact, reversibility is no longer an exception in legal matters. Sentences pronounced 'definitively' by the criminal judge thus often become reversible, if not temporary, as the concept of evolutionary sentences is developed. This, by extension of a law more 'normalising' than punitive, seems to characterise the current system and to herald the technique described here as 'evolutionary' sources.

Evolutionary sources

To speak of 'evolutionary' sources is to renounce both the past (custom) and the future (statute) in order to set the sources of law squarely in the present, which is by definition constantly changing. While custom can be evolutionary in its way (through the oral tradition that spontaneously adapts sources based on the past to the present), the system is more rigid with statute, which wants a hold on the future. Even with temporary laws, we must wait for them to disappear and be replaced by others before the rule changes, because the present indicative used in the wording of statutes has an imperative value that does not change by itself, unless it reverts to the simple indicative when, incorporating risk, statute becomes 'evolutionary'.

The process is rarely recognised as such. This concept of 'evolutionary sentences' does not appear in any criminal law. It is by arranging true correspondence (under the rubric of 'enforcement measures') between the guilty party's behaviour and the sentence laid down that statute manages, without ever explicitly saying so, to remove rigidity and immobility from the conviction, despite the principle of *res judicata*, which appears to be preserved. Sentencing is already involved in a certain interactive, and thus evolutionary, aspect with the technique of probation that 'suspends' execution either on the convicted person's good behaviour for a predetermined period, or on the condition of certain accompanying measures (surveillance, review, sometimes public-interest work or aid). The evolutionary and reversible nature is even more clear with the various forms of early release that is granted to prisoners in exchange for 'good behaviour' (sentence reduction) or 'social reclassification' (conditional release). Here there is a clear link between the transformations described earlier, from guilt to dangerousness, and this new conception of time that detaches the penalty from guilt based on the offence committed and encourages amendment of the penalty by taking into account the behaviour that follows conviction. This is a conception that is, after all, very complex in its application and therefore difficult for the penitentiary administration to implement; it is also difficult for the convicted to understand, because the variety of regimes and the frequency of their modification are such that they lead to unacceptable disparities, depending on the conviction date. The British system, which is more transparent, goes all the way to reversibility of the sentence by granting, upon entry into prison, a certain number of days by which the imprisonment may be reduced, which the convict loses only in the case of a disciplinary incident. This system coexists with the much-criticised use of the 'indeterminate sentence', which consists of sentencing for life so as to let the administration modulate the real length of the sentence in relation to the convict's behaviour, with any early release being, by definition, 'temporary' because the initial sentence is sufficient to justify reimprisonment, decided by the administration on a discretionary basis. Clearly, liberty is not always favoured by the use of reversibility.

That said, even though it is of legislative origin, the evolutionary process does not declare itself as such and does not directly affect the source of law. Statute is evolutionary only in the consequences it brings with it, by combining texts on sentencing and those on execution. There are, however, some areas of law where the source modifies itself.

First, administrative law, where new random relationships are taken into account. But this 'administrative law of the random' must be distinguished, to use the provocative phrase of André Hauriou,[10] from situations in which the administration simply provides a remedy for a random event or foresees the effects of a hazard that could occur – in short, 'plugs the leaks' – a theory of the unforeseen that civil liability law, on the contrary, rejects, and which allows the administrative judge to shift the balance of a contract in the case of economic upset. Only techniques such as price indexing for long-term contracts, or economic criteria defining an illicit agreement according to its effects on the market, operate such that the rule itself varies automatically if the referential data change (with the progressive increase of prices or changes in the market, for example), and the legal framework itself thus evolves without requiring a new law. This makes interpretation especially difficult, and leads to the creation of a veritable 'economic bench' able to understand all the elements of the economy that control the decision (Council on Competition, Commission on Stock Exchange Operation and so on).

But the preferred area of evolutionary sources is, without a doubt, European law. Thus, Community law, via Directives from the Council or the European Commission, imposes the result that is to be obtained without setting the legal means to reach it, thus inciting the states to adapt their laws to the economic data of the moment.

If one looks at the Council of Europe rather than the European Community, what is even more surprising is the openly evolutionary conception of the European Convention on Human Rights in the interpretation given to it by the Commission and the ECHR. Basing its interpretation on the text of the Convention's preamble itself, which sets the Council of Europe's objective as being the preservation 'and the development' of human rights and fundamental liberties, the jurisprudence forcefully affirms the Convention's evolutionary nature, and therefore the need to interpret it while taking into account the data provided by the different member states of the Council of Europe. Thus, for example, the evolution of society provides support for its greater tolerance for finding that the criminal indictment of homosexuality between consenting adults that still existed in Great Britain was contrary to the principle of protecting privacy. While it had rejected all such petitions

[10] 'Le Droit administratif de l'aléatoire', in *Mélanges Trotobas* (LGDJ, 1970), pp. 197–225.

until the 1980s, the Commission sustained the argument for violation of privacy and the Court condemned the United Kingdom in 1981 and the Republic of Ireland in 1988.[11] Almost identical in both cases, its reasoning (cited here from *Dudgeon*) was based on the idea of evolution itself:

> As compared with the era when that legislation was enacted, there is now a better understanding, and in consequence an increased tolerance, of homosexual behaviour to the extent that in the great majority of the member states of the Council of Europe it is no longer considered to be necessary or appropriate to treat homosexual practices of the kind now in question as in themselves a matter to which the sanctions of the criminal law should be applied; the Court cannot overlook the marked changes which have occurred in this regard in the domestic law of the member states.

The approach is much the same for transsexualism, equally tied to respect for privacy: a transsexual petitioned the ECHR after the state refused to modify the petitioner's civil status. Setting aside the violation of the right to privacy invoked in the petition, the Court, however, qualified its decision with a sort of warning: 'for the time being', it said, we must leave it in the hands of each state to determine how far it can go in satisfying the demands of transsexuals. Nevertheless, 'The Convention has always to be interpreted and applied in the light of current circumstances', and the Court concluded with genuine, legal recognition of the evolutionary nature of the question raised: 'The need for appropriate legal measures should therefore be kept under review having regard particularly to scientific and societal developments.'[12] Later, in a French case decided in 1992,[13] the Court sustained the violation, but without using the petitioner's argument, which was, precisely, that scientific data had evolved. More prudent still, the Court considered it 'undeniable that attitudes have changed, science has progressed and increasing importance is attached to the problem of transsexualism'; none the less, it also considered 'that there still remains some uncertainty' regarding the profound anatomical, biological, psychological and moral nature of the

[11] *Dudgeon v. United Kingdom*, ECHR, 22 October 1980, Series A, No. 45, and *Norris v. Ireland*, ECHR, 26 October 1988, Series A, No. 142.

[12] *Rees v. United Kingdom*, ECHR, 17 October 1986, Series A, No. 106.

[13] *B. v. France*, ECHR, 25 March 1992, Series A, No. 232–C; see also D. Salas, *Sujet de chair et sujet de droit: la justice en face au transsexualisme* (PUF, 1994).

questions related to transsexualism and its definition, adding 'there is as yet no sufficiently broad consensus between the member states of the Council of Europe' to lead the Court to conclusions that would oppose those of its prior decisions. In fact, it is only because of the major differences between France and England with regard to the law and practices in the area of civil status (more restrictive in France) that the Court considered the French situation 'not compatible with the respect due to her private life', and it was in the name of 'the fair balance which has to be struck between the general interest and the interests of the individual' that it agreed that a violation of the Convention had been sustained.

Finally, the question of confining the mentally ill gave the Court the opportunity to go further and preclude *any* definitive interpretation of a concept inscribed in the Convention on Human Rights. It affirmed, first of all, that one cannot detain a person as insane 'simply because his views or behaviour deviate from the norms prevailing in a particular society', thereby clearly distinguishing the insane from the dissident, the marginal or the deviant. To this was added the phrase, surprising in a judicial decision, that the term 'insane' itself 'is not one that can be given a definitive interpretation'. That is to say that the notion of insane is evolutionary by its very nature. As the Court explained it: 'it is a term whose meaning is continually evolving as research in psychiatry progresses, an increasing flexibility in treatment is developing and society's attitude to mental illness changes, in particular so that a greater understanding of the problems of mental patients is becoming more widespread'.[14]

Thus, the factors of evolution are the same as for transsexualism: scientific progress and tolerance by the community. The evolutionary direction is clearly indicated: toward 'a greater understanding of the patients' problems'. To be evolutionary, the concepts inscribed in a Convention that protects human rights must none the less obey the dynamic of expanding these rights. Evolution is therefore not abandoned to completely discretionary judicial interpretation. Judicial autonomy is still considerably increased, however, which explains the difficulty in accepting the idea of evolutionary sources itself, because it calls into question the traditional organisation of relationships between statute and judge, or, more broadly, between the transmitter of the norm (statute, administrative

[14] *Winterwerp v. Netherlands*, ECHR, 24 October 1979, Series A, No. 33.

regulation or international convention) and the receiver responsible for its application (judge or administrative authority). Unlike temporary sources, which do not modify the normative order, evolutionary sources openly free the receiver in relation to the transmitter of the norm. More visible when the transmitter acknowledges in a more or less explicit manner in the initial text the evolutionary nature of the norm, the phenomenon is also present, though covertly, at the heart of all jurisprudence that creates law. For example, through their evolutionary interpretation of the *Code civil* since the late nineteenth century, tribunals have made a strong contribution to the advent of a social law that favours solidarity over responsibility. Similarly, the term 'jurisprudential about-face' clearly indicates the reversibility that can stem simply from the interpretative process, and therefore from the receiver of the norm, even though the transmitter neither wanted nor foresaw this potential for reversal.

Not only is temporal relativity tied to spatial relativity, it also touches on the 'conceptual' question of the normative order and, precisely, on norm generation. Taking the monopoly away from statute and granting the judge – and, more broadly, the receiver – an autonomous (or partially autonomous) power to generate law inevitably heightens the variability of sources. We should therefore not be surprised that the destabilisation of normative time is accompanied by the appearance and development of non-legislative sources.

A 'delegalised' order: legislative and non-legislative sources

In systems following the Roman-Germanic tradition where Roman law left its mark, the majestic statute dominates the landscape. Law and statute are not identical because only statute, completed by regulatory acts (decrees and orders) containing details for execution, sets out the rules of law. The judge applies them in each particular case, but he or she is simply 'the mouth of the law'.[15] Echoing Montesquieu's famous line, the *Code civil* prohibits judges 'from pronouncing by general and regulatory avenues' (article 5).

In contrast to so-called common-law systems, where the authority of Roman law was never recognised and where statute is only a secondary

[15] *L'Esprit des lois*, book 11, ch. 6.

source of law that corrects and completes a jurisprudential body of rules, systems following the Roman-Germanic tradition appear to exclude sources other than those of legislative origin or, more broadly, written law (statutes and regulations).

Of course, the French Constitution of 1958 restricts the domain of statute by a definition limiting the subjects reserved to it, all other subjects having a regulatory nature. But it maintains the hierarchical subordination of regulation to statute – with the exception of invalidity (*illégalité*), which provides for allowing a refusal to apply a regulation that is contrary to statute and for voiding it based on it having overstepped its powers. In addition, it limits judges in their function as interpreters of statute to simple judicial 'authority' and not judicial 'power', which would compete with legislative or executive power.

At first glance, the generation of law appears to be organised according to a linear and unilateral conception that leads only one way – from the norm's transmission (statute) to its reception (the judge). I am talking here about a hermetic conception as well, that places the process of generating law in a purely normative field, isolated from any symbolic context. By overestimating statute's place, or more broadly, that of the norm's transmitter, this conception, however seductive in its simplicity and apparent rationality, hides a double omission: the omission of the Other, the interlocutor, who receives the norm and, in determining what meaning to give it, participates in the normative function, and the omission of Others, namely the symbolic field of values where the general legal principles that guide the norm's transmitter and receiver develop and are nourished. There is a sort of implicit cultural code – 'a rule of law that is expressed silently', according to Gérard Timsit[16] – that produces a legal conscience after a process difficult to understand because it obeys neither a hierarchy, nor an explicit causality: 'The principles are at all times whole in the rules that apply them, without ever exhausting themselves in any of these rules.'[17]

This is a double omission that I will try to correct by showing in turn the judge's role in generating law – namely the interaction between the text and its interpretation – and the place of general legal principles where the context produces a legal conscience.

[16] G. Timsit, *Les Noms de la loi* (PUF, 1992), p. 151.

[17] Ewald, *L'Etat-providence*, p. 508.

Text and interpretation: the judge's role

Interpretation begins with the text. But there are several ways to conceive of the relationship of one to the other: antagonistic, between the text, which tries to subjugate the interpreter by providing definitions as precise as possible without room for manoeuvre, and the interpreter, who slips into the interstices of the text, spots the failures or gaps, and finds in them the power to create law; complementary, like a couple belonging to the same mental universe and working together to generate law; or, to use Ronald Dworkin's metaphor, like a team of authors writing the same text with several hands, each writing a chapter in turn, respecting what precedes and announcing what follows. Such would be the judge's role as imagined by Dworkin: 'Her/his decision is part of a story that s/he must interpret, then continue, in keeping with her/his judgment on what will make it as good as possible.'[18] This is where the difference resides between common-law systems, where judges openly participate in the process of creating law, and Roman-Germanic systems, where only textual failures offer them such a possibility.

But this analysis accounts for neither the reconciliation of practices belonging to one or the other system, nor the common tension between the constraints exercised upon the interpreter and the freedom he or she is left by his or her margin of appreciation.

On the one hand, constraints are strong and are not limited to textual semantic precision alone. Judges are sometimes bound by the interpretation that the real transmitter of the norm – not parliament, but the government that wrote most of the laws – takes care to specify through interpretative texts such as circulars or ministerial responses to questions written by members of parliament. Once published, circulars can be cited to the administration. In civil matters, judges are not required to apply them, but do occasionally take inspiration from them. As for ministerial responses, which are officially devoid of any obligatory force, they are none the less invoked frequently by litigants and sometimes incorporated into the judge's decision, which indicates their real influence on the work of interpretation.

[18] P. Bouretz, 'Prendre le droit au sérieux: de Rawls à Dworkin', in P. Bouretz (ed.), *La Force du droit* (Editions Esprit, 1991), pp. 59ff.

Beyond interpretative texts, the judge's task is also framed by general rules of interpretation. While judges are prohibited 'from pronouncing by general or regulatory avenues' (*Code civil*, article 5), they are none the less required to judge: 'A judge who refuses to judge, claiming that the statute is silent, obscure or insufficient, may be pursued as guilty of denying justice' (article 4). Moreover, judges must 'provide a reasoning for' their decisions, that is, they must specify why and according to what rule it is rendered. Reasoned decisions facilitate Supreme Court review (and therefore encourage jurisprudential consistency) and incite stability as judges habitually use the same reasoning, which thus becomes a rule. To this is added a slew of interpretative principles, effectively 'meta-rules' that guide the interpreters' choices among various methods: linguistic principles that, via the so-called 'clear meaning' doctrine, are directly based on the meaning of words (*a fortiori* or *a contrario* reasoning, for example) or on their order in a sentence (role of punctuation, singular or plural); systemic principles that place the text within a system taken as a whole (encouraging the judge to avoid redundancy or inconsistency, for example, which will help choose between *a contrario* and *a fortiori* arguments); and, finally, functional principles that favour the purpose of the rule of law in society. This interpretation is itself historical or teleological when it refers to preparatory works and aims to finalise the text by reference to legislative intent, but it can also be based on avoidance of the absurd, which allows for setting aside a literal interpretation when it obviously leads to a result contrary to the one sought.

The very diversity of these principles provides the interpreter with a wide margin of discretion, which is, of course, increased when the text is incomplete (judges are required to judge) or the norms are in conflict (in which case the judges are required to make a decision).

In the end, it is paradoxically as if the judge, or, more broadly, the norm's receiver, were freed by this multiplication of texts, which increases the margin of appreciation and confers on him or her the status of source of law. Long a hidden source of law, jurisprudence is now officially recognised as such, even in systems with a strong legalistic tradition such as that of France and those of the Roman-Germanic family. This is why the historic opposition between these systems and those of the common law is diminishing – to the extent that the European Court of Human Rights now affirms that we 'would be wrong to exaggerate the distinction between common-law countries and continental countries'.

Pointing out that 'case law has traditionally played a major role in continental countries, to such an extent that whole branches of positive law are largely the outcome of decisions by the courts', the ECHR concludes that 'in a sphere covered by written law, the "law" is the enactment in force as the competent courts have interpreted it'.[19]

Yet one must consider the context that may herald a reconstruction of the landscape by placing both the transmitter and receiver of the norm under the control of general legal principles, which would create a shared legal conscience that would help them determine the meaning of rules and limit their discretionary power.

Context and legal conscience: the place of general legal principles

General legal principles have a surprising status. 'Custom of learned origin' according to some,[20] 'rule of judgment' within the Aristotelian definition,[21] these principles appear to be 'suspended within the spirit of our law'.[22] From 'the spirit of our law' they simultaneously catch moral inspiration (the principle of good faith, the adage *fraus omnia corrumpit* or the rule *nemo auditur propriam turpitudinem suam allegans*), legal technique (principles of two-tiered jurisdiction, contradictory debate, or respect for the right to a defence) and political philosophy. This philosophy is inscribed in the liberal tradition of 1789 (principles of equality and individual, political and economic liberties, and the separation of powers), enriched by the creation of social rights (right to health care, right to strike, right to freedom of association) and fed by pragmatism (state unity and a long history of public service).

This very sketchy list shows not only the heterogeneity of these general principles, but also the difficulty in distinguishing them from simple rules of law. Perhaps it is the case that (being aware of the tautology), the difference between precise rules and general principles is precisely the degree of generality of the latter. Of course, a rule is, by definition, general and abstract, but it fits within a specific branch of law – a rule relative to family law, criminal law or labour law. A principle, however, is the expression of a legal conscience that, set apart as a whole, as

[19] *Kruslin v. France*, ECHR, 24 April 1990, Series A, No. 176a.
[20] J. Carbonnier, *Introduction au droit civil* (PUF, 1990); *Code civil*, arts. 139ff.
[21] Ewald, *L'Etat-providence.* [22] J. Carbonnier, *Introduction au droit civil* (PUF, 1994).

an overview, unites the various parts of law, crossing the borders separating them. Thus, the right to a defence extends from civil procedure to administrative or criminal procedure, while the principle of equality inspires family law as well as contract or tax law, and fraud corrupts the legal relationship (*'omnia' corrumpit*) in every area of law.

It is therefore by their generality and their heterogeneity itself that these principles, derived from areas as diverse as morality, legal technique and even political philosophy, unify (or, more precisely, harmonise, as they do not require identical rules) a legal system or family of systems such as fundamental rights of the European Community or principles originating with the Council of Europe, such as 'pre-eminence of the law', or even the international community ('general principles of law recognised by civilised nations', to which the Statute of the International Court of Justice expressly refers).

Yet the principles play their harmonising role at the price of a surprising cacophony. General principles, whether regarding their origin, their legal support or their value in the hierarchy of norms, challenge all efforts to classify them.

As regards their origin, they are inspired (as is natural law) by an ideal of justice, but are incorporated into positive law as soon as they emerge from existing rules and can be invoked to support a legal argument. They are supported by domestic as well as international law, as the examples we just cited show. Even more remarkable, general principles escape the division between written and unwritten law. Written, we can find them outside the text per se. Thus, it is the Preamble to the Constitution of 1946 (to which that of 1958 refers) that 'solemnly reaffirms the rights and liberties consecrated by the *Déclaration des droits de l'homme et du citoyen de 1789* and the fundamental principles recognised by the laws of the Republic'. Moreover, it 'proclaims', as 'particularly necessary to our times', a certain number of the political, economic and social principles it enumerates (equality between men and women, right to asylum, right to work, freedom from discrimination, freedom of association, right to strike and so on). Similarly, it is in the Preamble to the European Convention on Human Rights that the principle of 'pre-eminence of the law' appears. It is also mentioned in the founding articles of the Council of Europe, while the Preamble to the UN Covenant on Civil and Political Rights refers to the Universal Declaration of Human Rights of 1948 and the principles laid out in the United Nations Charter by targeting the 'recognition of the inherent dignity . . . of all members of the human family'.

The fact that general legal principles, written or not, can thus occupy a variety of places in the hierarchy of norms is a phenomenon even more troubling because it is becoming coupled with the question of conflicts between principles of apparently equal value. Two solutions are recommended. The most frequently used consists, in the Conseil constitutionnel, in seeking a compromise, a sort of flexible dose established according to each text referred to it, acknowledging to the legislature the possibility of restricting one of the principles in order to save the other. This is how, for example, the Conseil constitutionnel acknowledged, in 1981 and 1986, the validity of a few hours' detention in order to allow identity checks to be carried out by the police, considering that the legislature must, in effect, 'reconcile' the freedom to come and go and individual freedom with the needs of finding offenders and protecting public order (persons or goods) from attack.

The other solution is proposed by legal scholars and underlies certain decisions, without being openly acknowledged by the Conseil constitutionnel. It concerns establishing a gradation,[23] a hierarchy between norms of constitutional value that would result, for example, in subordinating complementary rights (such as equality 'before the courts') to fundamental rights (such as the principle of equality). Alternatively, principles inscribed in the *Déclaration* of 1789 could be favoured because they are prior in time: the Preamble of 1946 could only complement the *Déclaration* of 1789 without ever contradicting it, unless it is acknowledged that, though later, the special provisions of the Constitution waive the more general provisions of the *Déclaration* of 1789. Thus, the lawfulness of misdemeanours and sentences, proclaimed in a general way by the *Déclaration*, would not apply to violations specially set aside by articles 34 and 37 of the Constitution.

Reaching such subtleties shows that the very idea of a hierarchy of norms would perhaps be, if not overwhelmed, at least caught in an even more complex muddle, such that the metaphor of the pyramid would no longer suffice to describe such a fragmented landscape.

[23] B. Genevois, 'Normes de valeur constitutionnelle et degrés de protection des droits fondamentaux', *RFDA* (1990), p. 317.

It is as if, with fewer landmarks and more sources, it is becoming impossible for a single metaphor to symbolise the principle that organises the landscape and presides over the generation of norms – as if, in fact, this ineluctable movement has, at last, redrawn the lines on the map of the legal landscape.

3

Redrawing the lines

Despite the reservations discussed in the previous chapter, the various levels of the system were clearly laid out according to a hierarchical principle. It was a pyramidal conception to which Hans Kelsen, the Austrian jurist, remains linked for having announced it in its 'purely theoretical' form: the norms of a legal order do not, he wrote, form a 'complex of norms in force one next to the other, but a pyramid or a hierarchy of norms that are superimposed or subordinated, one to the other, superior or inferior'.[1] This means that each legal order is composed exclusively of a set of norms that are derived from each other by virtue of a hierarchical principle, a supposed fundamental norm assuring the unity and validity of the whole.

Such validity, according to Kelsen, must be accompanied by a minimum of effectiveness, defined as the fact 'that the norm is effectively applied and obeyed, or followed'.[2] To the static conception of the system, he thereby adds a dynamic conception, allowing those organs responsible for applying law – the norm's receivers (but he does not use this term) – a margin that renders each act of application an act of creating law: 'All legal acts are both the application of a superior norm and the creation, governed by this norm, of an inferior one.'[3] Thus, whether it relates to the transmission or reception of the norm, the chain is uninterrupted from the top of the pyramid to the bottom – continuity, or 'transitivity' to use Gérard Timsit's term,[4] of the normative order.

Continuous and stabilised by hierarchical constraints, the generation of norms would also be linear, because hierarchy is unidirectional, even in terms of relations between, not state norms, but between national and international law or between national and local law. From one system

[1] H. Kelsen, *Théorie pure du droit* (Dalloz, 1962), p. 266. [2] *Ibid.*, p. 14.
[3] *Ibid.*, p. 315. [4] G. Timsit, *Thèmes et systèmes de droit* (PUF, 1986), p. 575.

to another, the relation can be only independence or *sub*ordination, according to Kelsen: a monist conception of law that accepts only one alternative and ignores any idea of *co*-ordination.

As reassuring as it might be, the metaphor of the pyramid does not easily account for the landscape we see. Largely incompatible with the instability of normative time due to its very permanence, such a metaphor also adapts poorly to spatial heterogeneity: where should international norms be placed in relation to constitutional norms? And how shall Community law norms and those of the European Convention on Human Rights be situated in relation to each other? The question is even more difficult when it concerns sources that do not necessarily have a written support. Of course, jurisprudence is formed according to a hierarchical principle, unified by the existence of supreme courts placed at the summit of both the judicial (Cour de cassation) and administrative (Conseil d'Etat) orders. But there is discontinuity both in relation to the Conseil constitutionnel and between the two supreme courts. Hence, if there is a pyramid, we must use the plural and add a specific qualifier, namely 'incomplete pyramids'.

There remains the almost insurmountable difficulty, however, of situating within this – or these – normative hierarchy(ies) the general legal principles that were described earlier as being both outside the system as natural law and incorporated into it because they are positive law, domestic and international law, written and unwritten, both superior and equal in importance to statute, and finally both equal and unequal to each other. In such a whirlwind, the image of the pyramid gives way to strange loops that evoke 'leaves of an eternal garland' by which, bringing together mathematics (Gödel's theorem), painting (Escher's engravings) and music (Bach's fugues), the mathematician Douglas Hofstadter shows how consciousness mocks hierarchies.[5] In addition to the tangles he describes – those that 'spring up when systems turn on themselves, for example when science studies science, when the government looks into governmental offences, when Art breaks its own rules and, finally, when human beings reflect on their own minds and spirits' – I would be

[5] D. Hofstadter, *Gödel, Escher, Bach: an eternal golden braid* (Penguin, 1979). See also the metaphor of the rhizome in G. Deleuze and F. Guattari, *Mille plateaux* (Minuit, 1980), especially pp. 13ff., where the authors list 'a few of the approximate characteristics of rhizomes': the principles of connection and heterogeneity, multiplicity, non-detrimental rupture, cartography and transfers.

tempted to add those that spring up from law's many sources when law calls rights into question.

To summarise, while not all hierarchy has disappeared, it has been altered. Instead of a continuous and linear hierarchy expressed by the pyramid image, there appear discontinuous hierarchies, like so many incomplete pyramids, and confused hierarchies that form 'strange loops', to use Hofstadter's image.

Discontinuous hierarchies and incomplete pyramids

As just seen, the discontinuity of the norm-generation process, no doubt reinforced by the variability of normative time, stems primarily from the retreat of statute and the advance of unwritten law (jurisprudence in particular), and from going beyond the state to international law, especially with the appearance of European sources, where written law in fact rubs shoulders with an extremely active and creative jurisprudence.

The best illustration of the interruption of the normative chain, both for domestic and European law, is the coexistence of autonomous and non-hierarchical supreme courts. In French domestic law, there is a gap in the chain between the Cour de cassation (the Supreme Court) and the Conseil d'Etat, and also between both these jurisdictions and the Conseil constitutionnel; in European law, the gap is between the Court of Justice of the European Communities and the European Court of Human Rights; finally, from domestic to European law, there is a gap between the Conseil constitutionnel and the European courts, unless this is regarded merely as a temporary discontinuity expressing only the incompleteness of the process of 'constitutionalising' and 'internationalising' norms.

While one cannot predict the future, it is enough for the time being to show how, given the current state of the law, the discontinuity is both constitutional and European.

Constitutional discontinuity

Such discontinuity is not inevitable, as is shown by the diversity of systems created during Europe's fairly recent efforts to constitutionalise norms by implementing procedures to review the constitutionality of norms.

It is doubtless not by chance that the pyramid image was first postulated in Austria, one of the very first European countries (preceded only by the Swiss Federal Constitution of 1874) to adopt a system for reviewing the constitutionality of laws (right after the First World War). The movement has grown since the Second World War, first in countries such as the Federal Republic of Germany and Italy, the most affected by the totalitarianism of the 1930s. The constitutionalising of law then accompanied the return to democracy in the 1970s in the south (Spain, Portugal and Greece), and in eastern Europe in the 1990s after the fall of Communism. The case of France is more difficult to situate, because the Constitution of 1958 created a mechanism for constitutional review with the Conseil constitutionnel, but limited its impact through a procedure that reserves the right to refer the Conseil to the president of the Republic, the prime minister and the presidents of the two parliamentary assemblies. It was only after 1974 that, by expanding the right to petition to a group of sixty deputies or senators and thus opening it up to the opposition, a simple procedural reform practically changed the entire system, as is shown by a few figures regarding the years 1958–99: the Conseil constitutionnel's activity increased more than tenfold if the first period (1958–1974), during which nine decisions bearing on the constitutionality of laws were rendered, is compared to a second period, slightly shorter (1974–99) but richer in decisions (416). It still has some way to go to reach the some 4,000 decisions of the Italian court or the 50,000 of the German court.

But the difference is not only chronological: it is also a result of the system introduced in France, which limits review of the constitutionality of a law to *a priori* review (before the text's promulgation) and precludes all possibility of *a posteriori* review, whether exercised by the supreme courts of the judiciary branch (Cour de cassation), the administrative branch (Conseil d'Etat) or by the Conseil constitutionnel itself. An extension was considered in 1989, but the draft revision, which would have permitted the Cour de cassation and the Conseil d'Etat to petition the Conseil constitutionnel after verification of the seriousness of 'the unconstitutional exception', failed in the Senate and the revision, revived by a draft lodged in February 1993, has been shelved for the moment.

The current discontinuity is thus maintained and is, moreover, splitting further, depending on whether we consider the norm of written law (statute) or unwritten law (jurisprudence).

European discontinuity

The European discontinuity is two-fold, because there is not only a partial break in the normative chain between domestic law and European law, but an almost total break between European Community law and that of the European Convention on Human Rights.

There is a hierarchy from domestic law to European laws, and the European norm carries over domestic statute. The Cour de cassation recognised this primacy in 1975 and has since applied it to every French statute, even those posterior to European texts.[6] However, the Conseil d'Etat waited until 1989 to admit the superiority of a European text over a later statute. The hierarchy has been fully recognised since 1989, including for Community regulations and directives, which are law 'derived' from the Treaty of Rome,[7] especially since the action for interpretation, which has been instituted by the ECJ and adopted (though not yet instituted) by the European Court of Human Rights assures a certain interpretative consistency.

This normative continuity is not, however, absolute. Contrary to the situation described regarding the constitutionality of laws, *a priori* European review does not exist, which means we cannot censure a law that does not respect a European text that appeared prior to its promulgation. The violation may be invoked only to contest its application, after the fact.

The possibility of an *a priori* review was in fact invoked in 1975 regarding the law on abortion. The Conseil constitutionnel was petitioned for violation of the European Convention on Human Rights, which guarantees the right to life (Article 2). Since the Constitution confirms the superiority of treaties over statute, the Conseil constitutionnel, by applying the Constitution, could have reviewed the compliance of the law with the European Convention. It set this argument aside, however, invoking the fact that the superiority of treaties over statute is strictly conditional, 'provided, for each accord or treaty, that it is applied by the other party' (article 55 of the Constitution).

This decision has been strongly criticised because European treaties, especially the European Convention on Human Rights, are not ordinary

[6] *Jacques Vabre*, Cassation mixed ch., 24 May 1975 (Dalloz, 1975), p. 497, Touffait conclusion.

[7] *Nicolo*, CE, 21 September 1989, *recueil* 190; Boisdet, CE, 24 September 1990; *Société Rothman and Philip Morris*, CE, 28 February 1992.

treaties, precisely because they escape this condition of reciprocity. This was clearly decided by the European Court of Human Rights in a matter between Ireland and the United Kingdom: 'Unlike international treaties of the classic kind, the Convention comprises more than mere reciprocal engagements between contracting States. It creates, over and above a network of mutual, bilateral undertakings, objective obligations which, in the words of the Preamble, benefit from a "collective enforcement".' Moreover, Article 60(5) of the Vienna Convention on the Law of Treaties expressly excludes all reciprocity regarding 'provisions relating to the protection of the human person contained in treaties of a humanitarian character'.[8]

By thus sending the question of compliance of statutes with the European Convention toward an *a posteriori* review carried out by ordinary judges, the Conseil constitutionnel renounced settling possible divergences (such as that evoked regarding disciplinary sanctions) that might result from the interpretations by the Cour de cassation and the Conseil d'Etat of various European texts – divergences that weaken the system and are even considered by some authors as an 'offence to law' and a 'genuine fault in the theory and practice of the rule of law'.[9] But the contrary position, according to which the Conseil constitutionnel could review, *a priori*, the compliance of laws with European texts, raises other difficulties and presents other risks of divergence, this time between the Conseil constitutionnel and the European courts. The only solution is for the Conseil constitutionnel to yield and consider itself bound by the European courts' interpretations, which would amount to its recognising a jurisdictional hierarchy that few constitutional courts have been willing to accept to date. There is no sign of such capitulation in France.

Finally, the discontinuity between domestic and European law also results from the uncertainty regarding the place of the European norm in relation to the constitutional norm. They are both 'supra-legislative', but in the event of conflict, given the current state of law, it seems impossible that the Constitution could be subordinated to an international, or even a European, treaty, which would result in accepting the

[8] *Ireland v. United Kingdom*, ECHR, 18 January 1978, Series A, No. 25.

[9] D. Rousseau, 'L'Intégration de la Convention européenne des droits de l'homme au bloc de constitutionnalité', in *Conseil constitutionnel et Cour européenne des droits de l'homme* (Sciences et techniques humaines, 1990), pp. 117ff.

abrogation or implicit modification of some of its provisions by the treaty. In practice, member states try to avoid conflicts by revising their constitutions prior to European-level ratification. Thus, with regard to the Maastricht Treaty, the Conseil constitutionnel clearly decided that authorisation to ratify the treaty could be given only after a constitutional revision bearing on the two questions considered to be incompatible with the constitutional text then in force – the shared monetary policy and the measures concerning aliens moving to France from other countries of the Community.

As for treaties that are already ratified, not all the problems have been solved. For example, the French government chose, in referring to the Schengen *acquis*, to undertake a constitutional revision on the right to asylum. Meanwhile, the German Constitutional Tribunal and the Italian Constitutional Court had decided – in less sensitive areas, it is true – that the primacy of Community law over domestic law was subordinated with respect to fundamental principles established by their constitutional systems. These decisions in fact resulted in the Court of Justice of the European Communities incorporating into its jurisprudence a certain number of general legal principles inspired by the constitutional traditions of member states, and sometimes by the European Convention on Human Rights, which, perhaps, is a way to initiate a response to the other weakness in the normative chain. More than a simple gap, it is a true break that separates Community law from that of the European Convention on Human Rights, because there is no hierarchy between the two European organisations, simply a juxtaposition of one to the other. The only link between them, beyond the fact that the Union and the Council of Europe position themselves in the same movement toward European integration, is that the fifteen states of the EEC (now the European Union) ratified the European Convention.

It is true that the symmetry between the two systems is but an appearance. One constitutes a true supranational legal order – the Community order – the primacy of which over domestic law is expressly established by the Treaty of Rome itself. The other, the European Convention on Human Rights, plays a subsidiary role in relation to national legal orders: it does not supplant norms, but merely tries to complete and, if need be, correct them, without creating a true legal order of its own. However, the difference tends to blur as the jurisprudence affirms the interpretations of the Commission and the European Court of Human

Rights. These are creative and, as seen above, evolutionary interpretations by which the often vague text of the Convention is progressively completed and enriched, such that we arrive at a set of rules that seems more and more to be that of an as yet unnamed supranational order (the European order of human rights?) whose place in relation to the Community order must be defined, as they may both be invoked regarding the same questions.

Here again, the situation has evolved. When the first European treaties were adopted in the 1950s, the sectors of activity seemed perfectly distinct, without risk of overlap: the economy and the market on one side, ethics and human rights on the other. But we are now discovering to just what extent the issues are related, as for example in the area of biotechnologies, or copyright as discussed above, or even in the case of abortion, considered not only in relation to the right to life, but also, in Community law, from the angle of freedom of services. There is also conflict with regard to the rights of aliens, which arise from both the principles of free movement and non-discrimination within the European Community and the respect of the ensemble of rights and liberties established by the European Convention on Human Rights. This double normative attachment is in fact evidenced by the jurisprudence of the two European courts, which is so abundant that it could set off real normative conflicts, as I show in Part III.

Hence the idea to have the European Convention on Human Rights ratified by the Community (now the European Union) as an entity distinct from the states comprising it. This would signify the supremacy of this Convention over Community norms, and thus make clear the obligation of the Community jurisdictions to apply it and, if necessary, follow the interpretations given by the European Court of Human Rights. This idea, proposed in a memorandum by the Brussels Commission in 1979 and taken up unanimously by the European Parliament in 1982 and then again in 1991, was in the end included neither in the Single European Act of 1986 nor in the Treaty on European Union of 1992, both of which merely cite the European Convention for the same reason as the constitutions and laws of the member states: as a source of inspiration that does not legally bind the Community. Moreover, in an Opinion of 26 March 1996, the European Court of Justice decided that the Community was not competent to make such a decision given the treaties' status, and the Amsterdam Treaty adopted in 1997 did not alter the situation. This treaty, instead, provides for greater automatisation of fundamental rights with the Charter on Fundamental Rights of the European Union adopted in Nice in December 2000.

It is certainly the case that the European Community's ratification of the Convention would pose several problems of a political, legal and even practical nature, considering the risk of getting bogged down in procedures after a string of litigation that could last years. The Community system is already complex, because national jurisdictions can appeal to the Court of Justice in Luxembourg for an interpretation, which suspends the litigation under domestic law. If the solution finally accepted can later be contested for violation of the European Convention on Human Rights before the other European court (in Strasbourg), there would be reason to fear the establishment of a 'litigious society' in Europe that would overtake the American example by a wide margin.

Yet we do need to find a solution, now that the issue has been specifically raised, even if European judges still manage to evade it.

Conscious of the risk of the growth of litigation, the two European courts try, in a very pragmatic way, to avoid obvious contradictions by regularly exchanging information and a set of cross-references, which allows them to take the other court's jurisprudence into account provided they each follow their own reasoning. While the risks of divergence are not thus precluded, these practices are indisputable evidence of a desire for harmonisation between these two European organisations. In brief, there is currently an attempt to compensate for the discontinuity in the norm-generation process from one Europe to another by setting up real tangled hierarchies, of circular rather than linear generation, which belongs to a scheme different even from that of incomplete pyramids.

Tangled hierarchies and strange loops

From rectilinear to curved shapes, the landscape of the law is changing. The painter Juan Gris said, 'rectilinear shapes are more concentrated than curved shapes, which are more expansive', which is true if loops represent an interaction that, rather than making hierarchies disappear, leads to their entanglement, and thus to the appearance of new ways of generating law which differ from each other depending on what types of systems become entangled. If the tangle arises between independent, non-hierarchical systems, 'alternative' hierarchies are created that establish a certain continuity where the normative process was interrupted. If fully or partially hierarchical systems become entangled, the normative levels are reversed – the lower level participates in the determination of higher-level norms – thus tending to produce 'reversed' hierarchies.

Alternative hierarchies (relationship between non-hierarchical systems)

This process allows the avoidance of a complete break in the normative chain, compensating systemic autonomy with a set of cross-references. One could even be tempted to see here a phenomenon of pure interaction, without any hierarchy at all, thus joining up with the Luhman and Teubner German School theory,[10] which presents law as an 'autopoïetic' system, circularly organised and marked by its rejection of the hierarchical model in favour of a perfectly circular model with no centre or summit, no founding principle, no 'meta-norm'. But this theory postulates the enclosure of the entire system and its absolute autonomy, whereas here we are accounting for juridically different systems that are apparently independent of, yet related to, each other – for example, domestic constitutional law in relation to European law, or European Community law in relation to the European Convention on Human Rights.

Hence the analysis proposed here is in terms of 'alternative' hierarchies, which perhaps better evokes the set of cross-references between systems. These references indicate alternately the primacy of one, then the other, thanks to the interactive exchange that characterises general legal principles. It is their heterogeneity itself, in fact, that makes them unclassifiable in the classical pyramidal hierarchy but facilitates the transfer of messages that bind apparently autonomous systems to each other.

Yet we must distinguish between different situations. The idea of a hierarchy between national constitutional norms and Community law is not entirely precluded because of the primacy of the Community order over national legal orders. However, the French Constitution cannot be implicitly modified without a revisional procedure, nor is there any express reference from the constitutional jurisprudence to the Community legal order. On the contrary, the latter takes into account the national

[10] G. Teubner, *Le Droit, un système autopoïétique* (PUF, 1993); N. Luhman, 'L'Unité du système juridique', *Archives de philosophie du droit* 31 (1986).

constitutional traditions and refers to them: first, as seen above, through the jurisprudence of the European Court of Justice, which has taken certain general principles from these constitutional traditions and built them up into 'fundamental laws of the Community'; then by express reference in the Treaty on European Union (the Union shall respect the fundamental laws 'as they result from the constitutional traditions common to the Member States, as general principles of Community law' (Article 6(2)).

The interaction between national jurisprudence and that of the European Court of Human Rights is more clear.[11] The ECHR, on the one hand, in an often implicit and diffuse though identifiable manner, establishes general principles not included in the European Convention on Human Rights, such as accessibility and foreseeability of statute, or the law of proportionality. Many of these principles are borrowed from national laws because they are inscribed in diverse forms and to varying degrees in the constitutional jurisprudence of countries such as Germany, Austria, France, Italy and Switzerland.

Conversely, national constitutional courts borrow from the law of the European Court of Human Rights. While this is obviously facilitated in countries where the Convention is incorporated into the constitution – namely in Austria or, with subtle alterations, Spain and Portugal – this process nevertheless exists elsewhere. The reference can be explicit (about fifteen cases corresponding to seven countries were catalogued in 1989), or implicit (as in France, where the Conseil constitutionnel expressly refers to the European Convention only when it deems the dispute to be about elections and thus beyond its function of judging the constitutionality of statutes). Whether it concerns the rights of those in custody, the notion of a fair trial, the right to privacy or to freedom from discrimination, both the text of the European Convention and the jurisprudence, however evolutionary, of the Commission and the ECHR have inspired several hundred national constitutional court decisions,[12] including in France, where there have been 'jurisprudential signs favourable to integrating the Convention'.[13] Even if, unlike other constitutional jurisdictions (namely the Spanish Tribunal, which

[11] See M.-A. Eissen, 'L'Interaction des jurisprudences constitutionnelles nationales et de la jurisprudence de la Cour européenne des droits de l'homme', in *Conseil constitutionnel et Cour européenne des droits de l'homme* (Sciences et techniques humaines, 1990), pp. 137ff.

[12] *Ibid.* [13] Rousseau, 'L'Intégration de la Convention européenne', p. 117.

sometimes cites ECHR decisions at length within the body itself of its decisions), the French Conseil constitutionnel does not seem well disposed to renouncing its freedom to assess and interpret the Convention's provisions. This attitude could lead to new normative confusion, inasmuch as the national interpretation would in turn influence the ECHR interpretation. Even if the Convention is ratified by all the member states of the European Union, the absence of primacy of one European system over the other precludes any hierarchy, thereby accentuating discontinuity.

There remain to be discussed here the cross-references mentioned above; they are indicative of the appearance of new types of normativity where hierarchies are alternately made and unmade. Here again, it is the resort to general legal principles that serves as a vehicle allowing the European Court of Justice to apply the European Convention on Human Rights as an element of Community law. This is how the ECJ has, for the last twenty years, adopted various principles appearing in the Convention, but as Jean-Claude Bonichot noted, 'without ever going so far as to say that the European Communities would be in any way bound by the European Convention on Human Rights as such'.[14] As has been pertinently emphasised by the same author: 'To say so would naturally have led the Court to place itself under the authority of the Court of Strasbourg somewhat, whereas having recourse to general principles allowed it to remain master of their contents and to adapt them to the system in which they were applied' – hence the current formula incorporating the European Convention on Human Rights, like the constitutional traditions common to the member states, as general principles of Community law. This formula was first used in jurisprudence, then copied in the Treaty on European Union, which places the fundamental rights guaranteed by the European Convention on the same level as those resulting from constitutional traditions, and qualifying them both as 'general principles of Community law' (Article 6(2)).

The consequence of this incorporation into Community law is that the general Community interest and the objectives, primarily economic, of the Communities can legitimate restrictions on rights established by the European Convention. This leads to the maintenance of a partial

[14] J.-Cl. Bonichot, 'La Convention européenne des droits de l'homme et le droit communautaire', *RUDH* (1991), pp. 317ff., identifying about twenty significant cases.

autonomy, evidenced, for example, by the jurisprudence concerning radio and television programme advertising[15] or aliens.[16]

This said, beyond the interaction through the channel of general legal principles transposed alternately from one European system to another, it was envisaged that the European Convention principles rewritten in a simplified version entitled 'Declaration of fundamental rights and freedoms' would be directly incorporated into a Community text. This declaration was approved by the European Parliament on 12 April 1989 and adopted by its Resolution of 12 December 1990. However, the Treaty on European Union did not take it up, and, as seen above, merely ratifies earlier jurisprudence by granting the status of general principles of Community law to the fundamental rights guaranteed by the Convention (but for the same reason as shared constitutional traditions). This perhaps avoided adding a duality in the drafting of the principles to the duality of textual interpretation, but maintained the uncertainty as to whether the principles have been incorporated into Community law or not. The debate may open now that the Nice Treaty has been signed (December 2000) with the possible incorporation of the Charter on Fundamental Rights of the European Union currently under discussion.

Lastly, and in a more fragmentary fashion, it is to be noted that, at the level of the EC member states, the Community occasionally adopts Conventions on international co-operation that have been conceived in the framework of the Council of Europe but which, contrary to the European Convention on Human Rights, are rarely applied because of the low number of ratifications. Such is the case, for example, for the Convention relating to the application of the principle '*non bis in idem*', which, in criminal matters, prohibits pursuing the same person twice for the same offence within the Community; traditionally, the prohibition was limited to the national space.[17]

This all demonstrates that, while it is originally of greater complexity, and thereby more prone to arbitrariness, the set of alternative hierarchies

[15] ECJ, 29 April 1988 (Dalloz, 1990), p. 401, Edelman note; see also examples given by Bonichot, 'La Convention européenne' and the analysis in Part III, below, pp. 178–80.

[16] See F. Massias, 'Police des étrangers', in M. Delmas-Marty (ed.), *Raisonner la raison d'Etat, vers une Europe des droits de l'homme* (PUF, 1989), pp. 51ff. See also the analysis in Part III, below.

[17] See M. Massé, 'Souveraineté pénale et modèles d'intégration dans l'Europe de l'Ouest', *Souveraineté et intégration* (Collection of papers from the Joint Poitiers and Montreal Faculty Colloquium, May 1992) (Thémis-Montreal, 1993), pp. 47ff.

allows, in fact, for expanding the process of norm generation by creating a confusion of norms between non-hierarchical systems. Ideally, on the contrary, when a hierarchy already exists, it should block such entanglements, unless it undergoes a true reversal of normative levels.

Inverted hierarchies (relationship between hierarchical systems)

'Inverted hierarchies' are nevertheless hierarchies because there are still different levels, but they are inverted because the norm is determined by the lower level, which is placed in a commanding position relative to to the upper level, whether it concerns a general norm (a law in relation to a national constitution, or a regulation in relation to a law), or an individual one (a particular decision in relation to the norm that it supposedly applies).

While reversal can thus occur within a hierarchical system, international practices show that it can also appear between two systems enjoying a partially hierarchical relationship between them, as with national laws confronted with European laws.

In both cases, the hierarchy is 'inverted' only if the lower level effectively determines, at least in part, the direction of the norm. The traditional conception of law precludes this inversion. The hierarchy is absolute within each national system: regulations must respect statute, which respects the constitution, and the judge is merely 'the mouth of the law', to borrow once again Montesquieu's famous line.[18] On the international level, hierarchy is either completely excluded (sovereignty of states) or it is absolutely guaranteed according to one of Kelsen's two models: primacy of a state legal order that determines the international order's validity, or the opposite, primacy of international law that determines the validity of state legal orders.

Such a conception precludes the inversion of hierarchies, because it postulates that between each point of the pyramid of norms there exists an absolute determining relationship. Even Kelsen himself, however attached he may have been to the monist conception of law that the pyramid metaphor expresses so well, admits that such is not always the case, at least in domestic law, where he acknowledges the indeterminacy of the

[18] *L'Esprit des lois*, book XI, chapter 6.

superior norm. Whether it stems from the imprecision of the language or is desired and inscribed in the norm itself (for example, when the criminal statute leaves the judge the power to determine the length, and sometimes the nature, of the sentence), there inevitably remains, he writes, 'a margin, narrow or wide, for the discretionary power game'. In fact, the higher-level norm is, in relation to the act of norm creation or of its physical execution, merely a frame to fill via this act.[19]

It is just this notion of 'margin' recognised 'within a frame to fill' that commands the entire process of inverting hierarchies because it expresses indeterminacy of the norm and, at the same time, transfers the power to determine it to the lower level. Already perceptible on a national level (but generally camouflaged because it is within an apparently unified system), this process becomes more visible on the international level, especially with the European Convention on Human Rights, which does not even pretend to incorporate national laws into a unified, supranational order.

On the national level, margins of appreciation that limit the review performed by the higher authority appear all along the normative chain. Yet one must distinguish the hierarchical relationship between a general norm and a particular decision (margin of appreciation of higher jurisdictions in relation to the statute, or lower jurisdictions in relation to the Cour de cassation and the administration in relation to the Conseil d'Etat) from the relationship between two norms that are of general application, such as statute and regulation or, even more clearly, constitution and statute.

The same is true on a European level, where recognition of a 'national margin of appreciation' perhaps enables acceptance of the movement towards the internationalising of law, since it partially preserves national sovereignty. It was the European Commission on Human Rights, chaired by the British judge Sir Humphrey Waldock, that took the initiative to grant states a margin of appreciation, beginning with the *Lawless* case judged by the ECHR in 1961.[20]

However, it was only with the Belgian linguistic case that the ECHR expressly reserved interpretation to competent national authorities and specified the foundation of its doctrine. In this case, the Court remarked

[19] Kelsen, *Théorie pure du droit*, pp. 454–5.
[20] *Lawless v. Ireland*, ECHR, 1 July 1961, Series A, No. 3.

at the outset that it 'cannot disregard those legal and factual features which characterise the life of the society in the State which, as a Contracting Party, has to answer for the measure in dispute. In so doing it cannot assume the role of the competent national authorities, for it would thereby lose sight of the subsidiary nature of the international machinery of collective enforcement established by the Convention.'[21]

The granting of a national margin of appreciation thus rests upon the Convention's provisions, specifically Article 35, which sets out the principle (of both domestic and international law) known as 'double jurisdictional competence'.[22] Since the national judge is competent to apply the Convention, and since he or she necessarily judges before the European authorities do (as an action may only come before the ECHR, according to Article 35, after 'all domestic remedies have been exhausted'), it would seem reasonable to take into account the interpretation brought by this national judge, inasmuch as he or she may have (as the Court occasionally recalls) a better understanding of certain situations proper to his or her country.

That said, there is merely a *power* of appreciation, not a *sovereign* state interpretation; and the ECHR regularly recalls that 'it goes hand in hand with a European supervision, embracing both the legislation and the decisions applying it, even those given by an independent court'.[23] Thus, in the *Handyside* case, 'Article 10, para. 2 [of the Convention] leaves to the Contracting States a margin of appreciation . . . Nevertheless, Article 10, para. 2 does not give the Contracting States an unlimited power of appreciation . . . The domestic margin of appreciation thus goes hand in hand with a European supervision.'[24]

The same is true in the *Klass* case regarding a law authorising administrative wire-tapping designed to prevent terrorism: 'The Contracting States enjoy an unlimited discretion to subject persons within their jurisdiction to secret surveillance. The Court, being aware of the danger such a law poses of undermining or even destroying democracy on the ground of defending it, affirms that the Contracting States may

[21] Belgian linguistic case, ECHR, 6 February 1967, Series A, No. 5 and 23 July 1968, Series A, No. 6.

[22] See W. J. Ganshof Van Der Meerch, 'Le Caractère autonome des termes et la marge d'appréciation des gouvernements dans l'interprétation de la Convention européenne des droits de l'homme', *Mélanges Wiarda* (Carl Heymanns Verlag, 1989), pp. 201ff.

[23] *Lingens v. Austria*, ECHR, 8 July 1986, Series A, No. 103.

[24] *Handyside v. United Kingdom*, ECHR, 7 December 1976, Series A, No. 24.

not, in the name of the struggle against espionage and terrorism, adopt whatever measures they deem appropriate.'[25]

While the notion of a margin of appreciation can thus soothe national sensitivities by limiting review by European authorities, it can also, on the contrary, extend review (as shown above with regard to the Conseil constitutionnel) into areas that apparently escape the European Convention on Human Rights and appear to be within national sovereignty only. One can cite, for example, the resort to disciplinary or administrative sanctions not explicitly addressed by the Convention, but upon which the European jurisprudence none the less exercises marginal review, considering sanctions close enough to the criminal category to threaten individual freedoms to be a 'criminal matter' within the meaning of the Convention (Article 6).

In either case, the margin (national margin of appreciation or European margin of review) results in substituting a pluralist concept for the traditional monist conception of law – even more overtly than in domestic law because European law, one must remember, does not aspire to unification. The concept of law discussed here is pluralist in the sense that it leaves room simultaneously for two legal orders that are neither totally independent of, nor totally subordinate to, the other. Whether it concerns limited review, which could be called a 'relative European primacy', or extended review, which would be 'controlled national sovereignty', the process described shows clearly that between absolute sovereignty (independence or juxtaposition of both sets) and the primacy of European law (dependence or subordination of one to the other), it is possible to envisage co-ordinating the laws in such a way that would arrange the partially distinct legal orders, each in relation to the others.

Finally, whether entanglement binds systems that would otherwise be completely distinct and non-hierarchical (through alternative hierarchies), or whether it is found within already hierarchical systems that are unified or partially distinct (inverted hierarchies), it offers new possibilities and suggests the hypothesis that beyond the American theory of the plurality of 'spheres of justice' simply juxtaposed against each other,[26] there could be real legal pluralism.

[25] *Klass v. Federal Republic of Germany*, ECHR, 6 September 1978, Series A, No. 28.

[26] M. Walzer, *Spheres of justice* (Basic Books, 1983); see also his 'Droit et communauté', in P. Bouretz (ed.), *La Force du droit* (Editions Esprit, 1991), pp. 91ff.

This pluralism would be 'legal' provided that, with regard to criteria of juridicity that remain to be defined, it is sufficiently orderly that disappearing landmarks, emerging sources and redrawn lines do not mean simply disorder and deconstruction of the landscape, but herald a reconstruction, the guidelines of which are still to be understood.

This is the task before us, announced in the title of Part I, that cannot be completed until we provide ourselves with the means to 'build on multiplicity' in the various manifestations described here.

PART II

Building on multiplicity

It is between the lines, in the blanks or in the margins that the future of law, its decline or its renewal, is written.

Decline is a possibility because, by weakening the system's integration, the margins diminish its 'juridicity'. This conclusion is inescapable if we consider that juridicity resides 'in the degree of control exercised over decoding the norm', because it follows that 'the tighter this control, the more the norm's juridicity is accentuated and becomes absolute; on the contrary, as the degree of control diminishes, the juridicity of the norm itself diminishes'[1] – inescapable, that is, unless we hypothesise a 'spectacular turnabout' through which 'structural under-determination [becomes] an advantage enabling the institution of an inter-subjectivity based on imperfect communication'.[2] Such communication, because it is still poorly determined, allows 'more or less the same effects of meaning' to be shared, despite different histories and structures. It is in this interactive context that Henri Atlan finds the property of under-determination to be an advantage: 'this property namely means a stability, a robustness in [a] system's functioning, because systems with different connections can still produce the same functional states'. This is why, despite – or through – misunderstandings, exchange becomes possible 'without our having to forcibly condition ourselves to formal language's transparency and unambiguousness'.

Although Atlan's 'system' is the neuronal network (our brains), his findings are generally applicable to legal systems (social constructs) and bear the promise of the legal systems' revival – the reconstruction of the landscape – that would make communication from one system to the other, a condition of truly inter-national law, possible. But we must verify whether this is a sensible route to take, because we cannot let the goal of

[1] G. Timsit, *Les Noms de la loi* (PUF, 1991), pp. 187–8.

[2] H. Atlan, *Tout, non, peut-être. Education et vérité* (Editions du Seuil, 1992), pp. 162–3.

internationalising law call rationality into question, as it is essential not only as a pledge of legal certainty, but also as an instrument of resistance to the arbitrary.

This verification goes through the three steps that Gérard Timsit showed comprise the process of generating law: 'predetermination', which refers to the conditions of norm transmission (the legislature in the broad sense); 'co-determination', which results from the margin left to the receiver responsible for applying the norm (the judge in the broad sense); and finally, 'super-determination', namely the code of values imposed on the legal field (the legislature as well as judges). It is an implicit cultural code, or, as cited previously, 'a silently expressed rule of law'.

Traditionally, a system of law is highly integrated, and therefore fully 'legal', when norms are prescribed (in the broad sense, encompassing positive prescriptions, prohibitions and authorisations) precisely and unambiguously (high predetermination), when they are interpreted without discretion according to classical Aristotelian logic (low co-determination) and are legitimated by reference to a homogeneous cultural code (high super-determination).

It is true that, even in the traditional view, such a system belongs more to the classical ideal than to reality. But as a classical ideal it is hardly contested, and we try to reduce, or camouflage, any deviations from it. But the landscape is now so transformed that this system can no longer function, even as a classical ideal. The entire process of law-generation has been modified, not so much by the disappearance of old landmarks as by the emergence of new sources, in all their multiplicity and variety.

From precise rules to 'standards', 'general principles', 'guiding' or 'correcting principles', 'notions of variable content' and 'vague notions' – a whole new terminology tries to express, with certain confusion and redundancy, another legislative method. This method consists of establishing norms while accepting a margin of appreciation in their application, which leads, through the questioning of the hierarchical principle and the appearance of discontinuous, alternative and tangled hierarchies, to the transformation of the norm-predetermination process. This transformation corresponds to a less 'controlling' vision of the law, where legal norms 'constitute less rules of conduct than rules for action',[3]

[3] See A. Jeammaud, *Les Règles juridiques et l'action* (Dalloz, 1993), p. 207.

including judicial action. I nevertheless keep the verb 'prescribe' to designate the different legislative methods, because it clearly indicates the idea of a predetermination that, albeit weakened, subsists none the less.

By the same token, the work of interpretation must be reinvented, especially in the continental view.[4] As I have shown, the judge – freed from the legislature – contributes more and more, within the margin left to him or her, to the co-determination of norms. This increased share in normative power requires renewed legal reasoning methods: with vague or poorly determined notions, the laws of identity and the excluded middle upon which the Aristotelian syllogism's rigour is based are no longer pertinent, even as simple means of review justifying the decision after the fact: unless, that is, we renounce all logical reasoning – and thus ratify judicial discretion and resign ourselves to the decline of law. We must therefore look for a base other than classical logic on which to build a rationale that substitutes proximity for identity and compatibility for conformity.

This search is also called for by the changing process of legitimating systems of law. This process has been disturbed by the emergence of a 'law of human rights' that is neither the resurgence of natural law, nor a copy of positivism. Instead, it adds a kind of 'meta-legal' norm to the existing legal norm. This meta-legal norm is nevertheless one of positive law, as it can underlie a decision of censure (of a statute or of a state).

To silent super-determination, which imposes itself through the values to which each society adheres (even more strongly the less openly it expresses them), has thus been added (or has been replaced by) a more explicit (some would call it overly detailed) super-determination, which pits human rights against the authority of the state. The paradox is that this expansion of the legal framework (constitutional or supranational), now extended to statutes and states, is accompanied by a weakening of normative strength, because human rights rest, in large part, on notions

[4] The problem is not limited to the continent, however. In a discussion of domestic law and the dangers of a government of judges, the American Ronald Dworkin proposes a simple solution: application of a 'suitability criterion', which leads to choosing the optimum solution, and a 'political moral criterion', which leads to taking citizens' rights into consideration. Dworkin concludes that it is unlikely that we could thus miss reaching a valid solution in that it can be ascribed to 'the best possible justification in relation to all of the laws held to be acquired': Ronald Dworkin, *Une Question de principe* (translation of *A Matter of Principle*) (PUF, 1996), pp. 151ff.

that are themselves poorly determined and leave the legislature and states room to manoeuvre out of their obligations.

If reconstructing the legal landscape is thus marked by a certain underdetermination of prescribed norms, the question remains as to whether this phenomenon inescapably heralds the decline of law, or if it is preparing a revival – that is, another conception of law, where legal expansion combines with methods of interpretation diversified by the use of new rationales and with the increased exigencies of a legitimation founded explicitly on human rights.

Prescribe, interpret, legitimate: these are the signposts on the road to take in evaluating the conditions under which a pluralism that remains legal – that is, orderly – is possible.

4

Prescribe: from precise rules to vague notions

More than ever, precise, unambiguous rules of law seem to be necessary. Whether a norm emanates from parliament, the executive power or the judge, it must fulfil the 'quality of the law' conditions laid out in detail by the European Court of Human Rights:

> Firstly, the law must be adequately accessible: the citizen must be able to have an indication that is adequate in the circumstances of the legal rules applicable to a given case. Secondly, a norm cannot be regarded as 'law' unless it is formulated with sufficient precision to enable the citizen to regulate his conduct: he must be able – if need be with appropriate advice – to foresee, to a degree that is reasonable in the circumstances, the consequences which a given action may entail.[1]

In other words, the legislature must, by way of rigorous definitions, reduce the multiple meanings of ordinary language. More or less competent to do so – at the risk of provoking, as in Community law, veritable avalanches of normative prescriptions, the overabundance and minutiae of which weaken the readability of the law – the legislature thus guarantees predetermination of the norm.

At the same time and in the same space (national, but also infra- and supra-national), faced with the complexity of situations that law is supposed to resolve, lawmakers are compelled to call upon vague or poorly determined notions, but their imprecision creates blanks, or margins, that apparently weaken predetermination and strengthen co-determination.

But there must be agreement on the terms used. 'Vague' does not mean 'indeterminable'. To be inscribed in a system of law, a so-called vague notion must be determinable. It differs from a precise, unambiguous rule only in that its meaning is not determined intrinsically by the legal

[1] *Malone v. United Kingdom*, ECHR, 2 August 1984, Series A, No. 82.

text, but by reference to the context – that is, to other sets of norms, the extra-legal contents of which the interpreter will incorporate when determining the meaning of the norm. In other words, vague notions avoid legal systems isolating themselves and share an inter-normativity that enables positive law to incorporate other social norms.

The ever-present risk of arbitrariness stems from precisely the fact that these other social norms are themselves multiplicitous, heterogeneous and elusive: hence the need for 'signposts' to indicate to the interpreter which direction to take, depending on the nature of the norms to which he or she is referred. In this regard, a distinction appears essential, starting with the multiple meanings of the word 'norm': between the reference to technical or social normality (that is, to a system where the norm is defined as the average of acceptable, reasonable and fair behaviours), and the reference to an ideal or a must-be (that is, to a system that is normative but composed of extra-legal (political, economic or moral) norms). This is why the analysis of vague notions leads to separating standards that refer to normality, either purely descriptive (that which is) or dogmatic (that which is usually thought),[2] from guiding principles that refer to an extra-legal normativity. Born of general legal principles, and therefore also participating in the process of super-determination, guiding principles become distinct once they are inscribed in an explicitly prescribed norm.

Standards

Not all vague notions are standards. One must set aside notions that are neither specific nor determinable, namely the cases where, since the interpreter is given no direction, there can be no control over the use he or she makes of the margin of appreciation. Such is the case, for example, with the 'principle of expediency', which gives the prosecutor discretion to refrain from instituting criminal proceedings without having to justify the decision, which escapes all review. Similarly, in the current French *Code pénal*, extenuating circumstances are left to the complete discretion of the judge, without requiring supporting reasons or appellate review.

On the other hand, there are notions that, albeit vague, none the less bear indications that refer the interpreter to a 'standard' of normality.

[2] S. Rials, 'Les Standards, notion critique du droit', *Les Notions à contenu variable en droit* (Etudes Perelman, 1984), pp. 39ff.

From the *bon père de famille* (due care and attention) so dear to Roman law and who still permeates the law of civil liability, to the *bonnes moeurs* (good moral character) of the French *Code civil*, there is no shortage of standards in the Roman-Germanic tradition, however legalistic it may be.[3] But it is in the Anglo-Saxon countries that the idea of standards takes on full legal meaning, first with *equity*, a true branch of law that rivals *common law*, which it complements and alters according to the demands of 'conscience', and above all with the almost constant reference to 'the reasonable man', called the 'standard *par excellence* of English law'.[4]

That said, the extreme heterogeneity of standards encourages a return to the original idea: inter-normativity. Standards bind legal normativity to a technical or social normality. In this sense, they are by definition a mix of fact and law. It is at once their weakness, because they reduce norm predetermination, and their strength, because by incorporating other norms into the legal norm, they enrich law through their direct hold on the professional or social milieu. In addition, having broadened from national to international standards, they go beyond divergences between national legal systems, facilitating exchange through shared references to normality criteria.

National standards

National standards are more or less evident and more or less detailed depending on the case, which leads the judge to complete 'textual' standards with a battery of 'jurisprudential' standards.

Textual standards are numerous in certain technical areas where the legislature itself sets out normality criteria through a set of generally regulatory texts. In the area of the environment, for example, ministerial orders set many types of standards: acceptable emissions and manufacturing standards for incineration, combustion or heating plants; standards to protect the environment and fight against air pollution, specific to each branch of industry and applicable to specific classes of industrial plant; standards related to discharging waste into water, adjusted

[3] See *Revue de la recherche juridique Droit prospectif* 3 (1988), entitled *Les Standards dans les divers systèmes juridiques*. See also S. Rials, *Le Juge administratif français et la technique du standard, essai sur le traitement juridictionnel de l'idée de normalité* (LGDJ, 1980) and 'Les Standards, notion critique du droit'.

[4] Sir William Dale, 'The use of standards in the English legal system', *Revue de la recherche juridique* 4 (1988), pp. 887–94.

according to seasonal variations; and noise standards applicable to industrial activities. Similarly, consumer law is considered 'choice terrain for normalisation'[5] and hence for standardisation.

Required by regulatory texts that often refer to business practices, or proposed by the French standardisation association (AFNOR, which is state-controlled but based on voluntary professional membership), the standardisation of consumer goods (see Part I, above) expresses the point of intersection between that which is technically feasible for trade professionals (manufacturers or businesspeople) and that which is socially acceptable to consumers, who are now involved in the procedure for determining and accepting standards. It is in this area that the word 'standardisation' takes on its full meaning of approaching an average acceptable to everyone. While the standard is based on a vague notion – product acceptability – the texts do the work of determining the contents of this concept.

In other areas, the text either says nothing, or simply sets the standard without specifying its components, which are the work of jurisprudence. In French constitutional law, for example, where normative principles carry far more weight than normality standards, the Conseil constitutionnel sometimes couples its compliance decision with a statute containing interpretation directives that can be read as real standards laid out for judges. Similarly, when it bases its review on the principle of proportionality of penalties, one of the rare constitutional standards derived from the idea of a 'strictly and evidently necessary'[6] penalty, the Conseil limits its review to cases of 'manifestly disproportionate' penalties.[7] It thus introduces a kind of jurisprudential standard of acceptable or reasonable proportionality.

The Conseil d'Etat, meanwhile, in restricting review of the administration's exceeding its powers to 'manifest' error – that which is both apparent and serious – imposes a normality standard, seriousness, which enables it in practice to extend the framework of administrative action. First appearing in the dispute over public service and redistributing

[5] See G. Cas and D. Ferrier, *Traité de droit de la consommation* (PUF, 1986), para. 217.

[6] Decision of 19 and 20 December 1981, Conseil constitutionnel, 80–127 DC, JO, 22 January 1981, p. 300.

[7] M. Long, P. Weil, G. Braibant, P. Devolvé and B. Genevois, *Les Grands Arrêts de la jurisprudence administrative* (13th edn, Dalloz, 2001), pp. 27–35, 172–81 and 636–45; L. Favoreu and L. Philip, *Les Grandes Décisions du Conseil constitutionnel* (11th edn, Dalloz, 2001), pp. 427ff.

agricultural land, review of manifest error has spread to areas as diverse as urban planning, building permits and the upper echelons of the police. Initially applicable in the area of prohibiting publications in foreign languages or from foreign countries,[8] review of manifest error is now also exercised over the registration of aliens, namely over measures on deportation or escorting over the border, including when these measures are taken based on a 'state of emergency', another normality standard.

Even in criminal law, where Jean-Etienne-Marie Portalis reminded us that we need 'precise statutes, not just jurisprudence', the appearance of the 'individualised penalty' rule mentioned earlier has led to standards that are occasionally outlined in texts, but are most often fleshed out by jurisprudence. The 1975 German Penal Code thus contains 'principles governing calculation of the sentence' according to which the judge must first 'set the framework applicable to the sentence that he or she believes, in his or her soul and conscience, appropriate to the offence committed' (article 46(1)), and then 'assess in what way and how strongly the general and special criteria require inflicting a penalty at the lower or upper limit of the legal framework'(article 46(2)). The terminology clearly indicates the combination of the normative guilt criterion with seriousness criteria that refer to the average behaviour and normality specific to the standards. Listed in this article are: 'the offender's motives and objectives, the state of mind denoting a punishable offence and the purposefulness it expresses, the degree of non-performance of one's duties, the method of execution and the reprehensible effects resulting from the offence, and the offender's record, personal and financial situation, behaviour after the act and, more particularly, efforts to repair the damage'. Systematised by the German Supreme Court, which reviews judges' reasoned sentencing decisions, this set of criteria has resulted in standardised sentencing.

Such standardisation is found in English law as well, despite the distance separating the Roman-Germanic and British traditions (at least when juries are not involved, because juries never give reasons for their verdicts). The standard contained in the Criminal Justice Act 1991 restricts imposition of custody and controls the choice between other penalties (probation, community service, curfew, fines), as well as the

[8] *SA Librairie François Maspero*, CE Assemblée pléniaire decision, 2 November 1973, *JCP* II (1974), no. 17642, Brailbant conclusion, Drago note.

length of custody and the level of fines. The judge's discretion is thus apparently still very wide, unless a sort of self-restraint develops through resorting to real sentencing standards according to fairly flexible formulae. One such formula is based on a joint publication of the Home Office and the Judicial Studies Board of a guide, *The sentencing of the court* (1964, reprinted in 1990), that defines a set of standards related to the characteristics of both offence and offender compared with the goals of the penalty (dissuasion, prevention, punishment). In 1989, the Magistrates' Association also published a sentencing guide that even includes a 'price' gauge (amount of fine or length of imprisonment).[9]

Finally, a practice highly unusual in criminal law has developed in England based on guideline judgments: two or three times a year, the Court of Appeal pronounces such a judgment to provide judges with unofficial direction for sentencing in a given area (for example, reckless driving, drugs, theft or rape). Presented as narratives, these 'judgments' do not cover every possible case, but try to indicate the major attenuating and aggravating circumstances and their desired consequences on the sentence decided upon. The ambiguity of these diverse jurisprudential standards is that they are not mandatory, but exercise variable influence depending on their authors' authority and prestige. At the very least they clarify the contents of this extra-legal normality.[10]

The system in the United States, with sentencing directives for the primary misdemeanours established by either the legislature or a statutorily authorised commission, is more restrictive. These state or federal directives are real textual standards imposed on criminal judges, subject to discretion that varies from state to state.

The paradox is that without such standards, the criminal judge's powers are broadest in a country with a strong legalist tradition, such as France. Expressly established by the new *Code pénal*, these powers 'for personalising penalties' are organised according to various legal techniques – from different probationary categories to alternatives to imprisonment, from conditional release to sentence reduction and other variants in methods of carrying out sentences – and result in the disappearance of any imposed minimum. Given such a wide selection, criminal judges, especially in the area of corrections, can do just about

[9] See I. Bing, *Criminal procedure and sentencing in the magistrates' court* (2nd edn, Sweet and Maxwell, 1992).

[10] A. A. Ashworth, *The criminal process, an evaluative study* (Clarendon Press, 1994).

anything they want in determining sentences, provided they neither overstep the legal maximum nor invent a penalty not provided for by statute. However, unlike the German Penal Code or the English laws, the new French *Code pénal* contains no indicators for judges other than a reference to the 'circumstances of the offence' and the 'offender's personality' – too vague for these criteria, called 'methods for personalising penalties', to be considered to be true standards (new *Code pénal*, article 132-24).[11]

The only base upon which standards may develop is the requirement, which makes a tentative appearance in the new *Code pénal*, to provide reasoning for the decision when ordering a firm prison sentence. This could lead the French Cour de cassation, like the German Court, to review this reasoning and progressively establish criteria that give normalising content to the concepts of seriousness and proportionality that implicitly control the choice of the penalty of imprisonment (and, *a contrario*, that of other sanctions).

There is one other way in which standards may develop: if the stimulus comes from Europe. In the various areas of economic law, which are those most directly influenced by Community law, national judges must already respect the 'proportionality' imposed by the European Court of Justice in Luxembourg. Meanwhile, the Council of Europe's Comité européen pour les problèmes criminals, noting the disparities in sentencing decisions, recommends 'identifying the pertinent factors' and those 'that should not have any influence on the penalty', and creating a working party to 'systematise the decisions rendered' and propose 'general principles': some kind of European standards for determining penalties.[12]

International standards

In technical, environmental and consumer areas, standards are already being internationalised, either through organisations such as the

[11] See, on the new French *Code pénal*, *RSC* 3 (1993).

[12] 'L'Identification de principes généraux applicables au prononcé des peines, y compris l'examen des facteurs pertinents et des facteurs sans intérêt en la matierè', Strasbourg Working Group recommendation 1989, adopted by Council of Ministers 1992; Consistency in Sentencing (Recommendation R(92) 17), Council of Europe 1993; 'Disparités dans le prononcé des peines: causes et solutions', Council of Europe Comité europeén pour les problems criminels, 1989.

European and the International Committees of Standardisation, or by certain European Community Directives that expressly set normality criteria. For example, the 1985 Directive on dangerous products bases the manufacturer's liability not on fault (that is, it does not matter whether the manufacturer knew the product was defective or not), but on the fact of having manufactured a product that does not provide 'the safety one can legitimately expect' – wording that refers to a normality criterion.

This same observation can also be made in other areas, such as procedure, where the concept of 'reasonable time', inscribed by the European Court of Human Rights, really appears to refer more to normality than to the ethical norm that most 'human rights' presuppose.

The right to be judged within a reasonable time or to be 'released pending trial', when applied in a criminal trial to a person placed in pre-trial custody (European Convention on Human Rights, Article 5) is part of the ethical goal of respecting individual liberty. On the other hand, the same right is granted more broadly to 'everyone', in civil as well as criminal matters and, by extension, in certain administrative or disciplinary proceedings, and thus fully assumes its meaning as a standard referring to normality. No doubt inspired by the famous English standard of 'reasonableness', this prescription is of textual origin, but its contents have been progressively systematised by European jurisprudence. This is a method consisting of combining multiple criteria without setting a threshold figure (the same length of time may be found to be reasonable or not, depending on the case). In refusing to set a threshold, the jurisprudence renounces high predetermination, which would have the advantage of legal certainty but the disadvantage of a reductive rigidity in relation to the diversity of practices. The criteria are defined by reference to concrete data, however, such as the matter's complexity, the claimant's behaviour (namely the procedural initiatives taken) and the manner in which the judicial system has conducted matters (its inertia or, on the contrary, diligence in conducting the trial). Thus, the same battery of criteria can apply from one proceeding to another, from one state to another, and can even be used, with a higher requirement threshold, in cases where the claimant is incarcerated during trial. Called 'relative and complex',[13] this notion of 'reasonable time' therefore appears essentially

[13] See G. Cohen-Jonathan, *La Convention européenne des droits de l'homme* (Economica, 1989) p. 426.

to be a standard that refers to normality criteria. However, European jurisprudence considers that the states cannot take advantage of the 'usual' slowness of trials, nor of the 'abnormal' or 'excessive' cost of improving judicial organisation, to escape censure by European jurisdictions.[14]

The concept of 'reasonable' time is also one component of a 'fair' trial – a more normative concept that refers to an ideal of fairness and can be considered a guiding principle of the trial.

Guiding principles

In order to locate guiding principles, one must look back to general legal principles, which I showed above to be distinguished from rules by their broader generality and their heterogeneity. I noted that whether one considers their origin, their legal basis or even their legislative or supra-legislative value, they appear to defy all attempts at classification. Yet all the metaphors that refer to them refer to concepts of solidarity and consistency: 'armatures' of legal thinking, 'main girders'[15] of the system, 'federating' elements expressing 'underlying values'. General principles would further be, according to Neil MacCormick, 'the general norms that agents consider, given their generality and positive value, as having a justifying and explicative function pertinent to the rules of law in force', or even 'the general conceptualised norms by which the system's agents rationalise the rules'.[16] 'Justifying and explicative' function, 'rationalisation of the rules': such phrases move away from the prescriptive text of the norm to evoke more often the context that 'super-determines' the choices – those of the legislature as well as those of the judge.

This analysis only partially explains the current phenomena, however, because the place and function of general legal principles are particularly unstable. Unwritten principles, such as, more broadly, a system's set of consensual or conflicting values (what the turn-of-the-century jurist François Gény called the 'given'[17]), favour the super-determination

[14] See V. Berger, *Jurisprudence de la Cour européenne des Droits de l'Homme* (7th edn, Editions Sirey, 2000) regarding reasonable period; L.-E. Pettiti, E. Decaux and P.-H. Imbert (eds.), *La Convention européenne des Droits de l'Homme, commentaire article par article* (Economica, 1995), pp. 267–9.

[15] See J.-L. Bergel, 'Les Principes généraux du droit', in J.-L. Bergel (ed.), *Théorie générale du droit* (2nd edn, Dalloz, 1989), pp. 69ff.

[16] N. MacCormick, *Legal reasoning and legal theory* (Clarendon Press, 1978).

[17] *Méthode d'interpretation et sources en droit privé positif* (2 vols., 2nd edn, LGDJ, 1919).

function. But more and more frequently, the legislature itself uses certain principles as a way to prescribe, to associate these principles, which have become 'guiding', with the predetermination process: they direct the interpreter by indicating which road to follow. This road is not the normality indicated by the standards, but an extra-legal normativity – that is, a normativity defined by values taken from outside the legal sphere. Unlike standards – a mix of fact and law – guiding principles are a mix of law and meta-legal values, and harbour conflicts that result not from their poorly determined nature, but from the risk of divergent and sometimes antagonistic determinations, such as when the public political order opposes the public economic order. Even when they are antagonistic and conflicting, their function is nevertheless comparable to that of standards: inter-normativity in both senses – incorporating extra-legal norms into the law for national principles and, on an international level, reconciling various legal systems.

National guiding principles

The proposed distinction between general principles and guiding principles should lead to setting aside purely jurisprudential principles. Yet it is clear that where written law is little developed, as in French administrative law, the Conseil d'Etat performs a quasi-legislative task by prescribing, through jurisprudence, true guiding principles that are in fact considered an element of lawfulness, disregard of which by the administration is akin to a violation of a rule of written law. A 'particularly bold [theory] in a legal regime such as ours', these guiding administrative law principles have occasionally been presented – and justified – 'as an act of faith in the supremacy of law'.[18] This means that the legitimating function may in fact take precedence over that of prescription.

I will therefore discuss essentially written-law principles here.

First, constitutional principles. Unlike standards, of which there are few in constitutional law, guiding principles are numerous in this area. Setting aside the French *Déclaration des droits de l'homme* of 1789 (which, despite its constitutional value, is none the less part of the human rights law associated with the processes of legitimation and superdetermination), the Preamble to the French Constitution of 1958 refers to the Preamble of 1946, which declares two types of constitutional

[18] Letourneur, *Recueil Sirey* 3 (1948), p. 69.

principles: 'fundamental principles recognised by the laws of the Republic', a poorly determined notion because these principles are not enumerated but are identified by the Conseil constitutionnel in its jurisprudence; and political, economic and social principles 'particularly necessary to our times', enumerated in the Preamble, in greater or lesser detail depending on whether they are precise concepts, such as the right of asylum, the right to strike or freedom of association, or vague notions, such as the right 'to work and procure employment', the right to 'health care, material security, rest and leisure', or the right 'to instruction, professional training and culture'. As for the body of the Constitution itself, it is, for the most part, built around the 'institutions of the Republic' among which the powers are divided. While most European constitutions include a statement of 'fundamental rights' (Germany), 'fundamental rights and duties'(Spain, Portugal), 'individual and social rights' (Greece) or even 'fundamental principles' (Italy), this category of 'human rights' in the broad sense has constitutional value in France only because the 1789 text has been incorporated by the Conseil constitutionnel into the *bloc de constitutionalité*. Whatever the case, constitutional law is thus particularly open to this type of statement.

However, guiding principles of legislative origin are more rare, even if the phrase has tended to develop over the last twenty years. It has developed *either* to recall, at the beginning of a statute, a unique underlying principle such as respect for life (law of 1975 on abortion), the duty to preserve our natural heritage (law of 1976 on the protection of nature), the 'fundamental right to housing'(law of 1982 on the rights and duties of tenants and landlords), or the principle of the unavailability of the human body (draft bill of 1992 regarding the human body), *or* to write such a principle (such as public order – combined in the *Code civil* with the good morals standard – or the interests of the child, which predominates in French family law)[19] into the body of a law or code. Such a principle is thus an indication, a direction for the judge to follow in interpreting the rest of the statute, without the consistency or rationalising function evoked by MacCormick necessarily being fulfilled, given the diversity of practices and the technicality of the rules.

A better guide is the method of setting out, at the beginning of a statute or code, a set of principles that, when combined, provide consistency to the rules they co-ordinate by indicating to the interpreter how to

[19] J. Carbonnier, *Les Notions à contenu variable* (Bruylant, 1984), pp. 99ff.

determine their meaning. From the 'guiding principles' of the new *Code de procédure civile* of 1975 to the 'fundamental principles' proposed in 1990 by the French Criminal Justice and Human Rights Commission with a view toward reforming the *Code de procédure pénale*,[20] the two phrases are comparable, even if the meta-legal nature appears more clearly marked in the second, which results from the particularly close relationship between criminal procedure and civil liberties. Proposed to parliament by the advocate of the reform before the National Assembly,[21] these principles were finally abandoned due to the reticence of both the government and parliament. This reticence was slightly contradictory, because it expresses two fears: that such principles (which would already be applicable) are useless, and that excessive power would be transferred to judges. Too effective yet not effective enough, these fears indicate an attachment to technical rules and a distrust of poorly determined notions – but the law of 15 June 2000 on the presumption of innocence finally did establish them.

The goal of these criminal procedure principles was particularly ambitious: they were meant to highlight the procedural lines of force, 'of which the technical rules are merely the more or less intelligible reflection',[22] to inspire a more ethical and less formalistic application by defining 'the spirit' of the procedure, and finally 'to participate, as a first step, in the European effort to build, together, a criminal procedure system that is, if not unified, at least harmonised'.[23]

The primary virtue of guiding principles is perhaps their ability to reconcile different legal systems without necessarily requiring unification of the rules. They have a harmonising, or co-ordinating, property, which is the *raison d'être* of international guiding principles.

International guiding principles

Well before the European idea took legal shape, the search for common principles had come from comparative law. At the very beginning of

[20] See *La Mise en état des affaires pénales*, collection of reports (La Documentation française, 1991), pp. 111ff.

[21] See M. Pezet report, *Journal Officiel* (Assemblée nationale, September–October 1992).

[22] *La Mise en état des affaires pénales*, pp. 111–12.

[23] *Ibid.*, p. 112. See also M. Delmas-Marty, *Procès pénal et droits de l'homme. Vers une conscience européenne* (PUF, 1992), pp. 291ff.

the twentieth century, the comparative law specialist Raymond Saleilles imagined that 'comparative law, through the reconciling of Justices, [would] tend to become, in its outline, the common law of civilised humanity . . . while maintaining, for each country . . . absolute independence . . .'.[24] Others, such as Edouard Lambert, founder of the Ecole lyonnaise de droit comparé (the Lyon School of Comparative Law), thought there was a way to discover a 'hidden global law'.[25] Still others imagined a natural global law that would unite with positive law 'as the soul with the body, to constitute *itself*, specifically and progressively, as the artist's ideal thought is inseparable from the marble, the colour or the sound when constituting, *with* these instrumental givens, the work of art itself'.[26]

It is true that the transformation of the comparative study bearing on national laws into this common law of civilised humanity or this hidden global law is more a result of religious revelation or the mystery of artistic creation than of truly scientific instruments. Alongside codified and doctrinal national law, which 'remains in the forefront', Saleilles places, 'as a source of direction and scientific and judiciary evolution', a 'natural law of variable content'. This is a surprising phrase, borrowed in part from the German jurist Rudolf Stammler: the two components of the guiding principle are evoked, through its function of 'direction' and its poorly determined nature ('variable contents'), but they are still inscribed in the very ancient tradition of natural law.

It took the shock of two World Wars for positive law to develop the first legal instruments for international harmonisation. Beyond the simple affirmation of the 'general principles of law recognised by civilised nations' (Statute of the International Court of Justice, Article 38(1)) as a source of international law, the technique of recommendations, which is without restrictive force but is highly encouraging, enables the development of international harmonisation principles. Examples include the UN's minimum rules or the European penitentiary rules adopted in 1987 and, in the biomedical field, the declarations of the World Medical

[24] R. Saleilles, *Revue trimestrielle de droit civil* (1902), p. 112. See also R. Stammler, *Wirtschaft und Recht nach der Materialistischen Geschichtsauffassung* (1986 [1896]).

[25] Congrès International de Droit Comparé, *Théorie générale et méthode* (ed. R. Saleilles), congrès of 1 August 1900 (published in Paris by the Société du Legislation comparée, 1901), pp. 26–61.

[26] See Ch. Boucaud, 'Les Perspectives historiques et philosophiques du droit comparé', *Mélanges Lambert* (LGDJ, 1938), p. 308.

Association, namely the Helsinki Declaration adopted in 1964 and revised several times, which sets out the twelve 'fundamental principles' of biomedical research and provides inspiration for later works such as the recommendation concerning medical research on human beings with which, in 1990, the Committee of Ministers of the Council of Europe set out a series of sixteen 'principles concerning medical research on human beings'.

However, it is through the system of conventions and treaties that true international guiding principles have developed.

The Treaty of Rome of 1957, the founding act of the European Economic Community, sets out a certain number of principles inherent in the notion of a 'common' market: principles such as the free movement of persons and goods, freedom from discrimination, and 'Community preference'.[27] As for law derived from the Treaty, it is supported mainly by the enumeration of highly technical rules (regulations) and the definition of goals to be attained (directives), rather than by the elaboration of guiding principles. However, the need to fight against fraud that has been attacking the Community budget recently raised the question of harmonising administrative and criminal sanctions, which are part of national law; the use of guiding principles is envisaged in this perspective.[28] In fact, the definition of such principles is largely facilitated by the jurisprudential work of the European Court of Justice in Luxembourg, which, starting with constitutional traditions common to the member states, and later by reference to the European Convention on Human Rights, has identified an entire set of principles (of substance, such as proportionality, and of procedure, such as respect for the right to a defence) that, despite their deficiencies, pave the way for the adoption of common guiding principles. Without using this expression, the Maastricht Treaty on the European Union provides for adopting 'common positions' and 'common actions', on the Council's initiative, in the areas of justice and internal affairs defined as 'questions of common interest'.[29] It also establishes the notion of 'general Community law principles' by affirming that 'the Union shall respect fundamental rights' such as are guaranteed by the European Convention on Human Rights and such as result from constitutional traditions common to the member

[27] D. Simon, *Le Systeme juridique communautaire* (PUF, 1997), para. 249.
[28] See *Quelle politique pénale pour l'Europe?* (Economica, 1993), pp. 319ff.
[29] See Article 31 of the Treaty on the European Union, referring to Article 29.

states (see Article 6 of the Treaty on the European Union, ratified by the Amsterdam Treaty in 1997), which is indicative of the tight overlap, between European Union and Council of Europe, of guiding principles and human rights.

Human rights again appear in the forefront of harmonising principles in other regions of the world and in the United Nations, even if the importance of the phenomenon varies depending on the degree of review exercised by the competent international authorities (the Inter-American Court that applies the American Convention on Human Rights, the African Commission that implements the African Charter on Human and People's Rights and the UN Human Rights Committee that applies the the Covenant on Civil and Political Rights).

Human rights are inscribed in the super-determination process, which is inseparable from the legitimating function and is examined further below. One must nevertheless underline their recent mutation. Born as statements of principle, they have become true legal principles and function as such depending on the various regional or global groups mentioned here. This means they are carriers of certain prescriptions. It is true that many jurists criticise their vague and imprecise nature, complaining that they are too poorly determined. But they deserve closer scrutiny.

'Human rights', defined as true rules requiring that national practices mirror prescribed norms, do exist. The prohibition against torture and inhuman or degrading treatment is, in every Convention and Charter cited above, a text allowing no derogations no matter what the circumstances (even in case of war or the fight against terrorism) and is subject to no discretion. Similarly, the Sixth Supplementary Protocol to the European Convention on Human Rights imposes abolition of the death penalty with the clarity of a quasi-absolute rule, the only exception being war. There is also a prohibition against denying freedoms other than those enumerated precisely and restrictively by the European Convention on Human Rights (a restriction that is much more vague in the other texts – the American Convention, African Charter and UN Covenant), which applies with the rigour of a technical rule and without allowing any discretion.

A last example: the guarantees of a fair trial are enumerated with great precision by the various texts mentioned here (Article 6 of the European Convention, Article 8 of the American Convention, Article 7 of the African Charter, Article 14 of the UN Covenant). In these texts, human rights succeed in combining the effect of super-determination with high predetermination.

Having said all this, these rights, for the most part, stem in fact from poorly determined notions. Respect for privacy or for the freedoms of expression and assembly, for example, is set out by wording that evokes guiding principles more than rules, because it refers to ethical choices and a meta-legal normativity. However, while these norms are poorly determined in the text that prescribes them, they can none the less be determined according to multiple criteria that the interpreters – that is, the international authorities that review human rights – are led to explicate, or even discover.

Thus, the European Court of Human Rights gives an 'independent' and poorly determined meaning to the concept of 'criminal matter' in order to extend the guarantees of a fair trial to administrative or disciplinary sanctions that, without falling within 'criminal law', impose punitive sanctions. It thus obliges itself to establish the components of this concept, primarily by reference to the domestic-law qualification, but also to the nature of the offence and the severity of the sanction, especially in the case of a deprivation of liberty.

Similarly, to judge whether a restriction – on privacy (wiretapping) or on freedom of expression (lawsuits against journalists) – is compatible with the Convention (because acceptable 'in a democratic society'), the ECHR forces itself to establish the criteria of this notion of democratic acceptability, despite it being a classic example of an indeterminable concept.

Overall, from standards to guiding principles, the texts all provide the same process of prescription by norms that are poorly determined, but always determinable according to multiple criteria that avoid the reductive effect of rules. Rules differ from this in that rules either correspond perfectly to a simple situation and thus give a legal solution that is clear in terms of conformity/non-conformity, or do not correspond and become completely inoperable. But the work of balancing and combining these criteria usually precludes the principle of correspondence, because facts very rarely correspond perfectly to all the criteria. Hence the analysis is in terms of proximity and judging compatibility, not conformity. It is thus almost inevitable that the receiver of the norm will be granted discretion to set the threshold of compatibility supporting the decision. Inevitably, therefore, the receiver (the judge in the broad sense, but also the state for international norms) participates in establishing norms.

It remains to be seen whether this 'co-determination' is necessarily synonymous with discretionary power and, ultimately, with arbitrariness, or whether it is possible, under certain conditions, to build a logical and rigorous reasoning that incorporates multiple criteria and enables us to control the use of the margin of appreciation.

5

Interpret: from classical logic to 'new' logics

'When the statute is clear, we must follow it.' In other words, precision in the prescribed norm precludes judicial normative power. But Portalis immediately added a distinction: between criminal matters, where 'we need precise statutes, not just jurisprudence', and civil matters, where 'the task of the judge' is to 'understand the true meaning of the statutes, apply them with discernment, and supply them in cases [where they are missing]'.[1] As a distant echo, the French *Code pénal* approved in 1992 states that 'criminal statutes shall be strictly construed', thus reaffirming the allegiance the criminal judge is obliged to show the legislature (which was so evident in the nineteenth century that it is not even mentioned in the 1810 text). As for the *Code civil*, it has not changed in this regard, and affirms, as it did in 1804, 'The judge who refuses to judge on the pretext that the statute is silent, obscure or insufficient, may be prosecuted as guilty of denying justice.' Required to judge, a judge is, however, not authorised to take the place of the legislature: 'Judges are prohibited from pronouncing via general or regulatory provisions on the cases submitted to them.' Limited to the statute's prescriptions yet encouraged to fill in its gaps and clarify its obscurities, the art of judging, said Portalis, is 'to not expose oneself to the risk of being first slave, then rebel, and disobeying from a spirit of servitude'.

We thus discern today, close to 200 years later, the 'three faces of a judgment'[2] that underlie the *Discours préliminaire* to the draft *Code civil* (cited above). The first face is the 'loyal transcription, tedious copy, recitation and ratification of the statute by the judge'; then the judge's participation in determining the meaning of the statute in the case of omission or imprecision (co-determination, or 'transdiction' as

[1] *Discours préliminaire prononcé par Portalis, lors de la présentation, devant le Conseil d'Etat, du projet de Code civil, rédigé par la commission du gouvernement*, pp. 46 and 45.

[2] G. Timsit, *Les Figures du jugement* (PUF, 1993), p. 164.

I propose to call it to distinguish it from 'transcription'); and finally, transgression, the face of Portalis' 'rebel' judge, who encroaches on legislative power or even opposes the statute in the name of values to which he or she submits his or her sensibilities, history and personal ambitions, but at the risk of 'disobeying from a spirit of servitude'.

Of these three faces, only the first – 'of precise statutes, not just jurisprudence', namely high predetermination and no co-determination – belongs to classical logic. In fact, it imposes a 'syllogistic' model of reasoning that has been considerably enriched since Aristotle, but that is still based on the three laws he identified: identity (there is only one true or one false), non-contradiction (the true is not the false) and the excluded middle, or bivalence (all statements are true or false).

To apply these laws of interpretation to legal reasoning, certain conditions of method and structure must be met. The conditions of method are that the legal norms must be precisely defined and assembled in coherent groups (coherence symbolised by the codes). The conditions of structure are that these groups must themselves fall within a unique and hierarchical structure (a monist conception of legal systems, as illustrated by Kelsen's pyramid).

In domestic law, each legal order tries to meet these conditions, which are firmly rooted in the western tradition. Of course, imperfections of language are such that the legislature can never entirely eliminate imprecision, and the increasing number of norms increases the risk of incoherence, but the task of the legislature is to make certain the conditions of method are met as fully as possible. As for structure, it traditionally falls within the monist conception that is imposed when law is identified with the state. Hence, in domestic law, the syllogism remains a pertinent model of reasoning, except when faced with indeterminate or poorly determined notions, standards and guiding principles. The discretion reserved to the judge does not allow for the absolute exclusion of those practices that are not identical to the prescribed norm, especially since the resort to multiple criteria makes exact adherence to the requirement of identity almost impossible.

Appearing in domestic law, this inadequacy of the syllogistic model is seen even more clearly in international law, the paradox being that standards and guiding principles carry with them both the opportunity to facilitate reconciliation of national systems and the risk of disqualifying the syllogistic model even further. This risk stems primarily from the method. While even in human rights, and even more so in Community law, precise rules exist, many international concepts are in fact vague, indeterminate or even incomplete.[3] This results, no doubt, from their conditions of development: political conditions (which do not offend national sensibilities by enacting overly precise and thus apparently overly restrictive rules) and legal conditions (which use terms that are neutral in relation to the terminology of each domestic legal system).

Add problems of structure, and one no doubt touches on the veritable eccentricity of international (especially European) law, the structure of which is openly pluralist, not monist, and seems literally inconceivable according to the syllogistic model.

Certainly one must distinguish, as I have shown, between Community law, a component of a supranational legal 'order' hierarchically superior to national legal orders, and European human rights law, which merely marks, according to the Preamble of the European Convention, the recognition of a 'common heritage of political traditions, ideals, freedom and the rule of law'. However, from the Community legal order to the common heritage of the Council of Europe, the difference has a greater nuance than first appears. On the one hand, the Community order obeys more or less unified processes depending on whether the norm is based on a treaty, a Regulation or a Directive. Occasionally, it grants a margin to the states in the interpretation of exceptions based on national public policy. On the other hand, the European Convention on Human Rights does indeed institute, though only partially, a supranational legal order imposed on the states, thus partially preserving the monist conception of law.

But when this monist conception is set aside (which can happen in Community law, and much more frequently with the European Convention on Human Rights), the syllogistic model becomes clearly inadequate, because the indeterminate nature of prescribed norms is compounded by a plural normative structure that belongs to several non-hierarchically related and simultaneously applicable systems (national and European laws). This is why my analysis will concentrate on the example of guiding principles emanating from the European Convention on Human Rights. The goal is to show how the reasoning

[3] M. Melchior, 'Notions vagues ou indéterminées et lacunes dans la Convention européenne des droits de l'homme', *Mélanges Wiarda* (Carl Heymanns Verlag, 1989), pp. 411ff.

is built, starting with establishing the criteria, and to examine under what conditions control can be exercised over the use of the margin of appreciation.

In short, to avoid the appearance of the third face – transgression – it is necessary, given the inadequacy of classical logic, to determine to what other logics the judge's work of co-determination should be subjected.

Determining the criteria

Two examples will illustrate the European judge's work of co-determination based on indeterminate notions, or even omissions, in the European Convention on Human Rights. One touches on the notion of restrictive measures admissible 'in a democratic society', which is indeterminate by nature because it refers to the idea that the measures by which a state, in the name of public order, restricts fundamental rights and liberties (such as privacy, freedom of thought, expression or assembly) can be justified provided they remain compatible with the criteria of a democratic society. The other is based on a concept that governs the applicability of the guarantees of a fair trial in Article 6: 'criminal offence'. Not inherently indeterminate, this concept becomes so in European case law because it is interpreted more broadly in order to extend European control, at the margin of criminal law, into the areas of disciplinary and administrative sanctions (which are not expressly referred to in the Convention) and thereby fill certain textual gaps with an interpretation that is openly declared as being 'independent' of national laws.

I begin with 'criminal offence', the criteria of which are now better known by a large number of jurists and have already been transplanted, with some nuances, into domestic law.

'Criminal offence'

The term 'criminal offence'[4] appears in Article 6 of the European Convention on Human Rights where several guarantees of procedure,

[4] See M. Delmas-Marty, 'Code pénal d'hier, droit pénal d'aujourd'hui, matière pénale de demain', *Recueil Dalloz* (1986), p. 27, and *Le Flou du droit, du Code pénal aux droits de l'homme* (PUF, 1986), pp. 317ff. See also, by the research group Droits de l'homme et logiques juridiques, 'La Matière pénale au sens de la Convention européenne des droits de l'homme, flou du droit pénal', *RSC* (1987), p. 820.

generally described as the right to a 'fair trial', are provided for. These guarantees can be invoked by everyone in suits to determine his or her 'civil rights and obligations', or the merits of 'any criminal charge against him'. The authors of the Convention no doubt intended these two terms to refer to the well-known legal categories of civil and criminal law.

But the interpretation given by European courts has evolved. Perhaps influenced by the extension of administrative and disciplinary sanctions, these courts turned to an independent European interpretation of the legal categories referred to in Article 6 – so strongly independent, in fact, that an offence not qualified as 'criminal' by national law can none the less come within the 'criminal offence' of the Convention.

'Criminal' without being of 'criminal law', these new offences appear to set aside the laws governing classical logic: identity ('A is A', or 'the criminal system is criminal'), non-contradiction ('A is not non-A', or 'the criminal system is not non-criminal') and the excluded middle ('if B is not A, then B is non-A', or 'if the system is not criminal, then it is non-criminal').

The goal, which is more or less explicit depending on the decision being made, is to avoid the practice (which one could call 'fraud against the Convention') by which states use extra-criminal sanctions to avoid providing the procedural guarantees required by Article 6. To attain this goal, and thus fill in the gaps in the Convention, European judges try to define criminal offences by referring to criteria they identify primarily by comparing national systems. Designated in similar terms from one case to another, these criteria include: the 'qualification of the offence according to domestic legal techniques' (criterion A), the 'nature of the offence' (criterion B) and the 'severity of the sanction' (criterion C). But the work of 'co-determination' does not end there and, through their decisions, the European courts specify the components of each criterion and the way in which they combine with each other to lead to or to preclude qualifying an offence as criminal.

The components of each criterion (the sub-criteria) *sometimes* come from comparative law, and thus from a legal normativity outside that of the Convention (criterion A, qualification of the offence according to domestic law, in fact requires an examination of the nature and history of national texts, as well as their judicial practices and procedure); *sometimes* from a particular normality (the analysis of criterion B, the nature of the offence, is based on the addressees of the prohibitive norm, who are limited to a specific category in the case of a disciplinary offence, but who include the entire population for offences of a 'criminal nature'); and *sometimes* from an ethical normativity (which could be connected to criterion B if the court decided to systematise the idea that an offence is criminal in nature when it is defined as an attack on the values inscribed in the Convention), which appears above all in the determination of criterion C, because the sanction's severity is judged primarily by taking into account any possible deprivation of liberty – hence the Convention's protection of derogations from the respect for freedom of movement.[5]

This heterogeneity of criteria no doubt stems from referring only to comparative law, which could lead to what has been called 'backward indexing'[6] – that is, an interpretation unfavourable to fundamental rights and liberties.

This said, criterion A is decisive only if it immediately provides the answer: if the sanction is criminal in domestic law, it shall be qualified as 'criminal' in European law, no matter what the nature of the offence or the severity of the sanction. However, if the domestic qualification is extra-criminal (whatever the nuances resulting from the sub-criteria), it is the combination of criterion A with criteria B and C that determines the qualification of the acts.

An analysis of the cases retained under the qualification of criminal offence shows two different ways in which the criteria can be combined. The first corresponds to the *Engel* and the *Campbell and Fell* decisions, and consists of retaining the severity of the sanction as the preponderant criterion. It concerns military personnel sentenced to disciplinary sanctions of twelve days' mandatory aggravated arrest and three to six months' assignment to a disciplinary unit, and prisoners who, as a disciplinary sanction, lost 670 days' sentence reduction.[7]

With respect to this first scheme, two other decisions (*Oztürk* and *Lutz*) are difficult to understand, because the sanction was simply a small administrative fine.[8] In the *Oztürk* decision, the offence was none the

5 The detailed analyses of these criteria appears in the articles cited above in this chapter, in particular in the form of a table in the article published in *RSC* (1987).

6 O. de Schutter, 'L'Interprétation de la Convention européenne des droits de l'homme, un essai de démolition', *Revue de droit international des sciences diplomatiques et politiques* (1992), p. 83.

7 *Engel v. Netherlands*, ECHR, 8 June 1976 (military sanctions) and *Campbell and Fell v. United Kingdom*, ECHR, 28 June 1984 (penal sanctions).

8 *Oztürk v. Federal Republic of Germany*, ECHR, 21 February 1984, Series A, No. 73, and *Lutz v. Federal Republic of Germany*, ECHR, 25 August 1987, Series A, No. 123 (administrative sanctions ordered in a traffic case).

less qualified as criminal, and the government ordered to pay interpreter fees, but this was because of the other criteria:

(a) with regard to criterion A (qualification according to domestic legal technique), it appeared that the offence had long been considered criminal in German law and followed a procedure fairly close to criminal procedure: moreover, such offences continue to 'be classified as part of the criminal law in the vast majority of the Contracting States';
(b) with regard to criterion B (nature of the infraction), the ECHR insists on the protected order and emphasises that the rule of law transgressed 'does not address a determined group with a particular status – in the manner, for example, of disciplinary law – but all citizens in their capacity as users of the road'.

Even more clearly, the *Lutz* decision specifies that the last two criteria (nature of the offence and severity of the sanction) are 'alternative and not cumulative': 'For Article 6 to apply in virtue of the words "criminal charge", it suffices that the offence in question should by its nature be "criminal" from the point of view of the Convention, as in the instant case, or should have made the person concerned liable to a sanction which, in its nature and degree of severity, belongs in general to the "criminal" sphere.'

It is the first of the two schemes (which favours the criterion of severity of the sanction) that seems best to fulfil the European Convention's primary objective: to protect human rights, liberty and security. Whether criminal or not in domestic law, a sanction that deprives a person of their liberty – like all sanctions that heavily impact upon protected rights, such as the right to hold property or to exercise a profession (definitive confiscation of certain goods, very high fines, permanent or long-lasting prohibition from exercising a profession, etc.) – should, as a 'criminal' sanction, benefit from the guarantees of a fair trial. This means the judge's work of co-determination incorporates elements of superdetermination, inasmuch as the choices are imposed by the cultural code inscribed in the Convention.

The second scheme, however, by favouring the two other criteria, partially refers to comparative law (criterion A), but mostly to a fairly vague normality. As I demonstrated above, the nature of the offence (criterion B) was barely examined with reference to its contents – to the values it offends – but more by reference to the norm's addressees: traffic violations, unlike purely disciplinary offences, concern the entire populace. This variable weighting, which results in considering criteria B and C as alternatives, can therefore give the impression that the judge chooses one or the other according to the result he or she wishes to obtain: to retain or set aside the 'criminal' qualification. In short, that the judge favours his or her personal cultural code over the common ethic inscribed in the European Convention. In fact, in assimilating certain administrative sanctions into the criminal category, the second scheme allows for a reconciliation of national legislation and unarguably contributes to extending guarantees. Such extension, however, is not based directly on the text of the Convention itself, but on a kind of general postulate of the legitimacy of any extension of the scope of application of the Convention. More recently, the ECHR specified[9] that even if the criteria are not determinative in themselves alone, they can, when combined and compounded, confer the status of 'criminal' on the charge.

This example thus shows that the process of co-determination, by referring to multiple criteria, is not in itself a source of arbitrariness, because the first scheme examined above has a well-argued base. It becomes so, however, when the determination either of the criteria or of their respective values is based, not on the common ethic, but on more vague considerations mixed with discretion.

At first glance, this risk is lower with restrictive measures admissible 'in a democratic society', because the criteria are imposed by the Convention itself, but it reappears in other ways.

Restrictive measures admissible 'in a democratic society'

Restrictive measures admissible 'in a democratic society' are highly diverse and include both criminal and disciplinary sanctions that invade our privacy: repressing homosexuality, limiting a journalist's freedom of expression, or restricting a peaceful demonstrator's freedom of assembly. Wiretapping is another form of privacy invasion; measures limiting foreigners' family groupings or separating them from their families through expulsions or escorting them over the border are a form of interference

[9] *Bendenoun v. France*, ECHR, 24 February 1994, 18 EHRR 54.

with family life. From the point of view of the European Convention on Human Rights, all of these examples are analysed the same way: as restrictions on protected rights and freedoms. Such restrictions are justified if the measure is considered 'necessary in a democratic society', and censured if not.

One must thus recognise that not all rights have absolute value and admit that, in line with the French *Déclaration des droits de l'homme* of 1789, the exercise of one's rights has 'limits'. According to the *Déclaration*, such limits are those that 'guarantee to other members of society the exercise of the same rights', it being specified that 'these limits can be defined only by statute' (Article 4 on freedom). Article 10 adds a restriction on the freedom to express thoughts and opinions, which is recognised only on the less individualistic and more authoritarian condition 'that their manifestation does not disturb the public order established by the law'.

Like the *Déclaration* of 1789, but more systematically, the European Convention sets out the double criteria of the restrictive measure's lawfulness (criterion A) and the legitimate objective that supports it (criterion B). But it also adds a third criterion: necessity 'in a democratic society' (criterion C).

The concept of a restrictive measure admissible in a democratic society is thus a guiding principle, in that it imposes no precise rules, but indicates to the judge what direction to take when interpreting. By specifying the contents of each criterion and the way in which they combine, the judge exercises a power of co-determination.

The criteria must be distinguished from one another, however, because the legitimate objective (criterion B) is examined abstractly, by strict reference to the Convention's long but limiting list, which includes the prevention of disorder and crimes and the protection of public safety, health, morals, the rights and freedoms of others (Articles 8 to 11), national security (Articles 8, 10 and 11), the country's economic well-being (Article 8) and, finally, the authority and impartiality of the judiciary (Article 10). Thus, when it rules on the validity of a restrictive measure, the ECHR examines whether the objective stated by the state to support the measure corresponds to a case on the list. But the criterion is so broad that it has never yet supported a decision of censure. However, criteria A and C play a decisive role: hence the importance of case law in co-determining them.

A European judge can cling to a formal conception of criterion A (lawfulness of the restrictive measure), verifying only that the measure is provided for by a text of law. But in fact, he or she proceeds differently, moving away from this conception via an extension and an additional requirement. The extension consists of taking into account the diversity of national laws (*common-law* judge-made systems and legalist systems in the Roman-Germanic tradition) and their evolution – which leads to a certain reconciliation between the systems, as lawfulness 'encompasses both written and non-written law' – and applying this definition not only to British cases, but also to Swiss or French cases, thus to traditionally legalist systems. As mentioned earlier, the ECHR in fact considers that it would be wrong 'to exaggerate the distinction' between the two major legal systems, because 'statute law is also invested with importance in the former [common-law countries]; vice versa, case law has traditionally played a major role in Continental countries, to such an extent that whole branches of positive law are largely the outcome of decisions by the courts'.[10]

To this conception, which is extensive regarding sources of 'European lawfulness', Strasbourg case law none the less adds a narrow concept regarding contents. Inspired indirectly by the constitutional jurisprudence of certain states that require, particularly in criminal law, precise legislative texts, the European courts for the protection of human rights consider that European lawfulness also includes 'the quality of the law'. They thus require the law to be accessible to citizens and stated precisely enough for them, 'if need be with appropriate advice – to foresee, to a degree that is reasonable in the circumstances, the consequences which a given action may entail'.[11]

Finally, criterion C, 'democratic necessity', is defined progressively, decision by decision, beginning with highly diverse elements that we associate as much with normality (the state of necessity invoked by the state in question and the severity of the measure taken) as with an ethical normality that, above and beyond the European Convention, refers to what one could call democratic values.

The subjectivity of the judge colours his or her appreciation of each of these elements. Thus, the examination of the state of necessity usually

[10] *Kruslin v. France*, ECHR, 24 April 1990, Series A, No. 1760; compare *Sunday Times v. United Kingdom*, ECHR, 26 April 1979, Series A, No. 30.

[11] *Malone v. United Kingdom*, ECHR, 2 August 1984, Series A, No. 82.

leads to verifying the existence of a 'pressing social need' and whether the motives cited to support the restrictive measure appear 'pertinent and sufficient'. For example, in a case of administrative wiretapping (and thus, more generally, of measures that invaded privacy) the ECHR emphasised that 'democratic societies nowadays find themselves threatened by highly sophisticated forms of espionage and by terrorism, with the result that the State must be able, in order effectively to counter such threats, to undertake the secret surveillance of subversive elements operating within its jurisdiction'.[12]

This verification is not systematic, however, and the Court sometimes even dispenses with it entirely, particularly in drugs cases, as if the state of necessity were so obvious that the state in question need not explain its reasoning.[13] The judge thus implicitly subscribes to a conception of dangerousness that neither comparative law nor the European Convention seems to impose.

As for the severity of the measure, the judge examines its objective, breadth and methods. For example, the judge in the wiretapping case held that administrative wiretapping must be 'confined to cases in which there are factual indications for suspecting a person of planning, committing or having committed certain serious criminal acts', and that 'so-called exploratory or general surveillance is not permitted by the contested legislation'.[14]

Similarly, regarding the freedom of expression of a journalist sentenced for having criticised the Austrian chancellor, Bruno Kreisky, in an article, the judge noted that the sanction (confiscation and seizure of editions of the newspaper and publication of the conviction) had not prevented the journalist from expressing himself because his articles were already widely distributed. However, he considered that the sanction 'none the less amounted to a kind of censure, which would be likely to discourage him from making criticisms of that kind again in future'. The decision specifies that 'in the context of political debate such a sentence would be likely to deter journalists from contributing to public discussion of issues affecting the life of the[ir] community' and, similarly, that it 'is liable to hamper the press in performing its task as purveyor of information and public watchdog'.[15]

[12] *Klass v. Federal Republic of Germany*, ECHR, 6 September 1978, Series A, No. 28.

[13] *Lüdi v. Switzerland*, ECHR, 15 June 1992, Series A, No. 238.

[14] *Lingens v. Austria*, ECHR, 8 July 1986, Series A, No. 103.

[15] *Ibid.* See also *Sunday Times v. United Kingdom, No. 2*, ECHR, 26 November 1991.

Along with the intrinsic severity of the restrictive measure, the judge also took into account the possible existence of other, less restrictive yet equally effective measures (extrinsic severity) and noted, for wiretaps for example, that they 'can be prescribed only if establishing the facts by another method is doomed to failure or considerably hindered'. In other words, the measure's severity is acceptable in this case but, *a contrario*, it could also not be acceptable.

Democratic values are the final element of appreciation of whether a restrictive measure is or is not acceptable. European judges try to determine them by referring to ethical norms common to countries of the Council of Europe, even if they are not all a result of the European Convention.[16]

Democracy implies a review of the use made of the restrictive measures provided for by statute. The rule of law, to which the Convention's Preamble refers, requires, according to the ECHR, 'that an interference by the executive authorities with an individual's rights should be subject to an effective control which should normally be assured by the judiciary, at least in the last resort, judicial control offering the best guarantees of independence, impartiality and a proper procedure'. However, the Court allows judicial authority to be precluded when there is an existing review exercised by an authority whose members are 'independent of the authorities carrying out the surveillance' and 'vested with sufficient powers and competence to exercise an effective and continuous control'. The Court thus considered, with regard to a committee composed of members of the German parliament (competent, according to the German statute, to authorise administrative wiretaps and to review their application), 'that the democratic character is reflected in the balanced membership of the Parliamentary Board. The opposition is represented on this body and is therefore able to participate in the control of the measures ordered by the competent Minister who is responsible to the Bundestag.'[17]

Democratic values also imply what one might call 'a democratic spirit', a concept that is more political than legal, yet is included in European judges' reasoning, particularly in cases involving morals and the press. For example, in a British case where the editor of a 'little red book' on sexual education for schoolchildren was criminally convicted for outrage

[16] S. Marks, 'The European Court of Human Rights and its "democratic society"', *The British Yearbook of International Law* (Clarendon Press, 1995), pp. 209ff.

[17] All quotation in this paragraph is from *Klass v. Federal Republic of Germany*.

against morals, the ECHR examined this restriction on the freedom of expression by paying 'the utmost attention to the principles characterising a "democratic society"'. Noting that freedom of expression constitutes 'one of the essential foundations of such a society, one of the basic conditions for its progress and for the development of every man', it added that this freedom 'is applicable not only to "information" or "ideas" that are favourably received or regarded as inoffensive or as a matter of indifference, but also to those that offend, shock or disturb the State or any sector of the population . . . Such are the demands of that pluralism, tolerance and broadmindedness without which there is no "democratic society".'[18]

This definition is frequently reused, especially in cases involving the press, where 'these principles are of particular importance'. While the press must not cross the lines drawn primarily to protect a person's reputation, 'it is nevertheless incumbent on it to impart information and ideas on political issues just as on those in other areas of public interest. Not only does the press have the task of imparting such information and ideas: the public also has a right to receive them.' Were it otherwise, the press could not play its indispensable 'watchdog' role. In fact, according to the ECHR, 'Freedom of the press furthermore affords the public one of the best means of discovering and forming an opinion of the ideas and attitudes of political leaders. More generally, freedom of political debate is at the very core of the concept of a democratic society which prevails throughout the Convention.' This is why it adds 'the interests of open discussion of political questions' to the other components of 'democratic spirit'.[19] At the same time, the Court affirms, in areas as varied as trade union law and criminal repression of homosexuality between adults, its conflicting and pluralist conception of democratic spirit: 'democracy does not simply mean that the views of a majority must always prevail: a balance must be achieved which ensures the fair and proper treatment of minorities and avoids any abuse of a dominant position'.[20]

By comparing it to 'criminal offence', one can take stock of the enormous co-determination work done on restrictive measures admissible

[18] *Handyside v. United Kingdom*, ECHR, 7 December 1976, Series A, No. 24.

[19] *Lingens v. Austria.*

[20] *Young, James and Webster v. United Kingdom*, ECHR, 13 August 1981, Series A, No. 44; also *Dudgeon v. United Kingdom*, ECHR, 22 October 1981 and *Norris v. Republic of Ireland*, ECHR, 26 October 1988.

'in a democratic society'. This is a tedious job that sometimes refers to concepts that are difficult to determine, such as pluralism, which I noted above was 'intrinsically indefinite', in that its limits are always being pushed back as far as possible, to the point where peaceful co-existence of conflicting opinions and interests is no longer possible.[21]

With regard to pluralism and, more broadly, the 'democratic spirit', it is extremely difficult to distinguish what belongs to a common ethical normativity (that is, a super-determination based on the Council of Europe's cultural code) and what is the judge's personal choice. Is this arbitrariness, limited only by 'considerations of discretion, more particularly by the Court's constant effort to avoid shocking – to make its role acceptable not by the objectivity of its mission, but by the political timidity of its interventions'?[22]

The question must be asked. But the answer will not come from simply examining the contents of each criterion, nor from a single statement of 'principles of interpretation' that do not have equal roles, depending on whether they are filling a gap or interpreting a poorly determined notion.

I have noted the importance of 'independent' interpretation, via which the European judge identifies the applicable criteria him- or herself, when it concerned filling a gap in the Convention regarding a 'criminal offence'. I pointed out that the risk of arbitrariness came more from the weighting of the criteria than from their contents, since the existence of two different schemes to combine the criteria gives the judge complete freedom, depending on the decision he or she wishes to reach, to choose the preponderant criterion. With opposite effect, one can also see an invariability in the scheme combining the criteria with other restrictive measures (a poorly determined notion, the criteria of which appear in the Convention).

The Court systematically examines the three criteria for measures admissible 'in a democratic society' in the same order, which indicates the decisive weight of the first criterion, lawfulness. If the conditions for

[21] M.-L. Pavia, 'L'Exigence du pluralisme, fondement de la démocratie, jurisprudence constitutionnelle', *Revue administrative* (1990), p. 320. Regarding all the criteria identified in the European jurisprudence, see M. Delmas-Marty (ed.), *The European Convention on Human Rights: international protection versus national restrictions* (Kluwer, 1992), esp. F. Ost, 'The original canons of interpretation of the European Convention on Human Rights', pp. 283ff. and M. Delmas-Marty, 'The richness of underlying legal reasoning', pp. 319ff.

[22] See de Schutter, 'L'Interprétation de la Convention européenne'.

lawfulness are not satisfied, the restrictive measure is censured without the Court proceeding to an examination of the other criteria. The same is no doubt true in the hypothesis where the measure's supporting objective is judged to be illegitimate with respect to the list set out in the Convention. This means that 'democratic necessity' is merely complementary when the other two criteria are already satisfied, which then sends the most poorly determined and least determinable reference, 'democratic spirit', all the way to the end of the chain of reasoning, as the final element of the third criterion – hence circumscribing, even if not completely eliminating, the risk of arbitrariness.

In the end, the principal difficulty in the European's judge's work of co-determination is not the search for criteria to determine the meaning of the guiding principles 'criminal offence' and restrictive measures admissible 'in a democratic society': it is reasoning logically based on these criteria. It is a practical difficulty if we apply the syllogistic model and require, in relation to each criterion, strict identity: their very plurality risks leading to a dead end, because no legal system will escape censure on one point or another. And it is a purely logical difficulty if the examination 'of the whole', to which European judges claim to be very attached, leads them to evaluate each case in terms of proximity rather than identity (thus reconciling rather than unifying national systems), because proximity implies a margin between identity and non-identity and at the same time disqualifies the syllogistic model because the 'non-identical' is not always considered as the 'excluded middle'.

This is why the margin of appreciation, which appears to be indispensable in practice, demands the use of other logics to control its use.

Use of the margin of appreciation

On the one hand, the interpretation of concepts such as 'criminal offence' is independent of national laws, that is, it is predominantly European; on the other, a 'national' margin is granted to the states to evaluate the criterion of the 'democratic necessity' of restrictive measures. Occasionally emphasised,[23] the opposition between independent interpretation and the granting of a national margin of appreciation is only superficial, because the former is concerned with filling in the Convention's

[23] *Ibid.*

gaps regarding extra-criminal punitive sanctions and the latter interpreting an imprecise concept, the common goal being to determine the meaning of a guiding European principle by simultaneously referring to national law and taking into account the 'common heritage of traditions and ideals' evoked in the Preamble of the Convention. In other words, it means choosing a pluralist, rather than a monist, conception of law every time – pluralist in the sense that the same practice is simultaneously part of two different legal orders, the coexistence of which characterises a situation one could call 'controlled national sovereignty' or 'relative European primacy', depending on which of the two processes observed result from it.[24]

'Controlled national sovereignty' involves extending European supervision to practices that seem to belong strictly to national sovereignty, such as resort to administrative, disciplinary or penitentiary sanctions not explicitly cited in the European Convention, but upon which European jurisprudence none the less exercises marginal control, considering as a 'criminal offence', within the meaning of Articles 6 and 7, sanctions sufficiently similar to the 'criminal' category to threaten individual liberties.

'Relative European primacy' involves, on the contrary, a self-limitation of European supervision in the face of practices that are, in fact, explicitly placed under the Convention's umbrella, such as restrictions on fundamental freedoms (privacy, freedom of thought, opinion, expression, religion and so on), authorised only in so far as they are admissible 'in a democratic society'. This self-limitation is, moreover, also applied to derogations accepted in cases of war or other dangers threatening the nation's survival, but only temporarily and 'only as strictly required by . . . the situation' (Article 15). In these areas, the European courts consider that the system of restrictions and derogations rests on the evaluation of national interests first: Articles 8 to 11 enumerate the various objectives that can legitimate restrictions in the name of what is called, in domestic law, 'public order', and Article 15 is a sort of application of the theory of 'exceptional circumstances'. Thus, when asked to decide whether the exceptional measures taken to combat terrorism in Ireland (namely long-term confinement without trial) were excessive,

[24] See M. Delmas-Marty and M. L. Izorche, 'Marge nationale d'appréciation et internationalisation du droit: reflexions sur la validité formelle d'un droit commun pluraliste', *Revue internationale du droit comparé* 4 (2000), pp. 753ff.

the ECHR emphasised that the national authorities were 'by reason of their direct and continuous contact with the pressing needs of the moment . . . in principle in a better position than the international judge to decide both on the presence of such an emergency and on the nature and scope of derogations necessary to avert it'. It thus granted to the states a certain margin of appreciation, but immediately specified that 'the States do not enjoy an unlimited power in this respect'.[25]

Unlike either sovereign appreciation or European primacy, the doctrine of the national margin of appreciation, like that of the European margin of review, openly recognises (well before the phrase was taken up by the Maastricht Treaty regarding the European Union of the fifteen member states) the 'subsidiary nature' of the international collective-enforcement mechanism instituted by the Convention. Subsidiarity has meant abandoning the principle of hierarchy, and thus of the subordination of national norms to European ones, in favour of a process of co-ordination, which is politically more acceptable to the states.

At the same time, the three laws of classical logic are called into question again: the law of identity (the national practice need not be 'identical' to the European norm), the excluded middle (a national practice that differs from the European norm is not necessarily 'excluded' from the European systems) and even the law of non-contradiction (the same practice may be both criminal under the European system and not criminal under domestic law). This is how a different legal reasoning develops: the requirement of identity is replaced by a more limited requirement of 'proximity', which implies implementation of a gradation scale. Decision-making is thus changed, because only identity makes rendering a decision of conformity possible. Proximity, on the other hand, excludes the concept of conformity and cannot lead to a jurisdictional decision until after a threshold has been set, even implicitly, above which there is deemed sufficient proximity for the practice to be considered 'compatible' with the reference norm. Thus the identity–conformity pair is replaced with a proximity–compatibility pair characterised by referring to a gradation scale and setting a threshold for decision. It is therefore only after having analysed both of these pairs of concepts that it is possible to take sides regarding the risk of arbitrariness and the pertinence of new logics as a means to control the use

25 *Ireland v. United Kingdom*, ECHR, 18 January 1978, Series A, No. 25; also *Klass* and *Handyside*; see also *Brennigan and McBride v. United Kingdom*, ECHR, 26 May 1993, Series A, No. 258b.

of a 'margin' in legal reasoning. Here, it involves the national margin of appreciation and the European margin of supervision, but in French domestic law this can be the margin of parliament faced with a review of constitutionality, of the administration and the government faced with review by the Conseil d'Etat, or even of the expert faced with the judge and the judge with the law.

The gradation scale

The gradation is sometimes explicit in the reasoning of the ECHR. For example, in the German case cited earlier, it is clearly said that not all invasions of privacy through wiretapping are incompatible with the European Convention, because the qualification depends on the degree of invasion: 'The first question to be answered is *whether* and, in the affirmative, *to what degree* the contested legislation, by allowing such surveillance measures, can be analysed as an invasion in the exercise of the right guaranteed to the claimant under Article 8(1)' (emphasis added).

Similarly, in the *Handyside* case, the Court raised the absence of a uniform European conception of morals, and notes (with regard to the 'little red book' on sexual education mentioned earlier) that a national margin of appreciation must be granted because the state authorities 'are in principle in a better position than the international judge' to rule on the precise contents of moral requirements, and on the need for a 'restriction' or 'sanction' designed to satisfy them. On this occasion, the Court notes, with particular explicitness, 'Whilst the adjective *necessary*, within the meaning of Article 10(2), is not synonymous with *indispensable* (comp., in Articles 2(2) and 6(1), the words *absolutely necessary* and *strictly necessary* and, in Article 15(1), the clause *strictly required by the exigencies of the situation*), neither has it the flexibility of such expressions as *admissible, ordinary* (comp. Article 4(3)), *useful* (comp. the first paragraph of Article 1 of Protocol No. 1), *reasonable* (comp. Articles 5(3) and 6(1)) or *desirable*'[26] (emphasis added). In other words, restrictive measures are placed on a scale from 'indispensable' to 'desirable' via every degree indicated; it being noted that the term 'admissible', considered alone, is found by the Court to be more flexible than the term 'necessary', while the guiding principle of the restrictive measure

[26] *Handyside v. United Kingdom.*

admissible in a democratic society becomes a more precise concept when it is determined by the three criteria of lawfulness, legitimate objective and democratic necessity.

While the list mixes the normality of standards ('ordinary', 'reasonable') with the normativity of guiding principles, the scale nevertheless allows us to situate the proximity of each restrictive measure in relation to the European requirement of 'democratic necessity'. Without granting the states 'unlimited discretion', the national margin allows for some deviation within the limits of compatibility set by the Court.

However, this deviation concerns only the criterion of democratic necessity, because the lawfulness of the measure relates exclusively, as does the legitimate supporting objective, to the European norm as interpreted by the former Strasbourg Commission and the Strasbourg Court.

The gradation scale for determining what constitutes a criminal offence appears to be slightly different. The (more subtle) European margin of review allows for extending the criminal category beyond the strict definition of domestic criminal law. Despite the formula in the *Lutz* decision, which seems to limit the gradation scale to the sole criterion of the sanction – 'for Article 6 to apply in virtue of the words "criminal charge", it suffices that the offence in question should by its nature be "criminal" from the point of view of the Convention, as in the instant case, or should have made the person concerned liable to a sanction which, in its nature and degree of severity, belongs in general to the "criminal" sphere'[27] – it seems none the less that the gradation takes on each of the three criteria here.

When qualifying the offence according to the domestic legal technique, the European Court occasionally emphasises the proximity of administrative and criminal sanctions: 'no absolute partition separates German criminal law from the law on "regulatory offences"'; moreover, the provisions governing criminal procedure apply by analogy 'to regulatory proceedings'.[28] In other cases, it also notes the proximity between criminal and disciplinary sanctions, namely those that are decided in prison: 'certain parallels between Board of Visitors' proceedings and criminal proceedings were drawn'.[29]

Similarly, for the criterion of the nature of the offence, the Court notes that in prison-system cases, the circumstances surrounding the offences

[27] *Lutz v. Federal Republic of Germany.* [28] *Oztürk v. Federal Republic of Germany.*
[29] *Campbell and Fell v. United Kingdom.*

'do give them a certain colouring which does not entirely coincide with that of a purely disciplinary matter'.[30] In other words, there are various degrees between the merely disciplinary and the criminal. Moreover, the Court occasionally refers to the severity of the offence, qualified as 'petty' in the *Oztürk*[31] case and 'more serious', or being 'especially grave', in the *Campbell*[32] case.

Finally, the severity of the sanction, criterion C, implies in itself a gradation: of quality. An administrative fine 'appears less burdensome' than a deprivation of liberty;[33] however, the loss of a certain number of days of reduced sentence inflicted on a prisoner 'is related to a deprivation of liberty'. The phrase expresses clearly the concept of proximity to a criminal sanction, because 'there belong to the "criminal" sphere deprivations of liberty liable to be imposed as a punishment'. The gradation is also quantitative, for example when the Court invokes a sanction denying freedom, which may be 'of too short a duration' to be classified as a criminal sanction or, on the contrary, charges that 'did indeed come within the "criminal" sphere since their aim was the imposition of serious punishments involving deprivation of liberty' (a comment made in the *Engel* case involving military personnel, comparing two days' mandatory arrest to a sanction of twelve days' mandatory aggravated arrest or of three to six months' assignment to a disciplinary unit).[34]

Subject to the nuances, indicated above, the observation therefore leads to setting out the hypothesis of recourse, no doubt intuitive and imperfectly controlled, to a logic of gradation – which requires choosing among them.

Among the contemporary logics, one can, in fact, distinguish those that extend classical logic by respecting the same basic laws, particularly 'modal' logics, which bring into play modality operators bearing on propositions and phrases ('it is necessary that . . . it is possible that . . .') or deontological logic ('it is mandatory that . . . it is permissible that . . .'), and those that compete with classical logic by deviating from one or more of its laws, in particular the graduated logics, which, far from expressing a poverty of reasoning, express a need for more nuanced expression to describe gradual applications in relation to a given situation or norm, even if in a vague or imprecise way.

30 *Ibid.* 31 *Oztürk v. Federal Republic of Germany.*
32 *Campbell and Fell v. United Kingdom.* 33 *Oztürk v. Federal Republic of Germany.*
34 *Engel v. Netherlands.*

Without going so far as to represent the legal systems in Europe as open sets of a partially ordered topological space,[35] an initial, primarily mathematical, representation of the European Court's logical reasoning in the areas studied can be sketched from the theory of fuzzy subsets.[36]

Granted, the very idea of 'fuzzy logic' might trouble the reader, justifiably anxious to avoid arbitrariness and to ensure legal certainty, and therefore to set and apply norms that are precise and consistent on the one hand, unified and hierarchical on the other. But fuzzy logic is the basis for a reasoning that, far from being synonymous with arbitrary, has proved particularly adept in areas ranging from artificial intelligence to material strength.

Starting with a basic referential (a clear set that includes all the 'objects' of the universe being studied), a fuzzy subset is characterised by referring to an initial clear subset, itself defined by one or more criteria, using a function called 'belonging', which determines the degrees of proximity in relation to these criteria.

The belonging function therefore implies that the criteria of the initial referential subset are explicitly stated, whereas these criteria remain generally implicit in a syllogistic-type reasoning. In this sense, one can say that fuzzy logic requires an 'ontological' approach to concepts that classical logic is content to set as postulates. Thus, for example, the *Code pénal* does not define the criteria underlying the criminal nature of the behaviours it prohibits.

Under such conditions, the fuzzy subset constitutes a sort of gradual extension of the initial subset within the universe chosen as the basic referential.

This description indeed corresponds well to the process observed, which one can represent as the gradual extension of a clear initial subset, real (criminal law) or imaginary (measures restrictively admitted in a democratic society), into a broader fuzzy subset (criminal offence or

[35] See J.-R. Roisin, 'Topos', in *Encyclopédie philosophique universelle*, vol. II, *Les Notions philosophiques: Dictionnaire de philosophie occidentale* (ed. S. Auroux) (PUF, 1990), p. 2614.

[36] A. Kaufmann, *Introduction à la théorie des sous-ensembles flous* (Masson, 1977); D. Dubois and H. Prade, 'Les Logiques du flou et du très possible', *La Recherche* 22 (1991), pp. 1308–16; D. Dubois and H. Prade, *Théorie des possibilités* (2nd edn, Masson, 1987); T. Terano, K. Asai and M. Sugeno, *Fuzzy systems theory and its applications* (Academic Press Inc., 1992); M. L. Mathieu-Izorche, *Le Raisonnement juridique* (PUF, 2001), pp. 313–49 (chapter entitled 'De la logique des predicats à la logique flou').

simply admissible measures). Far from weakening legal reasoning, fuzzy logic allows for enriching it by defining the criteria of criminal law or restrictively admitted measures, and discerning with greater rigour the conditions in which the judge can go beyond the simple transcription of the norm to a true participation in its co-determination, without having to renounce all logic: 'The satisfying legal logic of hierarchy of norms, where the superior norm pre-empts the inferior norms, has had to give way to a "fuzzy logic" that seeks to balance the claims of simultaneous but conflicting imperatives, frequently expressed in terms that are imprecise or at least leave a wide margin for their interpretation and application to particular cases.'[37]

The elements of legal reasoning are those that characterise fuzzy logic: the basic referential (the reference concept defined by one or more criteria) and the belonging function, which determines the degree of proximity in relation to these criteria. They are easily locatable in the two areas considered.

On the one hand, a 'criminal offence' is in fact located in a universe that includes all legal sanctions applicable in each member state, and its meaning is defined by reference to the three criteria indicated; the belonging function seems to determine the various degrees of proximity in relation to these criteria.

On the other, restrictive measures admissible 'in a democratic society' are situated in a universe that includes all measures restricting the rights and freedoms enumerated in Articles 8 through 11 of the European Convention. This imprecise concept is defined using the three criteria stated in the Convention; the belonging function also determines various degrees of proximity, but in relation to the 'democratic necessity' criterion only. That is, despite, or because of, its complexity, the second concept or 'guiding principle' only partially obeys the fuzzy logic model and, for criteria A and B, obeys the syllogistic model.

In my discussion on determining the criteria, I positioned certain risks of arbitrariness that result from the various combinatory schemes for 'criminal offence' and the heterogeneous composition of 'democratic necessity' (the sole fuzzy criterion involved in the determination of restrictive measures 'admissible in a democratic society').

[37] D. Edward, 'The Community's constitution – rigid or flexible? The contemporary relevance of thinking of James Brice', *The Columbia Journal of European Law* 5(1) (1998–9), pp. 1ff.; see Delmas-Marty, 'The richness of underlying legal reasoning'.

Now we must add the risk of arbitrariness that comes from setting a decisional threshold because, in and of itself, the logic of fuzzy subsets does not allow us to decide on the legal qualification of such and such a practice. It merely positions it on a graduated scale, more or less akin to the reference subset, and therefore more or less akin to criminal law or a restrictive measure restrictively admitted in a democratic society. In fact, some authors have concluded that fuzzy logic is by nature 'indecidable'.[38]

However, this difficulty is surmountable, as the decisions analysed here show, by setting a 'compatibility threshold' beyond which the proximity to the reference concept appears a sufficient basis on which to found assimilation. In relation to this threshold, the decision is therefore binary (compatible or incompatible), like the decision taken at the end of a classical logic chain of reasoning (conforms or does not conform). It remains to be seen whether such a decision is not only possible, but also rational, and to identify the risks of arbitrariness tied to decision-making, and therefore to the choice of the threshold.

The decisional threshold

Here again, the risk of arbitrariness results less from the change in logic than from the temptation of independence that the complexity of the decision-making process can inspire in the judge. I showed, for 'criminal offence', how resort to a scale of gradation based on multiple criteria, themselves graduated, could lead the judge to change the qualification by adjusting the weighting of the criteria. Similarly, the temptation can be to vary the decisional threshold according to the result one wishes to obtain.

Especially visible with restrictive measures admissible 'in a democratic society', this variability in the decisional threshold results from the fact that, according to the ECHR, the reach of the national margin of appreciation 'varies with the circumstances, demands and context'. This phrase sheds light on the cases judged, and this decisional variability seems both 'circumstantial' (or synchronic) when it results from the circumstances specific to the case, and 'temporal' (or diachronic) when

[38] Word as used in J. Wroblewski, 'Fuzziness of legal systems', in *Essays in legal theory in honour of Karle Makkonen,* vol. XVI (Oikenstie de jurisprudentia, 1983), p. 326: 'The fuzziness of validity consists, then, in the indecidability whether the statement "R is a valid rule in the legal system" is true, or its negation is true.'

it takes into account the evolution of the 'context', particularly society's tolerance of certain practices.

Among the pertinent circumstances, geopolitical data, especially in eastern Europe, will in future be taken into account. For the moment, the nature of the objective invoked to justify the restrictive measure heads the list of variability factors retained by European judges. It is in any case in this regard that the jurisprudence expresses itself most clearly: 'the scope of the domestic power of appreciation is not identical as regards each of the aims listed in Article 10(2)'.[39]

More precisely, the distinction is the following: if the stated objective is the protection of morals (as in the 'little red book' case[40]), the margin is wide because, as the Court observed, 'the view taken by the Contracting States of the "requirements of morals" varies from time to time and from place to place, especially in our era'. Thus, 'State authorities are in principle in a better position than the international judge to give an opinion on the exact content of these requirements.' This means that the level of proximity required in relation to the European norm is low, or the 'fuzzy index' is high.

But the same is not true if the objective stated to support the restrictive measures is to guarantee 'the authority and impartiality of the judiciary'. In fact, according to the *Sunday Times* decision itself, 'the domestic law and practice of the Contracting States reveal a fairly substantial measure of common ground in this area' (it is reflected in a series of clauses of the Convention, including Article 6, which has no equivalent for morals). Hence this comment: 'here a more extensive European supervision corresponds to a less discretionary power of appreciation',[41] thus the requirement of a higher level of proximity, or a lower 'fuzzy index'.

We must none the less emphasise that, even when it is stated, the consideration of the legitimate objective is sometimes qualified by other factors. Thus in the *Dudgeon* and *Norris*[42] decisions, where the stated legitimate objective was to protect morals, the Court seemed to grant a narrower national margin of appreciation, and thus set a higher compatibility threshold, than in *Handyside*. It brought to bear another variable, that of 'the nature of the activities involved': 'However, not only the nature of the aim of the restriction but also the nature of the activities

[39] *Sunday Times v. United Kingdom*, ECHR, 26 April 1979.

[40] *Handyside v. United Kingdom*.

[41] *Sunday Times v. United Kingdom*. ECHR, 26 April 1979.

[42] *Dudgeon v. United Kingdom* and *Norris v. Republic of Ireland*.

involved will affect the scope of the margin of appreciation. The present case concerns a most intimate aspect of private life. Accordingly, there must exist particularly serious reasons before interferences on the part of the public authorities can be legitimate for the purposes of Article 8(2).'

It is true that in these cases relating to homosexual practices between adults, a third factor seems to have led to the acceptance of the petitions of Dudgeon and Norris when several analogous petitions had been refused earlier. The shift in jurisprudence is based, in fact, on the evolutionary nature of the social context:

> As compared with the era when that legislation was enacted, there is now a better understanding, and in consequence an increased tolerance, of homosexual behaviour to the extent that in the great majority of the member States of the Council of Europe it is no longer considered to be necessary or appropriate to treat homosexual practices of the kind now in question as in themselves a matter to which the sanctions of the criminal law should be applied; the Court cannot overlook the marked changes which have occurred in this regard in the domestic law of the member States ... In Northern Ireland itself, the authorities have refrained in recent years from enforcing the law in respect of private homosexual acts between consenting males over the age of 21 years capable of valid consent ... No evidence has been adduced to show that this has been injurious to moral standards in Northern Ireland or that there has been any public demand for stricter enforcement of the law.

Thus the evolution toward greater tolerance 'in the great majority of the member States' joins the objective of protecting morals and the nature of the activities in question. In other words, 'circumstantial' and 'temporal' variability is thrown in.

Inscribed at the heart of the European system for protecting human rights, the latter variable is expressed not only by the adoption of 'additional' protocols, but even by the Convention's Preamble: 'the aim of the Council of Europe is the achievement of greater unity between its members and that one of the methods by which that aim is to be pursued is the maintenance and further realisation of human rights and fundamental freedoms'. Maintenance and 'further realisation' is a phrase that is repeated by European judges in support of interpretations they are afraid to qualify as evolutionary themselves (see Part I, above).

Although difficult to reconcile with the syllogistic model, which requires absolute truths with stable contents, such an interpretation can, however, be inscribed in a logic of gradation that, due to this gradation, leads to a relative truth with variable contents.

But these evolutionary factors must be clearly indicated and must not reveal the predominance of the subjective preferences of the judge. Alongside society's tolerance, other factors appear, as seen with regard to transsexualism, noted above. Observing that 'the law appears to be in a transitional stage', the ECHR concluded in 1986 (in a case concerning the United Kingdom) that we must, 'for the time being', leave to the respondent state the job of determining to what extent it can meet the demands of transsexuals. But it added that 'the need for appropriate legal measures should therefore be kept under review', with regard, particularly, to 'scientific and societal developments'.[43]

In 1992 (in a French case), the Court noted a double evolution, even considering it 'undeniable that attitudes have changed, science has progressed and increasing importance is attached to the problem of transsexualism'. But it is still an incomplete evolution, because the Court notes: 'however, in the light of the relevant studies carried out and work done by experts in this field . . . there still remains some uncertainty as to the essential nature of transsexualism'. Hence the prudence of its conclusion: 'there is as yet no sufficiently broad consensus between the member States of the Council of Europe to persuade the Court to reach opposite conclusions to those in its *Rees* and *Cossey* judgments'.[44]

These few examples show how the variability of the decisional threshold allows case law to adapt more openly to reality, without having to modify the norm, nor the criteria determining its meaning, while by its rigidity, the syllogistic model imposes either repeated reforms (at the risk of legislative and regulatory inflation) or interpretations so extensive that they deform and lead, paradoxically, from high predetermination to uncontrolled co-determination.

However, despite the possibilities incontestably offered by the new logics (especially the logics of gradation) as compared to classical logic, it is still true that, even when explicit, the threshold's variability is but the reflection of the 'indecidable' nature of the threshold itself. It is, in fact, impossible to show why compatibility with the European norm is set at one degree of proximity rather than another, just as it is impossible

[43] *Rees v. United Kingdom*, ECHR, 17 October 1986, Series A, No. 106. See also Part I, above.

[44] *B v. France*, ECHR, 25 March 1992 (refering to *Rees* and *Cossey*, 27 September 1990).

to show, in classical logic, the postulate on which a syllogism's major premise is based – for example, that which describes a certain type of norm as criminal, another as administrative.

No logical model succeeds in eliminating the arbitrariness inherent in predetermining norms using the syllogistic model, or in co-determining them using gradation logics. While necessary, logic is not sufficient to guarantee the legal nature of norms. This is indicative of the importance of the super-determination process that bases the choices, of both the legislature and the judge, on a cultural code that is rarely explicit. Legitimate when it concerns a common cultural code, the decision becomes transgression when it is inspired exclusively by a personal, or minority, code.

Certainly, the personal qualities of those who 'decide the indecidable' (the 'indecidable' being, here, the democratic nature of the legislative process or the 'independent and impartial' nature of case law) can limit the risk. But it reappears with laws that express only the choices of a charismatic leader, as with judges who obey a political, economic or media power or who, supposedly to show their 'independence', make the decision depend on personal beliefs asserted as elementary givens or gospel truths.

The extreme care the ECHR takes to connect its choices to 'attitudes', to 'science', or to the existence or absence of a 'consensus' among the states, clearly shows the concern for legitimacy that pervades every legal system. This legitimacy is even more necessary when the decisional margin is wide, but even more fragile when the choices are open and diverse.

6

Legitimate: from general legal principles to a 'law of human rights'

Founded on 'implicit' values, on beliefs that are 'not expressly formulated' and on 'subjacent' ideologies,[1] the legitimacy of legal systems seems to escape all scientific treatment, since it is partially unexpressed and the basis for the choice cannot be argued with. Caught between the dream of an impossible-to-find natural law and the myth of a pure theory bearing with it the risk of reducing law to a 'mere exercise in domination',[2] the search for legitimacy seems to lead to an impasse – unless, that is, we can establish that it is possible, if not to prove the legitimacy of the choice between opposing values, at least to examine how values, whatever they may be, underlie the legitimacy of a legal system. Hence the usefulness of an analysis through which the meaning of a legal norm is 'not only predetermined by the norm's author and co-determined by its addressee, but is also super-determined by the norm's field of transmission and reception'.[3]

While acknowledging that the problem is 'meta-legal', Gérard Timsit offers a tool for treating super-determination through what he calls 'methods for objectifying' the cultural code underlying this process. The tool is built upon a distinction between the various forms by which the code 'expresses itself' and the double mechanism of 'gravitation' and 'expansion', by which it 'ingrains itself' in the normative order.

Here, however, the perspective is clearly different. In evoking the passage 'from general legal principles to a law of human rights', the title of this chapter chooses to favour another objective, which is not to study

[1] G. Timsit, *Les Noms de la loi* (PUF, 1991), p. 161.

[2] F. Ewald, *L'Etat-providence* (Grasset, 1986), p. 506.

[3] Timsit, *Les Noms de la loi*, p. 161; see M. Delmas-Marty, 'Le Rôle du juge européen dans la renaissance du *Jus commune* – signification et limites', in P. Mahoney *et al.* (eds.), *Protecting human rights, the European perspective. In memory of Rolf Ryssdol* (Carl Heymahns Verlag, 2000), pp. 297ff.

the process of super-determination itself, but to show that it is undergoing a profound change.

While general legal principles are identified one at a time, primarily by administrative judges, and never express more than a small part of the dominant cultural code (which essentially remains implicit), they do maintain, despite their diversity, a certain homogeneity with respect to the values that inspire them. The specificity of human rights, however, results from their extreme heterogeneity, which is even more pronounced when they are the subject of group statements (declarations, fundamental statutes or international conventions).

A true basis for multiplicity, human rights signal a break with other forms that 'express' super-determination. The paradox is that via this extreme heterogeneity, and despite the misunderstandings it causes, the mark of human rights is more deeply 'ingrained' because they have, like general legal principles but with greater intensity, effects that are not limited to producing a 'legal conscience', but that directly control the choices of the legislature or the judge: so much so that we can speak of a 'law of rights' that, meta-legally inspired, none the less combines rules and guiding principles, thus associating the three processes of norm determination into a veritable redistribution, or restructuring, of legal categories.

Heterogeneity of human rights on the one hand, restructuring into a 'law of rights' on the other: these are the characteristics of a change that, through interpretational logics, introduces multiplicity at the core of the concept of legitimacy itself.

Heterogeneity of human rights

Human rights first appeared, in no particular order, in domestic law. With Magna Carta granted by King John in 1215, the Bill of Rights of 1628, the *Habeas Corpus* of 1679 and the Bill of Rights of 1689, the United Kingdom of Great Britain and Ireland was the first, followed by the United States of America with its Declaration of 1787, to grant human rights a place in domestic law. Universal in nature, the *Déclaration des droits de l'homme et du citoyen de 1789* is nevertheless French. Completed much later by the Preamble to the French Constitution of 1946, which proclaims a certain number of economic and social rights, it eventually became mandatory in domestic law with its constitutional review of statutes (introduced in the 1958 Constitution but actually instituted by the law of 1974, which enables sixty parliamentarians to refer a matter to the Conseil constitutionnel).

After the Second World War, many other states established, either in the actual text of their Constitutions or outside it (as with the Canadian Charter on Rights and Freedoms), a set of 'fundamental rights' (German Constitution) or 'rights and duties of citizens' (Italian Constitution) the violation of which may be brought first before the common-law court, then, if necessary, before a constitutional tribunal or court.

If the phenomenon, as yet incomplete, of the 'constitutionalisation of law' described at the beginning of this book thus contributes to the emergence of human rights in domestic law, it is coupled, as we have seen, with an 'internationalisation' phenomenon begun by the Universal Declaration of Human Rights of 1948 and marked by the adoption of interregional conventions (the European Convention on Human Rights of 1950, the European Social Charter of 1961, the American Convention of 1969, the African Charter on Human and People's Rights of 1981) or, more broadly, international ones (UN Covenants of 1966, one regarding civil and political rights, the other economic, social and cultural rights).

Limited to generalised texts, the list shows that heterogeneity is not limited to support for human rights alone, as the phrasing itself varies: 'rights' or 'rights and duties'; 'human' or 'human and peoples'; 'civil and political' or 'economic, social and cultural' rights.

Beyond the underlying distinction between individual and collective rights, the recent evolution tends more broadly to inscribe human rights in the long term, with rights of 'solidarity' that position the individual in relation to his or her lineage (ascendants and descendants) and the community in relation to future generations (and thus to the human race or 'family').

This is a discomforting move. Traditionally, the legitimacy of a legal system was based upon a homogeneous cultural code that avoided or limited conflicts by making one value or a couple of values predominant. Individual liberty is predominant in liberal ideology; equality, consensual or imposed, predominates in libertarian and Marxist ideologies; and the 'we', incarnated by the nation or race (fascism), or by religion (fundamentalism), dominates in totalitarian ideologies. While the heterogeneity of human rights enables the introduction of a pluralism of values that is one of the criteria of 'the democratic spirit' according to the European Court of Human Rights case law cited earlier, it is at the risk of conflicts that make one doubt not only the universality of human rights (see Part III, below), but even their pertinence in defining a common cultural code. In short, instead of reducing the indeterminacy of norms by indicating the values imposed on the legislature when it prescribes, or on the judge when he or she interprets, human rights would seem to contribute to the decline of law by legitimating, in advance, each value and its opposite. Pluralism cannot be thought of as Manichaean. Without renouncing fundamental choices that require excluding their opposites, it introduces nuances. On the one hand, these nuances result from the differentiation between values, and therefore between the rights that express them, depending on whether they fall within an absolute protection corresponding to the rights called 'inviolable', or are relativised by the admission of derogations, exceptions or restrictions. On the other hand, pluralism leads, except for absolutely protected rights, to an interaction or an interdependence that replaces the alternatives conception – Manichaean in that it imposes a choice between one *or* the other – with a combinatory conception that leads to a search for the point of compatibility between one *and* the other.

Differentiation

Presented as 'a common standard of achievement' in the Universal Declaration of 1948, human rights are all proclaimed therein with the same force, without apparent restriction. However, Article 29(2) of this Declaration admits the existence of 'limitations', specifying that they must be 'determined by law solely for the purpose of securing due recognition and respect of the rights and freedoms of others and meeting the just requirements of morality, public order and the general welfare in a democratic society'.

This acknowledges that conflicts between the rights of one and the rights of another are possible; and it means above all laying out, in accordance with the collective values of order generally associated with the policy requirements of state authority, a wide open (given the terms used) space for negotiation: morality, public order and the general welfare. At the same time, the question arises as to whether all the rights enumerated are subject to such limitations, or whether certain of them escape, benefiting from absolute protection.

The Universal Declaration is not very explicit regarding this concept of variable protection, nor, therefore, does it provide a scale of values underlying human rights. This scale is, however, explicit in the UN Covenant on Civil and Political Rights, as well as in the European and American Conventions on Human Rights, though it remains implicit in the African Charter.

This scale operates on four levels, because each category is subdivided into absolute or quasi-absolute protection and strong or weak relative protection.

At the very top of the scale are a few rare, absolutely protected rights, that is, those for which no derogation, exception or restriction is allowed, even in the event of war or '[I]n time of public emergency which threatens the life of the nation and the existence of which is officially proclaimed'.[4] This means there is something more precious than life in the hierarchy of values, so precious that we dare not name it, other than through prohibitions: of torture and inhuman or degrading treatment, of slavery and servitude, and of mass deportations, to which the UN Covenant adds the prohibition against performing a medical or scientific experiment on a person without his or her consent, and the obligation to acknowledge the legal personality of every person everywhere. We can read between the lines of this list the expression of the value: respect for the 'inherent dignity of the human person' in the strongest sense. This is evoked, if not by the texts themselves, at least by certain Preambles, such as the ones to the Universal Declaration of 1948 and to the UN Covenants of 1966. Dignity, or even, according to the phrase in UN Secretary-General Boutros Boutros-Ghali's inaugural address at the World Conference on Human Rights (Vienna, June 1993), 'the irreducible human element', that is, 'the quintessential values through which we affirm together that we are a single human community'.

'The irreducible human element' is the supreme ethical requirement and there is an absolute prohibition on going beyond 'that point beyond which violence can no longer be redeemed by a desire for reciprocity

[4] See Article 4 of the UN Covenant on Civil and Political Rights and, similarly, Article 15 of the European Convention and Article 27 of the American Convention. The African Charter does not include an equivalent provision, no doubt because of the quasi-institutionalisation of the legislated exceptions.

and becomes the pure negation of the human'.[5] Jean Ladrière goes on: 'There is not necessarily negation of the human where there is an attack on life, but where, in one form or another, there is an offence to what we call, in serious and deep terms, *human dignity*, that is, that which enables human beings to assert themselves as beings of blood, to rise above their biological reality and declare themselves in words they can truly assume, in which they can truly express themselves.' Like an echo, the 1984 UN Convention against Torture provides this definition: 'Any act by which severe pain or suffering, whether physical or mental, is intentionally inflicted on a person.' Inflicted 'intentionally' and with a specific purpose: to obtain information or a confession, to punish, intimidate or coerce, or 'for any other reason based on discrimination of any kind'.

The goal is to define the absolute limit of the 'negation of the human' evoked by Ladrière: 'To reduce the body to the pure passivity of a disintegrative suffering is to attempt to dissolve the conscience into the flesh; it is literally to desire a metaphysical destruction.' Such a destruction, continues the philosopher, is

> unacceptable because it signifies the destruction of the entire human order, the negation of the effort itself through which the humanity of humankind exists. As for the rest, we can only pretend to justify without contradiction. Because any justification refers to a meaning of building, and this meaning can only be human accomplishment, however we conceive of it. In particular, the justification drawn from the overriding interest of the group, of the community, of the State, consists of making this interest an absolute cause; what enables us to make this into an absolute cause is the mediating function of the organised community with respect to the horizon of meaning, that is, the advent of the human. We cannot simultaneously desire this event in theory and deny it concretely in an effective practice.[6]

On the next level, after the 'metaphysical' destruction, should logically appear the prohibition on 'physically' destroying, the corollary to the right to life. But the question is really much more complex, first because of the difficulty in situating the beginning of such a right (which only the American Convention expressly places at conception) or the

[5] J. Ladrière, 'L'Ethique et les intérêts collectifs', in J. Verhagen (ed.), *Licéité en droit positif et références légales aux valeurs*, 10th Jean Dabin Legal Studies Day (Bruylant, 1982), pp. 115ff.

[6] *Ibid.*, p. 115.

moment when it ends (which varies according to whether it concerns preparing a civil certificate, permitting organ removal, or carrying out experiments without a therapeutic purpose or on a person in a persistent vegetative state); next, because of different concepts regarding permissible exceptions, such as legitimate defence, the death penalty or euthanasia.[7] Hypothetically, as already emphasised, the right to life is never absolutely protected, because an act of homicide is legitimate when it involves 'defending any person against unlawful violence' – and even the texts abolishing the death penalty all specify that it can be re-established or maintained in the event of war. In the most favourable hypothesis, the right to life therefore belongs to the category of rights with quasi-absolute protection – that is, protected without exception or restriction, but which can be temporarily suspended in the event of war or threat to the nation's survival (the derogatory or 'national security' clause in the earlier cited texts: UN Covenant, Article 4; European Convention, Article 15; and the American Convention, Article 27).

The right to freedom from discrimination belongs in this same category, as does the right to the presumption of innocence for persons 'criminally charged', and, more broadly, the right to a 'fair trial'.[8]

The other enumerated rights are granted relative protection: they can be subject to permanent, not just temporary, derogations or restrictions. This relative protection is strong for derogations that are listed exhaustively and are imposed without a national margin of appreciation. Such is the case, for example, for the right to freedom and security according to the UN Covenant (Article 9) and the European Convention (Article 5), but not according to the American Convention, Article 7 of which authorises detention in conditions left to the discretion of states ('for the reasons and under the conditions established beforehand by the constitutions of the State Party concerned or by a law established pursuant thereto'), nor according to the African Charter, Article 6 of which permits any deprivation of liberty 'for reasons and conditions previously laid down by law'.

This relative protection is weak when the exceptions or restrictions are left to the discretion of the states, it being noted that conditions are, however, imposed. In the case of exceptions to freedom as mentioned

[7] See J.-L. Baudouin and D. Blondeau, *Ethique de la mort et droit à la mort* (PUF, 1992).

[8] Unless we admit the interdependence between this latter law, procedural law and the question of substance that accompanies it.

above (the American Convention and African Charter), these conditions are lawfulness and a certain judicial guarantee that results either directly from the right to appeal to a judge or tribunal (American Convention), or indirectly from the more vague phrase by which the African Charter states that 'no one may be arbitrarily arrested or detained'. Also, in the list of restrictions permitted by the European Convention on Human Rights, we find a complete set of conditions studied with regard to the margin of appreciation: lawfulness; legitimacy of the stated objective, and the democratic necessity as a combination of proportionality to the objective and democratic implementation.

This latter category (weak relative protection) therefore includes the right to freedom of movement according to the UN Covenant (Article 12(3)), the right to respect for private and family life (awkwardly placed by the American Convention under the title 'protection of the honor and dignity of the person', which creates an ambiguity in relation to inalienable rights: those of the first category), freedom of thought, conscience and religion, freedom of opinion and expression, freedom of peaceful assembly and association, the right to hold private property, the right to a name and a nationality (specific to the American Convention) and the right to environmental quality (African Charter and an additional Protocol to the American Convention). To these 'civil and political' rights, there are added, sometimes in the same texts (American Convention and African Charter), sometimes in different texts (European Social Charter, UN Covenant), 'economic, social and cultural' rights, 'human', and also 'people's', rights, complemented, in particular, by the Declaration of the UN General Assembly on the Right to Development (adopted by the General Assembly in Resolution 41/128 on 4 December 1986), by which the UN affirms that 'the human person is the central subject of development and should therefore be the active participant and the beneficiary of the right to development'. This latter Declaration insists on the correlative obligations this right creates for the states: to co-operate with each other to promote international development policies and, domestically, to offer their citizens 'access to basic resources, education, health services, food, housing, employment and the fair distribution of income'.

Although not exhaustive, this list gives an idea of the heterogeneity of the rights recognised and the risks of conflict that cannot fail to arise. The scale's usefulness lies, for rights with relative protection (strong or weak), in its introduction of an interdependence between the values, and thus an interaction between the rights that express them.

Interaction

The most visible conflict is between civil and political rights, strongly marked by liberal ideology and western influence, and economic, social and cultural rights, which appeared later and are more particularly demanded by socialist and Third World states. The balance sheet established at the World Conference in Vienna in 1993[9] shows the magnitude of economic disorder on a worldwide scale: between 150 and 200 million children work in more than 50 countries; approximately 700 million people are either without work or are underemployed (the figure increases by about 38 million per year); approximately 750 million people, or close to 20 per cent of the population in developing countries, are undernourished; close to 1 billion adults have received no elementary education and are unable to read or write, or are denied their cultural rights; between 1 and 1.4 billion persons in the world live today in conditions of abject poverty and another billion on the edge of poverty; approximately 1.5 billion persons are without access to sufficient health services, while roughly 1.3 billion are without clean water and about 2.3 billion are without access to an adequate sanitation system.

The plea of Mr Ibrahim Fall, United Nations Under-Secretary-General on Human Rights and Secretary-General of the World Conference, is easily understood: 'With such a situation as a backdrop, we can only say that human rights are devoid of meaning where poverty and destitution reign.' And he adds: 'A man did indeed walk on the moon, but on Earth, daily life remains a difficult, dangerous, and often deadly enterprise.'

This bespeaks the indivisible link between economic, social and cultural rights on the one hand and civil and political rights on the other. In fact, this link appears in their shared dependence on human dignity, because the concept of human dignity implies the right to exist and the right to live in conditions offering a minimum of dignity, as is in fact emphasised in the UN Covenants of 1966 and, more recently, the 1990 UN Commission on Human Rights Resolution on 'Human Rights

[9] K. Chammari, Report on the functioning and stakes of the fourth session of the Preparatory Committee of the World Conference on Human Rights, Geneva, 19–30 April 1993.

and Extreme Poverty'. Similarly, the French declaration on the 'National priority to fight against extreme poverty and to guarantee fundamental rights to all citizens', unanimously adopted by the National Advisory Committee on Human Rights in 1990,[10] recalls that extreme poverty and social exclusion constitute a violation of human dignity, and insists on the necessity for an implementation of human rights 'in their indivisibility'.

But the challenge of extreme poverty to human rights is not entirely clear. For example, a petition maintaining that cutting off electricity to public housing in the dead of winter constitutes 'inhuman or degrading' treatment was rejected by the European Commission on Human Rights.[11] At least the question was asked explicitly and it is still likely that, for example, the expulsion of a family in the middle of winter without relodging in decent conditions would be judged contrary to the European Convention.

In less extreme cases, where relatively protected rights are involved, it is in recognising, in a spirit of pluralism, this interdependency between values, and therefore of interaction between rights, that enables us to legitimate legal systems. This is how, for example, concerning the right to a fair trial in a civil matter, the ECHR found a right to free legal aid for the most disadvantaged, which is not expressly included in the European Convention on Human Rights, by combining the Convention and the European Social Charter. The Court emphasised on this occasion that 'there is no water-tight division between civil and political rights and social and economic rights'.[12]

Similarly, there is relatively abundant case law that tries to reconcile various rights that have relative protection, such as the press's right to freedom of expression and the right of all persons to respect for privacy. There is, moreover, a right that the European Convention never imposes as such, but in combination with all the others – the right to freedom from discrimination: 'The enjoyment of the rights and freedoms set forth in this Convention shall be secured without any discrimination' (Article 14, which then lists the prohibited discriminations: 'sex, race, colour, language, religion, political or other opinion, national or social

[10] See the National Advisory Commission on Human Rights report, 'Exclusion et droits de l'homme' (La Documentation française, 1992), pp. 475ff.

[11] *Van Volsem*, HRC, 9 May 1990, *RUDH* (1990), p. 349, F. Sudre note.

[12] *Airey v. Ireland*, ECHR, 9 October 1979, Series A, No. 32.

origin, association with a national minority, property, birth or other status').

This interaction is therefore not limited to relatively protected rights. There are many examples other than that of non-discrimination (a right with quasi-absolute protection). In 1987, the Inter-American Court of Human Rights issued an Opinion having mandatory force considers that the judicial guarantees imposed by the American Convention (*habeas corpus* appeal, individual appeal for protection, or any other effective appeal before a magistrate or competent tribunal) are the necessary complement to rights with absolute protection, because when it concerns guaranteeing the full exercise of these rights (respect for dignity within the precise meaning indicated by the prohibitions enumerated above), the suppression or restriction of judicial guarantees 'entails the lack of protection of such rights'.[13]

In other words, the interaction between rights does not necessarily come into play in the sense of a reciprocal limitation. It can lead, by a sort of force of attraction, to strengthening the protection of one by the indirect influence of the other. Thus in 1990, the UN Committee on Human Rights came to recognise the link between procedural guarantees and the right to life, stating very clearly that, 'in the case of a trial that could lead to the death penalty, the duty of the States to respect rigorously all the guaranties of a fair trial stated in Article 14 of the Covenant is even more imperative'.[14] Under these conditions, the violation of the right to life can result not from the death penalty itself (permitted as an exception), but from the violation of the rules for a fair trial. Indeed, using similar reasoning, the European Court of Human Rights decided in 1989[15] that for a country that had not yet ratified the Protocol abolishing the death penalty (the United Kingdom, which recently ratified it after having abolished it by the Crime and Disorder Act 1998) to agree to extradite a person charged with an offence to a country (the United States) where he or she risked this punishment could constitute not a violation of the right to life, because the exception of the death penalty is provided for in Article 2 of the European Convention, but constituted instead 'inhuman or degrading' treatment within the meaning of Article 3. The analysis was limited, however, to the circumstances of the

[13] Advisory Opinion requested by the government of Uruguay, 8 October 1987.
[14] *Carlton Reid v. Jamaica*, 20 July 1990.
[15] *Soering v. United Kingdom*, ECHR, 7 July 1989, Series A, No. 16.

case and, in particular, 'to the very long period of time spent on death row in such extreme conditions, with the ever-present and mounting anguish of awaiting execution of the death penalty'. To this circumstance were added the interested party's age (eighteen at the time of the act), his mental state (a strongly altered personality at the time of the offence) and the possibility of seeing the matter judged in another country that had also requested extradition, and that had already abolished the death penalty (Germany).

These few examples obviously do not pretend to resolve all the conflicts that can arise from the heterogeneity of human rights. They are simply to show that a pluralist conception of legitimacy must necessarily be accompanied by a new method of argumentation. Just as the resort to indeterminate or poorly determined notions, like standards or guiding principles, requires a change in interpretive logic as the only way to assure co-determination that is not synonymous with transgression of the prescribed norm, the resort to a pluralist conception of values that super-determine legal systems requires a combinatory reasoning method that also calls upon a mutation of logics. The search for 'compatibility' between two rights, apparently contradictory yet members of the same category of protection, requires that a decisional threshold is set that allows sufficient proximity (but not identity) to *both* reference values.

This means that the transformation of legal systems, from simple to complex to multiple, excludes neither the process of co-determination, nor of super-determination, but requires an apprenticeship in 'new logics' that, contrary to what many jurists fear, do not create the phenomenon of complexity, and thus uncertainty and imprecision – these are inherent in life itself – but teach us to tame it, to control it through increased attention and rigour.

Only on this condition – and it is essential – can human rights become the instrument for restructuring legal categories into a 'law of rights', giving them the new, mixed status of meta-legal norms and guiding principles.

Restructuring into a 'law of rights'

This idea, this observation even, that human rights could launch a restructuring process, responds to the transformations in the legal landscape described at the beginning of this book as the heralding of a 'reconstruction', of a new order to come. This process is incomplete, but is already perceptible in two particularly sensitive areas: sanctions and, be they sanctions or other measures such as police, medical treatment or socio-medical measures, the arrests and detentions that deprive a person of freedom of movement.

In these two areas (which are scattered among legal disciplines as diverse as criminal, administrative, civil, disciplinary and medical law), human rights, despite their heterogeneity (or perhaps thanks to it), propose the first elements of a common legal framework – common to the various legal categories, and common also – already – to different legal systems.

Toward a common law of sanctions

With the first codifications, sanctions were differentiated, isolated from each other in their specific legal regimes: a simple juxtaposition of independent sanctions with nothing to prevent their being compounded with regard to the same acts. For example, the victim of an offence could be awarded civil damages, which could be compounded with the criminal sanction per se of fine or imprisonment of the offender. Such compounding poses no difficulties as long as the implicit foundation of each category is different: punishment (criminal sanctions), discipline (disciplinary sanctions), regulation (administrative sanctions), reparation (civil sanctions) or even reconciliation with mediation, which is a sanction in the broad sense.

It was the sociologist Emile Durkheim who, in his search for a method to determine 'the function of the division of work', first proposed a transversal study consisting of classifying legal rules according to the various sanctions attached to them.[16] This led to comparing repressive sanctions, those that 'consist essentially of pain, or at least a diminution, inflicted on the agent', with compensatory sanctions, which 'consist solely of restoring the status quo, of re-establishing normal relations' (for example, injunction to perform, damages or cancellation). According to him, this analysis leads to placing criminal sanctions in the repressive category, and all others in the compensatory category.

[16] E. Durkheim, *De la division du travail social* (9th edn, PUF, 1973), pp. 33ff.

In a very different context, the emergence of a law of human rights will, through other avenues, introduce a classification that recalls Durkheim's, but does not copy it. Here I limit the analysis to the example of the French *Déclaration des droits de l'homme* of 1789 and the European Convention of 1950.

The *Déclaration* expressly addresses only those penalties that traditionally fall within criminal law (Article 8). Requiring necessity (and thus proportionality), lawfulness and non-retroactivity of statutes, the *Déclaration* reflects well the liberal and legalistic ideology of the French revolutionaries.

Close to two centuries later, the European Convention on Human Rights takes up the principle of non-retroactivity – of 'law', not just statutes – with regard to convictions for 'offences', and thus the principle of criminal law (Article 7). But above all, it indicates the new importance attached to procedural rules by setting out guarantees for a 'fair trial' (Article 6). A two-fold area of application is defined for these guarantees: hearings to determine 'civil rights and obligations' (Article 6(1)) and 'criminal charges' (Article 6(1) to (3)).

By transforming these texts into true guiding principles, the jurisprudence is building a sort of general theory (even though it denies it). This theory is applied to sanctions 'having the nature of a punishment' in constitutional jurisprudence, broadened to 'criminal charges' and 'civil hearings' in European jurisprudence.

The constitutional analysis remains close to Durkheim's, because the function of punishment, even when it is exercised not by the criminal judge but by a regulatory body (such as the Stock Exchange Commission or the Conseil de la concurrence), leads by extension to the application of the guarantees of the *Déclaration des droits de l'homme* and, as an unwritten principle with constitutional value, the respect for the 'right to a defence'.

The European analysis does not reproduce this functional reference directly, with punishment or repression on one side and restitution on the other. For one thing, Article 6 does not apply merely to sanctions in the strict sense, but to the process that may lead to sanctions (a criminal 'charge' or a civil 'hearing'); for another, because 'criminal' and 'civil' are determined (as I showed earlier for criminal charge) by reference to an entire set of criteria that go beyond domestic legal categories (civil and criminal law) to analyse the nature of the rights concerned.

The result is a complete redistribution of legal categories. 'Civil' is used to characterise not only hearings governed by civil law because they determine rights of a purely private nature (such as the right to hold property, to enjoy a good reputation, to obtain reparation of a prejudice caused by a private party or to launch a paternity action) but also those that would be governed, under domestic law, by disciplinary law (such as those to determine the right to continue to exercise a profession), administrative law (cancelling a public-transport licence or contesting a land-redistribution operation) and even arbitration procedures. However, hearings involving purely public law (fiscal taxation, residency authorisations or deportations of aliens, the promotion or firing of civil servants) escape the 'civil' qualification.

Because of the lack of criteria to define 'civil' and to establish a scale of gradation between hearings involving purely civil law (undeniably governed by Article 6) and those involving purely public law (which are excluded), today's European jurisprudence barely sketches out this new and independent legal category of 'civil hearings'. While it is still far from the conditions required for logical reasoning (as in the gradation logics examined earlier), it has none the less begun a broad redistribution assuring minimum common guarantees (beyond national qualifications), ranging from procedural rapidity to publicity (traditionally precluded in disciplinary and regulatory matters) and the independence and impartiality of the jurisdictional authority (dubious when a mediator chosen by the parties or a regulatory body is involved: they are not always independent and are rarely impartial).

As for 'criminal offence', the discussion of legal logics, above, demonstrated the extent of the work performed by European judges. Unlike the French Conseil constitutionnel, which seems to extend the guaranties offered under the *Déclaration* of 1789 as soon as a sanction has a 'punitive function', the ECHR combines a set of criteria that refer to legal normativity (comparative law reference), to normality, and to the meta-legal normativity of human rights (the nature of the rights concerned by the sanction, and especially whether a deprivation of liberty is involved). Without repeating the analysis of the underlying logics here, it is worth repeating that 'criminal' groups together, around criminal law, sanctions that can be qualified by the states as administrative or disciplinary sanctions, without precluding the possible assimilation one day of certain 'private penalties' decided by civil-law judges, for example in the area of liability for dangerous products (awarding not only compensatory damages based on actual damages, but also dissuasive and punitive damages based on fault).[17]

In sum, it has become common to think that, except for measures of purely public law derived from the inherent power of the state, all procedures that might lead to a sanction must respect each person's fundamental right to a fair trial. This respect must be greater when a 'criminal law' sanction may infringe essential rights (beginning with freedom of movement).

In the same way, but more broadly because there are not only sanctions but all sorts of internment measures, whether they belong to criminal law or administrative, medical or socio-medical law, the respect for human rights requires the recognition of minimum guarantees common to all deprivations of personal freedom. The basis is that these sanctions or measures, whatever their legal nature, infringe a fundamental right: the right to freedom and security.

Towards a common law on arrest and detention

Deprivation of liberty is sometimes mistakenly thought to mean prison. However, the example of *lettres de cachet* (official writings by the king) indicates that, at a time when imprisonment was an exceptional punishment, there existed avenues other than criminal law to detain someone. Our era is particularly fertile and imaginative in this area. Whether it is to 'intern' mental patients, dangerous alcoholics, or even those suffering from contagious disease; to 'detain' a person for purposes of identity verification or an alien being deported or removed, or even to 'maintain' an alien in a transit zone; to 'place' a minor in a supervised educational establishment or a vagrant in a hospice; or to constrain a person to live within a space so limited that it strangely resembles a prison, there are numerous practices the common denominator of which is to deprive a person of his or her freedom to come and go.

While the *Déclaration des droits de l'homme* limits the risk of arbitrariness simply by requiring that the measure be lawful, the French Constitution of 1958 adds a judicial guarantee (Article 66) requiring

[17] See S. Galand-Carval, 'De la fonction de peine privée de la responsabilité civile', Ph.D. thesis, University of Paris I (1993).

judicial review when the measure lasts longer than a certain length of time, which varies depending on the type of arrest or detention and, more particularly, depending on the 'degree of constraint' exercised on the person concerned. For example, in 1992 the Conseil constitutionnel decided that keeping a foreigner in a transit zone 'does not constrain the interested party to a degree comparable to that resulting from his or her placement in a detention centre', but that it 'none the less affects the personal freedom of the person subject to it'.[18] The result is that judicial authorities may intervene later, but only in 'detention' cases, and they must do so within some undefined period of less than twenty days (the twenty-day statutory period having been judged excessive).

But here again, most of the guarantees come from the European Convention on Human Rights, which couples the right to liberty and security (proclaimed in Article 5) with an exhaustive list of exceptions, and thus precludes by the same stroke any incarceration or detention neither provided for nor found on the list, such as a so-called 'security detention' that might, for public order purposes, be imposed on a person considered dangerous, without a criminal conviction.[19] The Convention legitimates all the listed measures, however, including those that escape criminal law, whether they concern the registration of aliens, educational measures applicable to minors or socio-medical measures regarding persons with infectious diseases or those of unsound mind, alcoholics, drug addicts or vagrants.

This legitimacy is not recognised, however, unless a fair number of conditions are satisfied. Taken together, these conditions do indeed constitute a common law – or an outline of a common law – on incarceration and detention.

This regime, like that of sanctions, is split into a basic regime (a set of minimum guarantees common to all the listed measures) and a regime incorporating stronger guarantees for criminal trials. The basic regime rests in part on the measure's lawfulness (the term 'lawful detention' is used in several paragraphs), and in part on the recognition of specific guarantees and including, for any person deprived of personal freedom by arrest or detention, the right to be informed 'promptly and in a language which he understands', of the reasons for this deprivation of

[18] Conseil constitutionnel decision 92–307 DC, 25 February 1992.

[19] *Guzzardi v. Italy*, ECHR, 6 November 1980, Series A, No. 39.

liberty; the right to make a judicial appeal regarding the lawfulness of the arrest (so as to create what one might call European *habeas corpus*); and finally, the right to reparations in the event the deprivation of liberty was under conditions contrary to the Convention's provisions. As Professor John Spencer underlines, '[i]n the course of the last twenty years . . . various forms of indeterminate detention have been repeatedly attacked as contravening Article 5 of the Convention (the right to liberty). In most of the cases, furthermore, the Strasbourg court has upheld the complaint, taking the line that if a court orders a person to be locked up for an indefinite period, he or she must be able to get a court to review the detention at intervals, and the body with ultimate responsibility for deciding when he is let out must be not a politician but a judge.'[20]

The stronger regime, specific to criminal law, establishes two distinct rights in the event of arrest or detention, both of which limit the length of custody: the right to be brought 'promptly' before a judge, and the right to be judged within a reasonable time or released pending trial, which limits pre-trial detention to a variable extent dependent on the circumstances of each case. Though established in many European countries, the right to speak with an attorney is not expressly provided for.

At a time when detention and internment camps are multiplying, especially since they escape the social visibility and legal framework of prisons, we are starting to see the possible impact of restructuring our much-splintered, yet (for some) little-regulated, legal categories.

Beyond these few examples – to which one could add, for instance, that of measures that 'restrict' (rather than 'deprive of') the freedoms listed in Articles 8 to 11 of the European Convention (private and family life, freedom of opinion, thought, expression, assembly and association: see above) – the results are still unclear.

Legal systems remain clumsy at 'building on multiplicity'. Whether it concerns prescribing a norm or interpreting or legitimating it by reference to meta-legal values, our way of thinking is still strongly influenced by the Enlightenment. Jurists much prefer the precise rules, syllogistic reasoning and homogeneous values of a 'monological' order.

[20] J. Spencer, 'English criminal procedure and the Human Rights Act of 1998', *Israel Law Review* (2000); *X v. UK*, *EHRR* 4 (1981), p. 188; *Wilson, Thynne and Gunnell v. UK*, *EHRR* 13 (1991), p. 666; *Wynne v. UK*, *EHRR* 19 (1994), p. 333; *Hussain and Singh v. UK*, *EHRR* 22 (1996), p. 1.

But law does not belong to jurists. It evolves without them, sometimes despite them, toward a complexity that one must not simply be content to deplore, but must try to 'think through'. That is why this book proposes, before deciding on the decline or revival of law, to explore the hypothesis of an open and pluralist juridicity that would accompany this complexity with zones of norm sub-determination. Taken from Henri Atlan's analyses showing that the neuronal networks to various connections produce, thanks to their sub-determination, 'the same functional states' in one human brain as in another,[21] the hypothesis is that the different legal systems can produce, via their sub-determination zones, a common legal truth.

Jurists would thus join the mathematicians whose works show the 'classical' reasoning method to be 'solipsistic (there is only one observer) or totalitarian (there can be several observers, but they then must all see the same thing)',[22] and who proposed a mathematical theory equally rigorous, but that leads to relative truths.

In their way, human rights – clumsy, imprecise and occasionally a source of misunderstanding – could be one of the bases for a comparable mutation that would oblige us to renounce a certain totalitarianism.

The preparation for the World Conference in Vienna offered more examples of this with its plan to enumerate new rights, such as the right to self-determination and the right to eliminate foreign occupation. Demanded in Asia and refused by western countries, this enumeration had to be abandoned in the end to reach agreement on the general formula, 'identification of the obstacles to new advances in human rights', which does not express (though it does not exclude, either) the idea that 'foreign occupation' constitutes 'an obstacle to new advances in the area of human rights'.[23] In avoiding a split, this purposely imprecise and even ambiguous phrase enables recognised rights to be extended, while keeping the definition of their contents open.

This example also shows, however, the risk of arbitrariness inherent in sub-determination, which is a serious risk that any so-called legal analysis must take into account. Hence the detour through 'new logics', still little known and little used, even though they have proven themselves

[21] H. Atlan, *Tout, non, peut-être. Education et vérité* (Editions du Seuil, 1991), p. 163.

[22] J. Benabou, *Théorie des ensembles empiriques, Cahiers de poétique comparée*, EHESS seminar (1987–8), pp. 5–6.

[23] Chammari Report.

elsewhere and would doubtless, when combined with classical logic, be the means to impose increased transparency and rigour on legal systems that have become openly 'dialogical'.

A cultural revolution, no doubt, but less 'revolutionary' than many jurists think: firstly because, as I have shown, the primary tools are already in place; next, because classical logic would still play a non-negligible role in every area of law, including human rights, where part of the norms are, or are becoming, precise and univocal. Just as non-Euclidian geometry enriched rather than disqualified Euclidian geometry, the methods proposed for 'building on multiplicity' do not require abandoning traditional legal methods, but combining them with others in order better to master a reality that is itself diverse and changing.

It is an apprenticeship, and it will take time. But do we really have a choice, other than to return to self-enclosed, highly specialised, fiercely national legal systems? This is a constant temptation for societies that are unsure of themselves, but such an attitude is more and more difficult to maintain in a society where the techniques for both physical and intellectual communication have developed in an apparently irreversible way.

In any case, the premise of this book is that, if we give ourselves the means to 'build on multiplicity' in our legal reasoning, we will be able to go beyond that reasoning and reinvent a law that is, truly, common.

PART III

Reinventing common law

If we believe Pascal, 'nothing is more common than a good thing, it is simply a matter of discernment'.[1] But there are numerous obstacles or pitfalls that keep us from discerning the outlines of a truly 'common' law.

The first pitfall is to announce a 'return to law'. Although strongly desired by some, a return would primarily inaugurate an American-style promotion of legal professionals. Now more than ever, this corollary of a specialist society reserves knowledge of the law to the initiated, even if they seem to have changed from high priests (superior magistrates or professors) fighting for legal purity into legal engineers or 'merchants of law'[2] (members of transnational firms more concerned with efficiency than legal orthodoxy). The development of specialist societies seems to have modified the spirit of the law, without facilitating access to it. But at least the crisis it provokes seems to provide sociologists with the opportunity to study 'this world of the tacit and the unsaid, where sociology had until now been strictly relegated to an ornamental or ancillary function'.[3] The analysis shows, in particular, how internationalising the legal field places rights in competition, which reinforces specialisation. While specialisation guarantees competency in the grand marketplace of law, it also creates gaps through which non-jurists (and not just sociologists) can enter the fortress of national law, and jurists can, on the basis of internationalisation and increasing specialisation, search for common principles.

Faced with this *challenge of specialist societies*, Europe appears to be a sort of laboratory, not only because it is confronted with national and supranational norms, but also because the mercantile spirit is confronted here with emerging human rights. What is specific to the European case is

[1] Blaise Pascal, *De l'esprit géométrique et de l'art de persuader* (Gallimard, 1969 [1728]), p. 602.
[2] Y. Dezalay, *Marchands de droit* (Fayard, 1992). [3] *Ibid.*, p. 26.

that the internationalisation of law comes simultaneously from opening economic borders and recognising an international, and even supranational, law of human rights to which the member states have agreed to submit themselves, at the risk of each in its turn being condemned by the European Court of Human Rights.

It is a laboratory for a legal pluralism that has, through this accepted tension between the two areas of economic law and human rights, moved away from the American model. The tension is marked by the presence of two, non-hierarchically related European courts, one in Luxembourg and one in Strasbourg. The pitfall here is that the states open up to one another at the cost of closing European borders and, to create harmony between Community (now Union) members, reserve this law exclusively to themselves, or impose it unilaterally on other countries as both a condition of economic aid and a support for cultural and political domination.

But one of the most constant traditions in Europe is openness to the outside, to the world. In the fifteenth century, Pic de La Mirandole studied not only Greek philosophy, medieval scholarship and classical theology, but also Arabic and Hebrew, which gained him access to the Koran and the Kabbala. He chose to model himself on all the great philosophers, to examine every position and learn from each school, expecting that, by confronting them, 'that light of truth Plato mentions in his letters will shine in our souls like the rising sun'.[4] And in 1789, the French revolutionaries, inspired by the philosophy of the Enlightenment, set out in their *Déclaration* 'the natural, inalienable and sacred rights of Man'. The generality of this formula, compared to the abandoned, more specific 'rights of the French citizen', expresses the idea of universality.

Neither the nationalism born in the nineteenth century, nor its contemporary revival, has been able to dissolve the bond between the position of reason in European culture and this openness toward the world. As seen by a Japanese philosopher, this bond, which 'sometimes leads Europeans to take as universal that which is specific to them', can be explained by 'the autonomy that is the basis of the Kantian ethic and of most of modern Europe's ethical systems'. The result of such autonomy is that, 'even when one does not reason in entirely the same way as others,

[4] Pic de La Mirandole, 'Sur la dignité de l'homme', in his *Oeuvres philosophiques* (PUF, 1993 [1486]), p. 51.

one assumes one can always examine their reasoning and understand them'.[5]

Therefore, European legal practices will be considered experiments in the legal pluralism laboratory only if they consider the real *worldwide stakes*, those that incorporate 'others' on a worldwide scale.

In short, the difficulties encountered in the search for a 'truly common' law are not so much the result of obstacles, even formidable ones, but of the ambiguity underlying the approach. Internationalising law creates the illusion that law is becoming common, when in fact it bears with it the two-fold danger of making it even more opaque to non-jurists – thus strengthening the hegemony of legal professionals – and of imposing it on every country through economic pressure – thus strengthening the hegemony of developed countries. It would therefore be naive to believe that the internationalisation of law (and its accompanying increased complexity) will guarantee the birth of a law that is truly common.

But the project is not doomed to failure. Rather than fighting behind the lines jealously to preserve the traditional concepts of strictly national and state-based laws, the path of what one could call a realist utopia consists in using the current transformations as a basis for reinventing common law: 'common' in the strongest sense, establishing, without attempting to fix or circumscribe, the 'irreducible human element' in the name of which the 180-odd states present at the 1993 Vienna Conference reaffirmed the universality of the human rights proclaimed, by fewer than one-third that number, in 1948.

[5] H. Ishiguro, 'La Philosophie', *L'Esprit de l'Europe*, vol. II, *Mots et choses* (Flammarion, 1993), p. 184.

7

The challenge of specialist societies

The challenge of specialist societies is two-fold, because increasing specialisation distances law from the justiciable, or simply from the citizen, whereas the European Court of Human Rights has established that, as a condition of 'quality', laws must be 'adequately accessible' and that citizens must have 'an indication that is adequate in the circumstances of the legal rules applicable to a given case';[1] even the French parliament, in adopting a statute on legal aid, indicated the importance it attaches to 'access to justice and the law' (article 1(1) of the law of 10 July 1991).

The first challenge is to conceive of a law common to all, both jurists and non-jurists, that combines specialisation with access to law. The second is even greater, because it questions the very idea that law can be common to every branch of law and express in some way the spirit of rights. After Roman and canon law, civil law (in the Roman-Germanic tradition) and British common law were able to perform the highly symbolic function of 'western right of access to the laws of the species'. That is, beyond legal technique, a function that, through the 'bond of lawfulness', transforms the biological person into law's subject.[2] In openly asking the question, 'is civil law still inhabitable?', and in showing how 'moving toward the ethical' indicates, with the derailment of law, 'the shake-up of the psychosomatic conception of man [*sic*] in the west',[3] Pierre Legendre foresees an inevitable 'reinterpretation of the world and the subject *fixed* in the west's philosophical corpus'. But the west is not cut off from the rest of the world, and it is by integrating the phenomenon of the internationalisation of law that we can begin, if not the

[1] *Malone v. United Kingdom*, 2 August 1984 (cf. Part II, above).

[2] P. Legendre, *Les Enfants du texte. Etude sur la fonction parentale des Etats* (Fayard, 1992), p. 49.

[3] *Ibid.*, pp. 151ff.

'spring-cleaning' foreseen by Legendre, at least a little dusting off so that we can see, under the accumulation of texts and interpretations, the spirit that inhabits them – assuming they are still inhabited.

Access to law

A 'truly common' law is, first of all, accessible, and if possible, accessible to all. This requires legislative discipline, almost an ethic, given that 'among all the abuses of law our protective era has done its utmost to fight, the abuse of law to legislate will have deserved a place'.[4] The legislature should in any case concern itself with arranging for communication between the 'statute and the people' that Portalis said was necessary 'for the people to know or be able to know that the statute exists and that it exists as law'.[5]

While the first codifiers tried to follow this precept, it would be vain to pretend that the people of France know the names of the fifty-six codes in force in their country today, let alone the innumerable non-codified statutes, decrees and orders, or the European Community (Union) regulations and directives. In creating a 'Superior Commission on Codification' by decree on 12 September 1989, the French prime minister intended to reaffirm the principle that 'every user of law . . . can find a subject, in its entirety, in a code, in the simplest form possible'.[6] But the Commission's composition, predominantly representatives of ministries and of 'the state's highest administrative, judicial and financial authorities', leaves not the slightest bit of room for these 'users of law' for whom it supposedly works. This technocratic, if not bureaucratic, conception evokes a law factory more than the republican ideal of statute: 'the expression of the general will'.[7] The fact that two parliament members (members of the National Assembly and Senate Statutory Commission) are associated with this so-called 'superior' Commission merely aggravates the marginalisation of parliament, because their role is to enable, as the report says, reaching 'the decisive phase of voting on the statutes'

4 J. Carbonnier, *Essai sur les lois* (Defrénois, 1970), preface.

5 *Naissance du Code civil*, p. 103.

6 Statement by M. Rocard, *Revue française de droit administratif* (1990), p. 303.

7 Rapport de la Commission Supèriere de la codification (La Documentation française, 1989); see also in B. Oppetit, *Essai sur la codification* (PUF, 1998), pp. 71–88; Circulaire du 1er ministre relative à la codifications des textes législatifs et réglementaires (30 May 1996).

codification in the best conditions';[8] that is, as quickly and with as little debate as possible.

But nobody's fooled. The new *Code pénal* of 1992 (which entered in force on 1 March 1994) admits non-liability based on mistake of law, thus renouncing Portalis' 'invariable' rule that 'ignorance of the law is no excuse', and in instituting the Commission on Codification the prime minister was quick to admit, after tipping his hat to users of the law, that he did not mean to 'nourish the hope of a miraculously simple law, written with a vocabulary limited to 500 words and accessible to anyone who has learned to read'.[9]

Hence the importance of those who explain laws and inform users of their rights, and therefore of lawyers and, so that all may benefit from such advice, of legal aid for the most disadvantaged: 'Proclaiming human rights, an essential basis of democracy and the rule of law, is insufficient without guaranteeing rights; this can be effective only if equal access to justice is truly assured.'[10] Heading the Conseil d'Etat's report on legal aid, this phrase indicates the desire to substitute, beyond the first step taken with the law of 1972, the idea of state-funded aid (in fact required by international texts on human rights) for the traditional aid, granted and paid for by justice-system auxiliaries, primarily lawyers.

Sent to the prime minister in 1990, this report should have led to the previously mentioned law of 1991 that, in fact, provides not only jurisdictional aid (open access to justice for all, including aliens), but also aid 'to access to the law'. This includes both aid for consultations regarding 'rights and obligations relative to fundamental rights and to the conditions essential to the beneficiary's life' and assistance before non-jurisdictional commissions and the various administrations 'to obtain a decision or exercise a prior mandatory appeal'.

This reform follows closely after that of the legal profession which, by two statutes of 31 December 1990, created a 'new' profession from the fusion of those of barrister and solicitor. A 'free and independent' profession, indeed, but one that the 'new lawyer' can exercise not only as an individual or within a partnership or civil professional company, but also in a commercial company (limited liability company, corporation or limited partnership) whose articles of incorporation are

[8] Commission on Codification, Third Annual Report, 1992.
[9] Statement by M. Rocard.
[10] Conseil d'Etat Rapport sur l'aide juridique (La Documentation française, 1990).

simply rewritten as '*société d'exercice libérale*' (independent contracting company), or even as an 'employee' of a lawyer, a partnership or a company of lawyers. By establishing this commercialisation of the legal profession, the two laws of 1990 chose modernisation at the risk of two-tiered justice: for those who wield economic power, a 'tailor-made justice' sold in the 'supermarkets' that the large international firms became, where each specialty is represented and being over-equipped is a strategic choice to reassure clients and intimidate competitors;[11] and, for ordinary citizens, a 'mass' justice – some speak of 'slaughterhouse' justice – where general practitioners, small-scale craftsmen faced with the engineers of giant multinationals, try to help their clients within the limits of their competence, which cannot be universal.

From the manufacture of laws to legal supermarkets, the evolution is parallel in that it shares the objective of modernisation, is supported by the same management techniques, and obeys the same economic constraints. It remains to be seen whether the answers are the same in the search for a law that remains common.

Manufacture of laws

The concept of codes itself, like so many isolated and independent monuments, was built on the three-sided foundation of state space, stable time, and order based on statute. But one must not forget that the landscape has changed. With the multiplication and diversification of sources of law, marked by the appearance of non-state (primarily, but not exclusively, international), extra-legislative and evolutionary sources, the change, both quantitative and qualitative, demands completely new legislative methods. The great invention is this interrelation between texts and context or, more broadly, between the various normative groups that operate simultaneously – hence the utility of the Commission on Codification that, at the crossroads of all the codifications, is in a position to see the difficulty, which it raises in its third report: 'As work progressed, the Commission on Codification was more and more frequently confronted with the problem of understanding the

[11] Y. Dezalay, *Marchands de droit* (Fayard, 1992); see also 'La Production doctrinale comme objet et terrain de luttes politiques et professionnelles', in Centre d'histoire du droit et de recherches inter-normatives en Picardie et Centre universitaire de recherches administratives et politiques de Picardie (ed.), *La Doctrine juridique* (PUF, 1993), pp. 230ff.

relationship between the various codes, both those that exist and those being written.' We have yet to find an adequate response. When it began its work, the Commission chose to exclude merely cross-referencing from one code to another, without reproducing the articles concerned, because it 'is Sibylline and requires reference to several codes'.[12] Thus, to facilitate access to the law and to 'guarantee, in conditions of proper legal certainty, that readers are informed of the code', the Commission distinguishes a 'leader code' and one or more 'follower code(s)', explaining that 'the follower code(s) will indicate that the rules relating to a question are governed by the leader code articles reprinted [in the follower code]'.[13] While it denies doing so – 'naturally, qualification as a follower code implies no inferiority or subordination of the rules contained therein to the leader code, nor of the administrations responsible for them'– the Commission introduces a de facto hierarchy, which is undoubtedly not the best way to co-ordinate the various groups. Moreover, in its third report, the Commission itself expresses reservations regarding this method: 'The technique of leader and follower codes does enable us to surmount quite a few difficulties [of articulation between various codes], but the Commission is aware of the danger regarding the final text's readability that would result from generalised resort to this technique.' In addition, the Commission flags 'the impossibility for the French authorities to incorporate Community law other than by documentary appendices', emphasising that, 'while this approach is an improvement in the accessibility of these new norms for the citizen, the question of codifying European law will be asked in the near future with greater and greater insistence'.[14]

In the end, one can assume that computerisation will enable the incorporation of any and every normative set of texts into another set (national, infra- or supranational), without necessarily removing them from the original set, with each database having its own access code, thus excluding any de facto hierarchy. For example, a criminal–labour law provision would be accessible from both the 'criminal law' and the 'labour law' databases, and a Community directive regarding consumer rights would be accessible from the 'consumer law' and 'Community law' databases.[15]

[12] Commission on Codification, first balance sheet after a year of Commission activity, General Report for 1990.

[13] *Ibid.* [14] Commission on Codification, Third Annual Report, 1992.

[15] Regarding the proposed application of this method in criminal law, see M. Delmas-Marty, 'Le Nouveau Code pénal', *RSC* 3 (1993), pp. 439ff.

Despite the increasing complexity of law, physical access can be arranged. But the existence of references makes intellectual access, the ability to read and understand, particularly difficult. The manufacture of laws, no matter how perfect from a technical standpoint, simply cannot replace the general will. It has neither the competency nor the legitimacy to define the lines of force that, alone, will reinject coherence and readability into the set under consideration. This is where parliamentary debate can once again take on political and legal meaning – by expressing society's real choices through the adoption of guiding principles that would direct the interpretation of the various technical rules. Examples of such guiding principles could include: principles of decriminalisation, including a series of indicators of seriousness (fault, damages, amount protected) and usefulness (effectiveness and efficacity of existing or proposed sanctions) to direct choices between criminal and extra-criminal sanctions;[16] fundamental principles of procedure to lighten formalism and clarify the conditions of invalidity;[17] or principles of harmonisation on a European scale.[18] The search for such principles is no doubt one of the means to facilitate access to law, without necessarily reducing its complexity, which is merely the legal field's reflection of a social organisation that has itself become more interactive, and thus more complex.

In short, the answer is not to eliminate the manufacture of law and return to the heroic times of the Napoleonic codes, but, rather, to take inspiration from Matisse, looking for harmony in the colours on his canvas: 'When the second colour didn't seem to agree with the first, I added a third to harmonise them.'[19] Therefore, when the reference from one code to another does not create the sought-for harmony, adding guiding principles may create synthesis without renouncing the analytical tools of modern bureaucracies. That is, access to law does not necessarily equal access to all the technical subtleties of the legal rule, but does at least entail the possibility, knowing the underlying principles, of making a reasoned decision as a citizen and justiciable, according to the European Court of Human Rights in *Malone v. United Kingdom* (above), 'to regulate [one's] conduct' and to 'foresee to a reasonable degree in

[16] *Ibid.*, p. 444.

[17] See the Commission de justice pénale et droits de l'homme, *La Mise en état des affaires pénales*, collection of reports (La Documentation française, 1991), pp. 111ff.

[18] See M. Delmas-Marty, *Quelle politique pénale pour l'Europe?* (Kluwer, 1996), pp. 319ff.

[19] Jean Guichard-Meili, *L'Art de Matisse* (Editions Aimery Somogy, 1986).

the circumstances, the consequences which a given action may entail', 'if need be with appropriate advice'.

The need for appropriate advice must be effectively satisfied by the guarantee of equal access to justice and law. The Conseil d'Etat recalled this principle in its 1990 report on legal aid, which served as a reminder that was necessary but late, coming when competition between legal systems was hastening the changes in the legal profession wrought by the 1990 reform – to such an extent that some observers were already remarking that 'the national legal elite have renounced defending the old individualistic, sole-proprietor concept of law and are lining up behind the banner'[20] of big national or international firms: those whose watchwords – profit, profitability and efficiency, and the policy of diversification – in fact belong to a supermarket strategy.

Legal supermarkets

'When, as in the United States, legal services represent greater economic weight than the steel industry, when City law firms can pride themselves on contributing over £350 million to the British balance of payments, when opening a foreign office or buying computer equipment is figured in hundreds of millions of francs, it is clear that these professional organisations are also 100 per cent capitalist enterprises'[21] – deluxe supermarkets – and bear the same risks, as a few resounding failures and painful takeovers have demonstrated. They also have the same tendency as capitalist enterprises to develop: in addition to traditional legal or legal–financial (advising) and judicial (litigating) activities, big-business firms are themselves law producers, be it private justice through mediation and arbitration techniques, or state justice when, beyond the recent wave of major legal–financial battles, legislative or jurisprudential lobbying develops.

And yet the traditional lawyer, both *artisan* and *notable*, whose profession is 'a calling', has not disappeared. Jean-Claude Woog described the lawyer's profession thus, in 1987: 'At the very least, it calls for a person's complete commitment' and, beyond the prior and continuing acquisition of knowledge and savoir-faire, it requires 'respect for the moral rule and an emphasis on profound human qualities'. Hence this

[20] Dezalay, *Marchands de droit*, p. 230. [21] *Ibid.*, p. 224.

riveting shortcut: 'To be a lawyer is above all to love and devote oneself to others.'[22] From a calling to a supermarket is not simply a change, but a veritable earthquake that will shake the entire profession.

But we must consider this profession's capacity for resistance, both economic (takeovers and bankruptcies mark the limits of the development policy of the big national and international firms) and ethical. In France, the ethical tradition of bar associations has a long history, even longer than in the United States. Proof can be seen in the initial methods for implementing the laws of 1990 (the brand new Conseil nationale des barreaux (CNB – the national council of bar associations) was a driving force in their elaboration). Created by the law of 31 December 1990, elected in April and definitively organised in September 1991, this Council is original in being 'national', while the 180 bar associations had until then claimed regional independence (including the Conference of Bar Presidents, which included the presidents of all the bar associations except the one in Paris). Structured in commissions (professional education, international questions, access to law and justice, harmonising professional rules and practices, social commission), the CNB's primary function is to provide governmental representation for the profession. It supervises the harmonisation of professional rules and practices and educational programmes. It has thus formulated proposals and opinions on points as sensitive as the entrance-exam programme for regional legal education centres, the list of specialisations admitted and regulation of advertising.

In these three areas, the CNB's choices showed a certain, sometimes strengthened, attachment to the profession's traditional ethic, such as with the so-called *grand oral* (oral exam), the only part of the professional education entrance exam that cannot be satisfied with equivalent diplomas. The new order substituted, for the old elitist 'general culture' oral presentation, the both ethical and practical choice of an oral presentation on a subject relating to the protection of 'fundamental rights and liberties'.

As for specialities, which lawyers, like the former solicitors (*conseil juridique*), may now mention on their letterheads, a list was set by an order of the minister of justice, based on the CNB's proposals. While rubrics having an economic connotation predominate (tax law, economic

[22] J.-C. Woog, *Pratique professionelle de l'avocat* (LITEC, 1987), p. 6.

law, business law, corporations, enforcement law, real estate law and so on), the law of persons none the less appears as such, at the head of the list (including the law of the family and the child, as well as immigration law, followed by criminal law and completed by social law).

Finally, with regard to advertising, the CNB recognised its utility 'in a society dominated by the law of the market, by lively international competition, and the increased role of the media and consumer associations', but it also emphasised the necessary 'fidelity to certain principles . . . The profession of lawyer cannot be likened to any commercial activity whatsoever; a lawyer is not an entrepreneur like any other; nor simply a legal technician; the lawyer's *specificity*, which justifies a special status in our society, is the accomplishment of a mission *in the public interest, his or her participation in a public service*.'[23]

This is why, within the scope of its mission to harmonise the profession's rules and practices, the National Council edited a brochure entitled 'Personal advertising for lawyers', which sets out a certain number of prohibitions, such as proposing or offering services at home (solicitation and canvassing), of publishing a firm's fiscal results (except for those required for the new commercial companies of lawyers) or divulging a client's identity (except to develop activities abroad). Beyond the principles of utility, accuracy, discretion and respect for the dignity of the profession, the CNB imposes prior communication of the advertising support to the president of the bar 'so that he or she can make his or her observations known'. Finally, it specifies that distribution of information for publicity 'should be done only from the firm, with no allowance for placing the documents in public places or giving them to third parties to distribute'.

A fair number of ambiguities remain, none the less. In a society described as 'dominated by the law of the market, lively international competition, and the increased role of the media and consumer associations', the National Council has not necessarily succeeded in making 'public interest' prevail over the American model that already so influences part of the profession.

This might make us think that the reminder of ethical principles is merely incantatory – a derisory rampart in the face of international competition and certain national jealousies that tend to turn lawyers into

[23] U. Iannucci Report to the Conseil national des barreaux, 1993.

'law merchants'. The reality is no doubt more nuanced than that, and it is probably that the transformation concerns only a fraction of lawyers, which would herald not the deconstruction of the profession, but a major reconstruction, substituting a new bipartisan separation between business lawyers and personal lawyers in place of the academic cleavage between private and public law and the sociological classification of academics compared to practitioners.

While the question of access to law risks its very meaning being modified – a power on one side, a right on the other – the idea of a law common to the various legal disciplines is called into question at the same time, so much so that we doubt the existence of a common spirit ready to challenge this splintering into specialities with a harmonious, if not unified, ensemble called law.

The spirit of rights

Law becomes something ordinary and familiar when it is accessible: 'common', meaning a law placed within everyone's reach.

At first glance the search for a mental community in the face of splintering disciplines that partition themselves as they diversify seems to proceed from the opposite approach, because it is of academic inspiration,[24] as the resurgence of Roman law in Europe, from the Middle Ages to the Renaissance, shows. True, the resurgence was limited to continental Europe, because England rejected Roman law and invented, by developing the use of recourse to the royal courts, its own common law, which in fact played the role of Roman law in countries placed, at some point in their history, under English domination.

This is shown, also, by the drafting of the French *Code civil*, just when 'the Revolution was running dry in its strongly desired conquest of a common law',[25] a common law that would, in fact, like to be the peaceful synthesis of old French law and the Revolution:

[24] For an attempt to tie such an effect of 'democratisation of law' to the law of human rights, see the collective research by M. Delmas-Marty, W. Doise, A. Girardet, R. Lenoir and A. Percheron, 'La Perception des droits de l'homme dans la société contemporaine', Report of the Institut de droit comparé de Paris (1991); minutes in the *Archives de politique criminelle* 11 (1989), p. 35; and 'Discours juridique et discours ordinaire – premiers résultats de la recherche sur la perception des droits de l'homme', *Archives de politique criminelle* 12 (1990), p. 145. See also W. Doise, *Droits de l'homme et force des idées* (PUF, 2001).

[25] F. Ewald, *Naissance du Code civil* (Flammarion, 1989), p. 35.

> Too often, we think as if humankind will end and begin again each instant, without any sort of communication between one generation and the next. Generations, in succeeding one another, blend, entwine and become confused with one another . . . we have, in our modern times, loved change and reform too much; if, with regard to institutions and laws, the centuries of ignorance were the arena of abuse, the centuries of philosophy and enlightenment were too often but the arena of excess.[26]

Hence the Code writers' moderate tone: 'We have, if we may say so, concluded a transaction between written law and custom, whenever it was possible to reconcile their provisions, or to modify one by the other, without disrupting the unity of the system, nor shocking the overall spirit.'[27]

This is the paradox of the French *Code civil*, which unifies law within national boundaries and influences more than one national law, but none the less does not achieve the European unification sketched out by Roman and canon law. Granted, the universal pretension of the writers had almost disappeared with the final version's elimination of the *Livre préliminaire*, which opened with a declaration likely to worry Napoleon, who dreamed of imposing the Code as an emblem of France's hegemony in Europe: 'There exists a universal and unchanging law, source of every positive law text: it is but natural reason inasmuch as it governs all men.' The argument in favour of its suppression was easily found in the principle of a distinction between that which is 'science's share and that which belongs to legislation'. The *Livre préliminaire* became the *Titre préliminaire* of eight, highly technical articles organising 'the publication, effects and application of the laws in general'.

There remained, however, the symbolic force of a Code that was long considered by French jurists as the *jus commune* of the various branches of law, a sort of common trunk defining the method and principles applicable throughout the system.

This is indicative of the anxiety that grips many jurists at the thought that, through progressive marginalisation, the *Code civil* will become but one code among others (the fifty-five others catalogued in 1989 by the Commission on Codification) – anxiety because the *Code civil* has offered generations of interpreters an appropriate tool for exercising

[26] Portalis, 'Discours préliminaire au projet de Code civil', *Naissance du Code civil.*

[27] *Ibid.* Almost 200 years later, the new Civil Code of Quebec (effective 1 January 1994) also aspires to constitute a common law: see R. Cabrillac, *Le Nouveau Code civil du Québec* (Dalloz, 1993), p. 267.

their 'systematisation' function. This function is both instrumental and symbolic, as it maintains the belief in law's rationality, which tends to 'rebuild law as a coherent, integrated, monolithic set, all the elements of which hold and fit together harmoniously'.[28]

Now, the multiplication of more and more specialised branches, which themselves split off and which must be reconciled or combined, increases legal complexity, especially when it increases the quantity of texts. This phenomenon is a real challenge for 'the ideal logician'[29] to which most jurists are still attached, and is, for them, a source of uncertainty and disorder, especially now that law seemed to be in full expansion. Hence their confusion, which is expressed in the number of works devoted to the 'decline',[30] the 'crisis',[31] 'law's role in contemporary anxiety'[32] and 'law's regressive tendencies'.[33]

The ideal must be reinvented, because we must learn, as I said, to build on multiplicity, namely to know and master the tools of new logics: not to disqualify classical logic, but to complete it so as to treat problems beyond its reach.

But with what mindset? Logic enables interpretation of the norm (co-determination) without necessarily revealing the cultural code that inspires it (super-determination).

As described at the beginning of this book, the reconstruction of the legal landscape seems to be inspired by both the market mentality and the human rights mentality – two approaches that super-determine the choices within the system. It would be premature to liken them to the separation outlined earlier between business law and personal law, as these mentalities often haunt the same terrain.

[28] J. Chevallier, 'Les Interprètes du droit', *La Doctrine juridique* (PUF, 1993), pp. 259ff.

[29] J. Lenoble and F. Ost, *Droit, mythe et raison* (Facultés universitaires Saint-Louis, 1980), p. 297.

[30] G. Ripert, *Le Déclin du droit. Etudes sur la législation contemporaine* (LGDJ, 1949); H. Battifol, 'Le Déclin du droit, examen critique', *Archives de philosophie du droit* 8 (1963), p. 43; G. Burdeau, 'Le Déclin de la loi', *Archives de philosophie du droit* 8 (1963), p. 35. See also the critical analysis of A. Perrot, 'La Doctrine et l'hyphothèse du déclin du droit', *La Doctrine juridique* (PUF, 1993), p. 1815.

[31] P. Roubier, 'La Crise du droit et l'évolution régressive', *Théorie générale du droit* (Sirey, 1951), p. 330; F. Terré, 'La Crise de la loi', *Archives de philosophie du droit* 25 (1980), p. 17. See also Perrot's citations, *La Doctrine juridique*, p. 1815.

[32] J. Carbonnier, 'La Part du droit dans l'angoisse contemporaine', in LGDJ (ed.), *Flexible droit* (2nd edn, LGDJ, 1971), pp. 112ff.

[33] B. Oppetit, 'Les tendances régressives du droit', *Mélanges Holleaux* (1991); see also 'L'Hyphothèse du déclin du droit', *Droits* 4 (1986), p. 9.

The market mentality

While it may be true that the market mentality refers to 'all that, in the name of money, cannot be reduced to economy, pure and simple', or even 'that, in the market, cannot be reduced to a field that can be fenced in by a theory',[34] it encompasses much more than business law, and even property law. The old idea, contained in the French *Code civil*, that 'any obligation to do or not to do shall be resolved in damages, in the case of non-performance on the part of the debtor' (article 1142) is a simple and realistic idea (what better way to force people to fulfil their obligations?) that can none the less lead to a deviation, 'such that the decision to respect or renege on one's obligations can result from a monetary calculation, thus showing that the sanction of the rule of law is at least as important as the rule itself and that, in many cases, an economic calculation can lead to escaping one's obligations'.[35] This deviation is especially visible in tort, and not just contractual, liability, where damages enable the evaluation, by equivalency or substitution, of the price of a human life – and to discover its relativity.

First, relativity in time: human capital increases first with education, then with our first professional experience, and then diminishes as we age and exhausts itself on the eve of our death in old age. It is as if the price of human life followed a bell curve: zero at the beginning, rapidly increasing during our studies and then again a little more at the beginning of our careers, then diminishing with age to become zero again on the day we die.

Relativity in space also: at the time of Clovis, a Frank was worth, they said, two Gaulois,[36] and Rousseau's Sybarite, evaluated through reference to his consumption of various goods, 'would have been worth at least thirty Lacedaemonians'.[37] Today, private international law reveals that

[34] J. Derrida, 'Du sans prix ou le juste prix de la transaction' in R.-P. Droit (ed.), *Comment penser l'argent*? (Le Monde Editions, 1992), p. 386.

[35] See D. Cohen, 'Le Droit et l'argent, tout a-t-il un prix?' in Droit (ed.), *Comment penser l'argent?*, pp. 299ff.

[36] See G. Cottereau, 'Du Caractère relatif du prix de la vie' in Droit (ed.), *Comment penser l'argent?*, pp. 323ff. See also B. Moris, 'Nord-Sud, l'argent du riche et l'argent du pauvre' in Droit (ed.), *Comment penser l'argent?*, pp. 335ff.

[37] See J.-J. Rousseau, 'A discourse on the arts and sciences', in *The Social Contract and Discourses* (trans. G. D. H. Cole) (Everyman, 1973 [1750]) p. 19: 'The politicians of the ancient world were always talking of morals and virtue; ours speak of nothing but commerce and money. One of them will tell you that in such a country, a man is worth just as much as he will sell

each state applies its own rules and that indemnities are higher in France than in Italy, Spain, the United Kingdom or Germany (beyond the fact that moral prejudice, recognised in French law, is not considered on the other side of the Rhine).

But the principle of indemnity has been progressively detached from contract or tort. Chapter 1 showed how moving from liability to solidarity leads to recognising a right to indemnity where risk replaces fault as the generating factor: thus the entire area of accidents, and therapeutic accidents in particular, leads to such an expansion of the right to indemnity that it frankly raises the question of distribution of the corresponding financial burden in economic terms, whether the burden is borne in the end by social security, private insurance or indemnity guarantee funds.

Some commentators are beginning to raise the need for a halt to this evolution. According to François Ewald, the idea of 'precaution' should be expressed in a kind of synthesis between the past – 'we are no longer alone in the face of destiny' (that was foreseeing) – the present – 'we are all together in the face of destiny' (this is prevention) – and his recommendation for the future: 'We are moving toward societies in which there will be a social security base and an individual coverage base.'[38] However, the practices resist attempts to stop the system evolving. For example, in 1993, for the first time in France, the Conseil d'Etat, with the concurrence of the Assembly (and hence with particular solemnity), accepted the assignment of liability to a public hospital for an abnormal, exceptional and extremely serious accident that occurred without medical error.[39]

for in Algiers; another, pursuing the same mode of calculation, finds that in some countries a man is worth nothing, and in others still less than nothing; they value men as they do droves of oxen. According to them, a man is worth no more to the State than the amount he consumes; and thus a Sybarite would be worth at least thirty Lacedaemonians.' Note that Rousseau borrows word for word a text of Montesquieu's, without citing it by name or appearing to see the underlying irony. Referring to the *Political Arithmetic* of Sir William Petty, Montesquieu writes, in *L'Esprit des lois*, book XXIII, chapter 17, 'of Greece, and the number of its inhabitants': 'Sir William Petty, in his calculations, supposes that a man in England is worth what he would sell for at Algiers. This can be true only with respect to England. There are countries where a man is worth nothing; there are others where he is worth less than nothing.'

[38] Interview with F. Ewald, *Le Monde*, 21 April 1993. See also, regarding insurance practitioners' calculation methods, D. Kassler, 'Quelle est la valeur économique de la vie humaine?' in Droit (ed.), *Comment penser l'argent?*, pp. 310ff.

[39] See CE, 10 April 1993, Recueil des arrêts.

The future seems even more uncertain as the market mentality has gained on the law of the person not only through the end result of indemnity, but even, more profoundly, through its very means of expression – negotiation – which seems now to reach the hard and irreducible core of the person through moral rights (*droits de la personnalité*).

Discussion in Chapter 1 of the 'market of bodies' and of 'creative works' showed how these concepts have evolved by diversifying: from absolute unavailability to availability limited by a principle of gratuity, to having a pecuniary nature and finally to the search for profit. Thus, to varying degrees, the market mentality has been introduced into an area traditionally placed 'beyond lawful trade'.

The distinction between the law of persons and the law of goods, which is traditional in private law, has become somewhat blurred, and this blurring is more than a simple readjustment of disciplinary categories or a re-evaluation of hierarchies specific to the legal field. It is also affecting the *summa divisio* inherited from Roman law that opposes private law, which controls relationships between individuals, to a public law specific to the organisation of communities, including the state, and their relationships with individuals. This opposition results in the separation of judicial tribunals, placed under the authority of the Cour de cassation, from administrative tribunals, placed under the authority of the Conseil d'Etat. The market mentality, which is of private origin (merchants), is now contaminating the concept of public service, while, conversely, private economic operators who do not follow the rules of the market are subject to 'administrative' sanctions, thus public law. The confusion increases when a sanction decided by an independent 'administrative' authority, such as the Stock Exchange Commission or the Competition Council, is appealed to judicial, rather than administrative, jurisdictions.

This redistribution of the major legal disciplines is not only due to the market mentality, however. It is being imposed simultaneously under the pressure of human rights.

The human rights mentality

With regard to human rights, I showed above how legal reasoning, beginning at the moment of the declaration of these rights and their enforceability against everyone, including states, led to restructuring the major legal categories along common lines, of which I gave two examples: a 'common law of sanctions', which regroups administrative, disciplinary and civil sanctions, and even the various forms of arbitrage and mediation around criminal law; and a 'common law of arrest and detention', where police measures (detention or maintenance in a transit zone) applicable to aliens and various internment or medical, medico-social and medico-pedagogical placement measures applicable to the mentally ill, alcoholics, addicts, contagious persons, vagrants and minors, reside with criminal incarceration (that is, custody before or during trial, and post-conviction 'correctional' or 'criminal' imprisonment).

The human rights mentality could very well blend with the market mentality to super-determine the reorganisation of the legal world. This obviously does not mean they will combine with each other, but that, both coming from a phenomenon of openness and often internationalisation of the economy on the one hand, of reproof on the other, they produce a comparable effect of rebuilding the legal landscape.

How can we analyse such a relationship, which is at first sight self-contradictory? It is perhaps the Kantian distinction between dignity and price that best elucidates the comparison. Used by Jacques Derrida with regard to the market mentality, such analysis shows that these two concepts are neighbours, but heterogeneous, because 'dignity is an *unconditional* value; its absolute respect obeys an imperative law that is, in reality, the cause itself, the origin of the moral sentiment; this law is not negotiable, it is above the market; unlike dignity as an *incalculable* value, price is conditional, hypothetical, negotiable, calculable':[40] heterogeneous without being incompatible. In fact, one must, according to him, 'negotiate the non-negotiable . . . because it is the very possibility of money, of a price, even the principle of equivalency, that *also* enables us to neutralise the differences to reach a pure singularity such as dignity or universal law'. Hence the consequence that 'rejecting money or its principle of abstract indifference, the disdain for figures, can be in connivance with the destruction of morals, of law' – provided, that is, that the 'principle of abstract indifference' is respected: a Gaulois is worth a Frank and a Lacedaemonian Rousseau's Sybarite . . .

The case of the stolen hand imagined by a legal historian,[41] Jean-Pierre Baud, beyond the anecdote's provocativeness, fits within this

[40] Derrida, 'Du sans prix ou le juste prix de la transaction' (emphasis in original).

[41] J.-P. Baud, *L'Affaire de la main volée* (Editions du Seuil, 1993).

perspective. It is 'stolen' because, separated from the body, the hand became an object that could be appropriated, and taking it against the owner's will constitutes indeed a theft: 'the fraudulent taking of another's object' (French *Code pénal*, article 379; new French *Code pénal*, article 311-1). To sustain his argument that between the person and the body there exists a relationship of ownership because the body is a thing and not an extension of the person, Baud reminds the reader that the negation of this proprietary relationship enabled canon law to justify slavery. He adds the much more recent example of 'the man with the golden cells',[42] decided in 1990 by the Californian Supreme Court.[43] The case involved a patient who underwent surgery on his spleen, and whose blood contained antibodies with exceptional therapeutic properties. Without his knowledge, the doctors proceeded to draw his cells and patent them, intending to share in a market estimated at $3 million. After various twists and turns, the Supreme Court finally refused the patient the right to assert ownership of his cells and also refused to authorise the doctors to exploit them industrially.

From this double example, Baud draws the conclusion 'that human dignity means conferring the quality of thing on the body',[44] so as to 'negotiate the non-negotiable' and make the human rights mentality and the market mentality coexist in the *Code civil.* But this market is such that commercialisation will, in fact, be limited in the name of respect for human rights. To introduce such a limit, Baud proceeds to a sort of reinterpretation of the *Code civil.* He suggests incorporating the human body into article 1128, which sets out the concept of 'things beyond trade', but as a 'modern transcription of sacredness, because the concept of thing must not be likened to that of merchandise, which would engulf precisely these things beyond trade that sacred things are'.

Baud's analysis may appear seductive, but it merely puts off the problem, because it does not define the legal meaning of the category 'sacred

[42] A description coined by Bernard Edelman in 'L'Homme aux cellules d'or', *Recueil Dalloz* (1989), p. 225.

[43] *John Moore v. The Regents of the University of California*, 793 P. 2d 479 (Calif., 1990). For a critical analysis of the case, see B. Edelman and M. A. Hermitte, *'L'Homme aux cellules d'or'* (Edition Christian Bourgeois, 1988). See also Edelman, 'La Recherche biomédicale dans l'économie de marché' (Dalloz, 1991), p. 203, and M.-A. Hermitte, 'Réflexions d'un juriste sur le rapprochement des mots "économie" et "expérimentation"', in A. Marangopoulos-Yotopoulos (ed.), *Expérimentation biomédicale et droits de l'homme* (PUF, 1988); see Part I, above.

[44] Baud, *L'Affaire de la main volée*, p. 226.

things'. Neither the detour he takes by Mircea Eliade ('the sacred is the real *par excellence*'), nor his return to Pufendorf, who esteems people 'held to serve themselves with these sorts of things in a certain way',[45] indicates where the lines not to be crossed will be drawn when exercising an owner's prerogatives, traditionally summed up by the Roman trilogy of *usus* (usage), *fructus* (perceiving the fruits or revenue) and *abusus* (the right to dispose of a thing, for consideration or for free).

It is not enough to declare a person's ownership of his or her body as a thing to assure respect for human dignity. Proof of this is the development of various practices such as recruiting healthy volunteers for scientific experiments, or surrogate mothers for medically assisted reproduction, or even the donation of organs for transplant. Whether the subject is 'reimbursed for costs' or receives the 'price' of the sale or rental of his or her body, the difference is no doubt not essential. However, the basis for such practices is most often the law of supply and demand, which solicits persons from disadvantaged countries or social backgrounds to 'sell' their bodies. It is this predominance of the market mentality that, apparently, flouts the principle of equal dignity at the heart of human rights.

I chose to highlight the most extreme example, though there are many other practices that could be cited to illustrate the relationship between the market and human rights: a bilateral and interactive relationship as is shown by the frequency with which human rights are invoked in business law, where the problem is more visible and harder to avoid, thus encouraging the search for the legal means to respect effectively, and not just put on display, the principle of equal dignity. Such respect implies, in the case of a conflict of interest, the predominance of human rights over the law of the market, and above all the definition of lines that are not to be crossed, which calls for a set of applicable, and applied, sanctions. But the internationalisation of the market, whether it concerns the body or anything else, has taken on such a dimension that the problem can no longer be resolved by national law alone. Outlined on a European scale, the answer is part of the worldwide undertaking.

[45] M. Eliade, *Le Sacre et le profane* (Gallimard, 1989 [1957]), pp. 25–62; Pufendorf, *Droit de la nature et des gens* (Lyon, 1771), pp. 16ff.

8

The European laboratory

The dream of hegemony abandoned, no one can pretend to be the inventor of Europe. It is being built a little bit everywhere, growing like a living organism, with its own sources of energy and its own wounds, growths and folds.

It is not by choice, but by necessity and chance combined, that Europe is becoming a space with variable geography, partially orderly and partially chaotic, similar perhaps, to the topological spaces that mathematicians have discovered 'replace the static world of classical sets with an evolutionary world constituted of continually varying objects'.[1]

Europe is a partially, and diversely, ordered space, because there have indeed been attempts, since the Second World War, to create this European order that we now conjugate in the plural (there are now two Europes – the fifteen-member European Union and the forty-three-member Council of Europe). There were political attempts, from July 1948 onwards, to create a European Assembly composed of parliamentary representatives. British hostility to the plan resulted in the compromise that should have enabled the creation of the Council of Europe, the articles of which were signed in London on 5 May 1949; these were modest articles, limited to periodic meetings of a simple Committee of Ministers, named by the governments, and of a consultative assembly without any real power.

However, the Franco-Germanic quarrel over the Saar, a mining region and important metallurgical centre, steered the debate in another direction entirely. From the desire to avoid fresh conflicts was born the idea of putting the Franco-Germanic coal and steel production together under a common High Authority, in an organisation open to other European

[1] See J.-R. Roisin, 'Topos', in *Encyclopédie philosophique universelle*, vol. II, *Les Notions philosophiques. Dictionnaire de philosophie occidentale* (ed. S. Auroux) (PUF, 1990), pp. 2614ff. (cf. Part II, p. 118, above).

countries. The European Coal and Steel Community (ECSC) thus constituted an embryonic, six-party Europe.[2] Its institutions prefigured, with a few differences, those of the European Economic Community (EEC) and the European Atomic Energy Community (Euratom) that were created by the Treaty of Rome in 1957 after the failure of the European Defence Community (EDC). The progressive enlargement of the Common Market, from six to nine states in 1973, ten in 1981, twelve in 1986 and fifteen in 1998, was accompanied by a strengthening of European institutions, with the increasing use of the majority vote rather than unanimity for Council of Ministers decisions, the increased importance of financial resources specific to the Community, and the progressive autonomy of supranational organs such as the Commission, the Court of Justice of the Communities and, to a less pronounced extent, the European Parliament. The revision of the Treaty of Rome by the Single European Act (1986), the Maastricht Treaty on European Union (1992), the Amsterdam Treaty (1997) and the Nice Treaty (2000) mark the principal stages in this economic, legal, and entirely political integration.

Politically, the European space remains chaotic. Nationalist movements are developing in the west, especially in Northern Ireland and the Basque region, while the end of Communism in the east has 'revive[d] the question of borders',[3] and at the same time reactivated national, ethnic and religious violence and confrontations in the former Yugoslavia and USSR.

It remains to be seen if the method chosen, or rather imposed by the circumstances, will measure up to the ascribed objective: 'Europe', said Jean Monnet, 'will not be realised all at once, or through building a group; it will be made through concrete realisations, creating first a de facto solidarity'.[4] 'Making Europe means making peace'.[5]

To make peace, or, more precisely, to create conditions for preserving peace, it was indispensable to develop legal structures, and to make them as invisible as possible to avoid running smack into the principle of national sovereignty. This led to the appearance of devices that were at first almost hidden in the recesses of the two founding groups: on

[2] Belgium, Italy, Luxembourg and the Netherlands joined France and Germany.

[3] Y. Lacoste, 'La Fin du communisme ressuscite la question des frontières', in A. Compagnon and J. Seebacher (eds.), *L'Esprit de l'Europe*, vol. I, *Dates et lieux* (Flammarion, 1993), pp. 191ff.

[4] J. Monnet, *Clefs pour l'action* (Association des amis de Jean Monnet, 1988), p. 50.

[5] *Ibid.*, p. 51.

the one hand, the European Convention on the Protection of Human Rights, adopted in 1950 by the Council of Europe but ratified very slowly by the member states (by France in 1974); on the other, Community law resulting from the treaties relating to the European Community (now the European Union) and the texts derived from it. This is therefore a bipolar construction, the complexity of which is increased by the more or less independent satellites, such as the Benelux countries and the 'Schengen space' to the west,[6] and the Conference for Security and Co-operation in Europe (CSCE), with the participation of central and eastern European countries.[7]

Thus Europe has become an experimental laboratory in which, in the landscape of incomplete pyramids and strange loops described earlier in this book, one can study the proliferation of legal structures that perhaps indicate, through their simultaneous yet non-unified functioning, the birth of a 'legal' (that is, ordered) pluralism.

It is a difficult birth, requiring prior mastery of language's multiple meanings. It requires learning to say 'the same law for everyone' in several languages, without running into translation problems that only linguists can solve.[8] It is most assuredly difficult, since legal thought is frightened of multiplicity, which it associates with disorder and will continue to try to minimise, on the pretext of organising it, unless we reinvent this common thing that would, if not unite, at least harmonise this legal Europe. It would still be a 'common' law, but in a broader sense, encompassing the various traditions that make up Europe.

It is not my intention here to describe the legal situation in Europe, but to measure this coexistence of European orders – a plural that irresistibly creates disorder – to try to find the key to harmonisation.

[6] Benelux is the entity comprising Belgium, Luxembourg and the Netherlands resulting from the economic union of these three states. First thought of in 1944, with action taken as of 1948, this union is the fruit of a series of agreements that resulted in a treaty in 1960. More recently, the 'Schengen space' comprises thirteen signatory states of the Schengen *acquis* (14 June 1985 and the 'application' agreement of 19 June 1990), and two states that joined by treaty, which organises free movement within common borders and at the same time organises a system of co-operation between national police forces and the institution of an automated information file (the Schengen Information System).

[7] The CSCE dates from the conferences in Vienna (1989), Paris and Copenhagen (1990) and Moscow (1991), and from the outset marked the attachment of thirty-seven states (those of central and eastern Europe in their configuration at the time) to principles of common law, establishing the 'human dimension' as an essential component of security and co-operation in Europe. See *RUDH* (1989), p. 295 and (1990), pp. 339 and 490.

[8] P. Braselmann, 'Le même droit pour tous?', *Liber* 13 (1993), p. 4.

Coexistence of European orders

In current legal terminology, only Community law constitutes a legal order distinct from that of the member states, though both the European Commission and the Court of Human Rights are managing to build a supranational legal order based on the European Convention. In practice, the set of norms defined by the Convention and the former Commission and ECHR case law resembles more and more a system sufficiently independent to be defined as a 'legal order'.

However, the coexistence of Community law and the European Convention on Human Rights was initially helped by a certain partitioning of the respective competencies to fields that were thought at the time to be quite limited. In sum, each state remained sovereign over its territory, on the condition that it recognised the primacy of Community law in the economic field (which was thought to be narrowly delimited), imposed under the authority of the Tribunal and the European Court of Justice in Luxembourg; and on the condition that each state respect – but each was certain to be exemplary on this – all of the rights and liberties placed, by the European Convention, under the authority of the European Commission and the Court of Human Rights in Strasbourg. Luxembourg on one side, Strasbourg on the other, became the symbols of each jurisdiction's independence, and therefore of their peaceful coexistence. This coexistence was made even more peaceful as only the European Commission on Human Rights could have a matter referred to it by an individual claiming to be a victim of a violation of his or her rights, while the Luxembourg courts exercised only 'attribution' competency concerning the lawfulness of the Community authority's acts, a state's failures on a complaint from the Commission or another state, or the interpretation of Community rules on 'prejudicial' questions raised by national jurisdictions. It was also more peaceful because the states saw in it protection from unification attempts that might threaten their legal sovereignty.

This competition was supposed to be an efficient enough legal integration tool imposed, of course, a step at a time, but continuously – a new kind of integration, in that it combines classical logic (principle of hierarchy, requirement of identity, decision of conformity) with a logic of gradation (principle of harmony, requirement of proximity, decision of compatibility).

I have shown, in fact, how recognising a margin – national margin of appreciation to arrange national sensibilities, European margin of control to fill in the gaps in European texts – has transformed legal reasoning by introducing a gradation scale and a decisional threshold (the 'compatibility' threshold) that escape the rules of classical logic. I also laid out on what conditions this type of reasoning can obey another logic – of fuzzy subsets – that guarantees both rigour of reasoning and decisional flexibility. These conditions control the refutable – namely, the controllable and non-arbitrary nature of the judge's decision – and thus the admission of a process of norm co-determination that is neither the simple transcription of texts nor a revolt against them.

However, the examples studied above were deliberately chosen by reference to a single European legal order – in most cases, that of the European Convention on Human Rights, so as to limit it to the Europe/state relationship and avoid the problem of any possible Europe/Europe confrontation. Appearing more recently, such confrontation of various European legal orders is inevitable, however, as over time the areas where these two legal orders (the Common Market and human rights) are both competent to determine the applicable norm have proved numerous.

For example, the status of aliens and workers is governed simultaneously by the fundamental rights established by the European Convention on Human Rights and by the principle of free movement within the Common Market. The free movement of merchandise and services does not preclude recognising the right to hold property, the right to a fair trial in case of conflict, nor recognising various rights and liberties, such as freedom of expression in the face of a mass media, or the respect for dignity in the face of biotechnology.

Escaping the traditional opposition between the law of persons and the law of goods, this confrontation between the Europe of merchants and the Europe of human rights illustrates (transcribed in terms of systems) what sociologists call 'simultaneous polysystemy', defined by André-Jean Arnaud as 'the meeting of several legal systems in the same place at the same time',[9] but considered 'impossible in so far as a precise legal relationship cannot be subject to more than one rule'. Hence the need for a 'mechanism to solve this problem'.[10]

[9] See A.-J. Arnaud, *Dictionnaire encyclopédique de théorie et de sociologie du droit* (2nd edn, LGDJ, 1993), under 'Polysystémie'; see also *Pour une pensée juridique européenne* (PUF, 1991), p. 86.

[10] See references in previous note.

In looking for such a mechanism, one must first distinguish Common Market *and* human rights (the norms applicable under different scenarios appear compatible) from Common Market *or* human rights (they appear incompatible) – Arnaud's 'disjunctive' polysystemy – which imposes a choice even more painful as there is no legal hierarchy to solve the conflict.

Common Market and human rights

Two examples will illustrate this compatibility between the European legal orders.

First, there is the example of the status of aliens, at the crossroads of Community law (to which must be added, at the risk of incompatibility with human rights, the Schengen *acquis* upon its entry into force) and the European Convention on Human Rights (completed by Additional Protocols, in particular numbers 4 and 7). Of course, this is merely the crossroads of two ensembles that do not target exactly the same territory (Community on one side, national on the other), nor the same persons (Community members on the one hand, aliens of any national origin on the other). But there is a catch-all zone where both legal orders (apart from the Schengen *acquis*) apply simultaneously and, for the most part, compatibly.

Their compatibility stems first from the proximity of the applicable rules. Thus, Article 48 of the Treaty of Rome sets out the principle of free movement within the European Communities and Article 2 of Additional Protocol 4 of the European Convention on Human Rights guarantees to 'everyone lawfully within the territory of a state' the right 'to liberty of movement and freedom to choose his residence'. There is also proximity of limitations and restrictions that each system authorises, as, 'in the forefront of each State's sovereign prerogatives appears the right to determine unilaterally and with discretion the conditions for attributing its nationality, for allowing non-nationals to enter, and for evicting them'.[11] More broadly, in effect the states largely remain masters of their criminal policy or their immigration policy, whether it concerns extraditing an alien accused of having committed an offence subject to the jurisdiction of another state that asserts it, turning back illegal aliens at the border or deporting them once they have entered the

[11] D. Lochak and F. Julien-Laferrière, 'Les Expulsions entre la politique et le droit', *Archives de politique criminelle* 12 (1990), pp. 65ff.

territory, or finally, deporting an alien whose presence in the national territory constitutes a threat to public order. However, the states must respect the rule of non-discrimination, established in both the Treaty of Rome (Article 7) and the European Convention (Article 14) and take into account the guarantees introduced by Community law (Directive 64/221 of 1964) with regard to human rights (Additional Protocol 7). These guarantees require them, under the supervision of each of the European courts, to limit the reasons for their decisions to the accepted criteria and to respect certain procedural rules.

In addition, for citizens of member states of the Community, the right to family grouping is established by several Regulations of the Council (of 1964 and 1968, modified in 1976 and 1992), accompanied by a Directive of 1968 (modified several times).[12] More broadly, in granting every person the right to respect for family life (Article 8), the European Convention can be an obstacle to a decision of deportation if, regardless of the other merits of its argument, it deprives the person of all family contact.[13]

But compatibility is more than just proximity of the applicable rules, which one could call 'positive compatibility'. It also results from their complementarity, namely the fact that the rules set out by one of the ensembles can fill in the gaps in the other: a sort of 'negative complementarity' that expresses primarily the applicability of all the rights and liberties established by the European Convention on Human Rights to aliens, as a complement to Community law. This is how Article 3, for example, which prohibits torture and inhuman or degrading treatment or punishment, can be invoked when deportation results in sending a person to a country where there is a risk of such treatment.[14] There is

[12] See Articles 5 to 9 of Directive 64/221 and the ECJ case law, in particular decisions Case 36/75, *Rutili*, 28 October 1975 [1975] ECR 1219 and Case 98/79, *Pecastaing*, 5 May 1980 [1980] ECR 691; see also Article 1(1) of Protocol 7, setting out the procedural guarantees except in emergencies (Article 1(2)). See also F. Massias, 'Control of aliens' in M. Delmas-Marty (ed.), *The European Convention for the Protection of Human Rights* (Kluwer Academic Publications, 1992).

[13] See the decisions *Berrahab v. Netherlands*, ECHR, 21 June 1988, *Moustaquim v. Belgium*, ECHR, 18 February 1991, and *Beldjoudi v. France*, ECHR, 26 March 1992. See also P. Kayser, 'Le Regroupement familial dans le droit communautaire, la Convention européenne des droits de l'homme et le droit interne français', *JCP* I (1993), p. 3679.

[14] See, for the European Commission on Human Rights, *Amekrane v. United Kingdom*, 11 October 1973, and, for the Court, *Soering v. United Kingdom*, 11 July 1989, Series A, No. 161. See, however, the decision of the Conseil d'Etat (CE, 15 October 1993, *JCP* (1993), Actualités no. 43), granting extradition to the United States on the simple promise of the American prosecutor not to seek the death penalty.

also a prohibition (Article 4 of Additional Protocol 4) against collective deportation of aliens, based on the same 'absolutely protected' principle (see Part II, above) of respect for the dignity of the person (in the strongest sense of the word).

Leaving room for the differences specific to national practices, and especially to the states' constitutional jurisprudence,[15] the proximity of norms and their complementarity are sufficient temporarily to assure, if not complete protection, at least compatibility between the two European legal orders regarding the status of aliens.

As for the second example, the law of goods, the compatibility between legal orders appears at first sight to be due more to their complementarity than to the proximity of applicable norms. In fact, Community law especially, with its goal of transforming the 'common market' into a 'single market', attempts to guarantee the free movement of merchandise and services by prohibiting 'quantitative import restrictions, as well as all measures having an equivalent effect'.[16] This prohibition is interpreted broadly by the ECJ, to the extent that it occasionally neutralises certain provisions of domestic criminal law, either when the sanction is 'so disproportionate' to the seriousness of the offence that it hinders free movement, or when the offence itself is judged to constitute a measure with an effect equal to an import restriction.[17]

Setting aside the more difficult questions of procedural rules for disputes involving goods and those involving people (see below), the European Convention on Human Rights and its Additional Protocols offer less protection for the movement of goods, the very essence of the market, than for the right to own property, which is simply a restatement of 'Every natural or legal person is entitled to the peaceful enjoyment of his goods' (Article 1 of Additional Protocol 1). There is thus complementarity with a text that specifies the conditions in which the right to hold property may be restricted or regulated.[18]

[15] See, e.g., in France, recent decisions of the Conseil constitutionnel regarding the law on nationality (CC, 22 July 1993) and the law on the conditions for aliens to enter and stay in the country (CC, 93–326 DC, 11 August 1993).

[16] Article 28, Single European Act 1996.

[17] See, in particular, the well-known examples of the price of books and of petrol, ECJ decisions, 10 (Case 229/83 *Leclerc v. Au blé vert* [1985] ECR 1) and 29 January 1985 (Case 231/83 *Henri Cullet et Chambre syndicale des réparateurs automobiles et détaillants de produits pétroliers v. Centre Leclerc à Toulouse et à Saint-Orens-de-Gameville* [1985] ECR 305).

[18] The right to own property is attacked by measures that deprive a person of his or her property 'in the public interest and subject to the conditions provided for by law

However, the ECJ has several times considered that the right to hold property is an unwritten fundamental principle 'guaranteed in the Community legal order in accordance with concepts common to the constitutions of the member states, reflected in the first protocol of the European Convention'.[19] The set of cross-references between the two European orders is dealt with below; here only the proximity and complementarity of the principles expressed are addressed.

This proximity also comes from the concept of proportionality, which is used in Community law as well as in the process of jurisprudential interpretation of Additional Protocol 1. This process is similar to that studied with regard to restrictions necessary in a democratic society (see Part II, above), even though the Protocol envisages not only the regulation of the right to hold property, which can be analysed like so many other restrictions, but also true 'deprivations', such as expropriation or nationalisation. In fact, the Strasbourg authorities, while recognising here again a wide national margin of appreciation, considering the 'great latitude' the legislature enjoys in social policy and economic matters,[20] control the proportionality between the public utility or interest invoked to support the measure and the gravity of the infringement of the right to hold property. This control has brought the Strasbourg Court to introduce a principle of indemnity that is, however, not expressly included in the text, other than by deduction from the general principles of international law cited in Article 1(2) of the European Convention. This principle would in any case be imposed in the name of the enforceability of the protected rights as, in the absence of its recognition, 'Article 1 would assure but an illusory and inefficient protection of the right to hold property'.[21]

and by the general principles of international law': Article 1(1) of Protocol 1. It is regulated by restrictive measures taken 'in accordance with the general interest or to assure the payment of taxes or other contributions or penalties': Article 1(2) of Additional Protocol 1.

19 See Case 44/79 *Hauer v. Land Reinhard-Pfalz*, ECJ, 3 March 1978, [1980] 3 CMLR 42.

20 *Mellacher v. Austria*, ECHR, 19 December 1989, and comments of L. Sumat, *Gaz. Pal.*, 24–5 April 1991. For a more precise study of the national margin of appreciation and its variations from one decision to another, see F. Massias, 'L'Influence de la Convention européenne des droits de l'homme sur le droit de propriété', *ERPL* 2 (1994), pp. 47–78.

21 See *James v. United Kingdom*, ECHR, 21 February 1986, and *Lithgow v. United Kingdom*, ECHR, 8 July 1986, Series A, No. 102. See also B. Stern, 'Le Droit de propriété, l'expropriation et la nationalisation dans la Convention européenne des droits de l'homme', *Droit du commerce et des pratiques internationales* 17(4) (1991), pp. 394ff.

Finally, there is proximity in the possible combination, which at times controls the review of proportionality, of the right to hold property with the right to non-discrimination, which is also affirmed in the two legal orders. There may therefore be a violation, if not of Additional Protocol 1, at least of the European Convention (Article 14) and of Community law (Article 7 of the Treaty of Rome), when a state permits different treatment with regard to property without any 'objective and reasonable' justification (based on birth out of wedlock, for example[22]).

However, the Court of Human Rights admits that different treatment between nationals and aliens has, with regard to indemnity, an 'objective and reasonable justification', because aliens are 'more vulnerable' to domestic legislation and there may be a legitimate reason to demand 'a greater sacrifice' from nationals than from aliens.[23] If an alien who is a Community citizen is involved, the solution of the ECHR can be found to be in conflict with Community law, which, in its area of application, prohibits 'any discrimination on the basis of nationality'. Similarly, in the case of a trial, there may be a conflict between the procedural guarantees admitted by the two legal orders.

The coexistence of different but simultaneously applicable normative systems, the 'simultaneous polysystemy' discussed by Arnaud, cannot function unless the two systems are compatible, either through complementarity or through proximity of the norms they determine. Lacking that (that is, in the case of incompatible norms), conflict appears inevitable.

Common Market or *human rights*

Not evident in the texts themselves, the conflict can arise, more or less explicitly, in the jurisprudence. I consider here only two examples that, on the surface, concern neither persons nor goods, but are at the crossroads of the two categories: the provision of services and procedural rules.

The Amsterdam Treaty expressly addresses the concept of services. Under the title 'Free movement of persons, services and capital' (Title III

[22] See *Inze v. Austria*, ECHR, 23 October 1987, and, for other examples, Massias, 'L'Influence de la Convention européenne'.

[23] See *James v. United Kingdom*, and the comments of Massias, 'L'Influence de la Convention européenne', and of Stern, 'Le Droit de propriété'.

of the Treaty), Community law requires the abolition of restrictions on the free provision of services within the Community 'in respect of nationals of Member States who are established in a State of the Community other than that of the person for whom the services are intended' (Article 49(1) of the Amsterdam Treaty). It thus more precisely concerns cross-border services, which the Treaty also specifies must give rise to remuneration (Article 46). However, free movement is subject to measures that would be justified 'on grounds of public policy, public security or public health' (Article 56(1)).

While it is clear that public order cannot serve as an alibi for purely economic considerations, which would lead to authorising restrictions designed to protect states from foreign competition, it is difficult to determine with certainty the contents of this 'concept of variable dimensions that refuses to be defined by an exhaustive list'.[24]

This is where conflict may arise: respecting the rights and liberties protected by the European Convention on Human Rights can lead to two, diametrically opposed situations: either the respect for human rights appears to justify a restriction that Community law prohibits in the name of free movement, or conversely, it leads to prohibiting a restriction that Community law permits, in the name of public order.

Far from being classroom scenarios, such situations can be illustrated in two very different areas: a cable television broadcast and communication of information on the possibilities for abortion abroad. They illustrate different points, but both are considered 'services' within Community law, and both are confronted with the principle of freedom of expression within the meaning of Article 10 of the European Convention on Human Rights.

In the first case, an association of publications challenged the Netherlands on prohibitions on advertising and subtitling radio and television programmes broadcast from other member states into the Netherlands. Despite various controversies regarding the concept of cross-border services under the EC Treaty and on the concept of remuneration (obvious for the transmitters, who are paid directly by the advertisers, but more arguable for the broadcasters, who are paid by their subscribers), it was held that services were indeed provided within the

[24] See S. Poillot-Perugetto, 'Ordre public et droit communautaire', *Recueil Dalloz* (1993), p. 177.

meaning of Articles 49 and 50 of the Amsterdam Treaty, which raised the question of whether the prohibitions were justified.

The Dutch government argued for a public order exception, emphasising that the objective of their regulation was to assure financing, through collective advertising receipts, for various organisms designed to 'maintain a regime of pluralist and non-commercial radio broadcasting, as well as a pluralist and independent press'. The ECJ set this argument aside, citing the rule of proportionality and reasoning that there are 'less restrictive and non-discriminatory means to realise the targeted objectives'.[25]

The final question before the Court was whether Article 10 of the European Convention on Human Rights imposed obligations on member states, 'independently of the applicability of written Community law provisions'. This question was judged 'not applicable' and left unanswered, though the Court had dealt with the question more explicitly in 1985, in the *Cinétique* case (regarding the exploitation of cinematographic works in theatres, then on videocassettes or videodisks). The Court held that it was required 'to assure the respect of fundamental rights in the field specific to Community law', but that it was none the less not held to 'examine the compatibility with the European Convention on Human Rights of a national law that lies, as in the present case, in a domain within the national legislature's appreciation'.[26]

The European Court of Human Rights does indeed hesitate to exercise control over freedom of expression in audiovisual communication matters, trying especially to avoid 'disarming the states in the face of attempts to escape the requirements of both domestic and international telecommunications regulations'.[27] But at least it consistently and unequivocally affirms that freedom of expression is one of the essential foundations of a democratic society, one of the primordial conditions of its progress

[25] See ECJ, Case C-352/85, 26 April 1988, *Bond van Adverteeders et al. v. the Netherlands* (Dalloz, 1990), p. 401, Edelman note. See also ECJ, 25 July 1991, chroniques Carton, 'La Radio et la télévision devant le droit communautaire', *Les Petites Affiches* 24 (16 October 1991), p. 20.

[26] ECJ, 11 July 1985 (Dalloz, 1986), IR, 244, note by T. Hassler (cited by Edelman in note on *Bond van Adverteeders et al.*, p. 401).

[27] P. Wachsmann, 'La Cour européenne des droits de l'homme et la liberté d'expression: renforcement ou affaiblissement du contrôle?', *Mélanges G. Apollis* (PUF, 1992). Compare especially these decisions: *Groppera Radio AG v. Italy*, ECHR, 28 March 1990, *Autronic AG v. Switzerland*, ECHR, 22 May 1990, *Informationsverein Lentia et al. v. Austria*, ECHR, 24 November 1993.

and the fulfilment of everyone.[28] Hence the resulting application of this law to every person, including any profit-generating commercial company,[29] and to any 'message', including 'programmes whose content – mainly light music and commercials – could raise doubts as to whether they were "information" and "ideas"'.[30] There is also the consequence that freedom of expression is valid not only for information or ideas received favourably or considered inoffensive, but also for those that offend, shock or disturb. Here again is the reference, made with regard to restrictions necessary in a democratic society, to the 'democratic spirit' that results from pluralism, tolerance and openmindedness.

Now, the complexity and richness of the Strasbourg case law and its extension into the area of business and advertising make it difficult to maintain for long the polite indifference exhibited in Luxembourg. Certainly, there are already points on which the two courts converge, such as the common requirement of proportionality between restriction and cited objectives, the exclusion of any economic justification, and the adoption of a comparable attitude of reserve regarding the maintenance of a strict state monopoly.[31] Similarly, there are cross-references in more recent texts regarding television without borders (Directive 89/552 of 3 October 1989 and European Convention on Transfrontier Television of 5 May 1989) indicating the effect of competition and also the attempt to increase compatibility between the two European legal orders, as I show below. But there is still a danger of incompatibility, especially since the progressive extension of the fields of application of each of these orders is multiplying the sources of conflict, and the Charter of Fundamental Rights of the European Union, approved by the Convention on 2 October 2000, and adopted at Nice on 7 December 2000, further increases them.

Proof of this can be found in another area, in the way in which the question of abortion was raised. Strictly prohibited in Ireland, where the

[28] G. Cohen-Jonathan, 'The European Convention on Human Rights', *JCI Europe* 2 (1992), fasc. 6522.

[29] *Autronic AG v. Switzerland* (see note 27, above).

[30] *Groppera Radio AG v. Italy* (see note 27, above).

[31] See Cohen-Jonathan, 'The European Convention on Human Rights', pp. 24ff. Compare ECJ Case C-260/89, *Elliniki Radiophonia Tiléorassi AE and Panellinia Omospondia Syllogon Prossopikou v. Dimotiki Etairia Pliroforissis and Others* [1991] ECR I-2925, 18 June 1991, and HRC, 15 January 1992, declaring five petitions receivable against the Austrian government denouncing the monopoly system and the absence of regulations permitting the operation of private radio or cable television broadcasting companies.

Constitution protects life even of the unborn, information regarding the possibilities for pregnant women to practise abortion abroad could not be distributed because such information had been prohibited by injunction by the Irish Supreme Court. This was the contested point.

First, the ECJ examined the issue from the perspective of free movement of services. Even though it considered, in effect, such information as a 'service' within the meaning of Article 49 of the Amsterdam Treaty, the Court none the less held, in its decision of 4 October 1991,[32] that the services did not come within the Community sphere because they were free and included no advertising. In this way, the Court avoided all risk of conflict with the European Convention on Human Rights, and more specifically on the principle of freedom of expression, which was, in fact, invoked shortly thereafter in Strasbourg.

In Strasbourg, the European Court of Human Rights concluded on 22 October 1992 that there was a violation of Article 10 of the Convention.[33] Despite the national margin of appreciation, which is particularly important when protecting morals is involved (see Part II, above), the Court deemed the interference 'too broad and disproportionate', primarily because of the 'absolute' nature of the Irish Supreme Court's decision, which did not consider the age, state of health or reasons for which these pregnant women sought advice and information on abortion.

Refusing, as the Commission had,[34] to be dragged into a controversy over Article 2 of the Convention and the possible protection of the life of an unborn child, the Court indicated, however, the incompatibility between the restriction imposed by the state and the respect for freedom of expression, leaving open the question of whether, for its part, the Court of Justice in Luxembourg would have admitted the restriction on the free movement of services on the basis of national public order.

Inversely symmetrical to the preceding case, the Irish case shows the complexity of conflicts that can arise from the triangular relationship between national legal norms confronted simultaneously with the Community order and the European Convention on Human Rights.

[32] *Society for the Protection of Unborn Children Ireland Ltd v. Grogan*, ECJ, 4 October 1991 (Dalloz, 1991), IR 255, *Revue trimestrielle de droit européen* (1992), p. 163, note Gaudemet-Tallon.

[33] *Open Door et al.*, 29 October 1992, see comments by G. Sudre in 'Chronique d'actualité – droit de la Convention européenne des droits de l'homme', *JCP* I (1993), p. 3654.

[34] See *X v. United Kingdom*, HRC, 13 May 1980 (compare with *Brugeman v. West Germany*, HRC, 12 July 1977, in which German women contested, conversely, the strong repression of abortion in Germany as an infringement of their right to privacy).

Finally, the rarest case, which will no doubt become less rare, must be examined. The case involves a direct conflict between Community law and the European Convention on Human Rights with regard to the procedure applicable to sanctions that Community law applies to economic operators who do not respect the rules.

This is the rarest case because Community sanctions were for a long time limited to the area of competition, where the Commission could intervene in cases of practices incompatible with the Common Market, such as agreements between companies or other concerted practices likely to affect business between member states and to restrict or throw away the game of competition, or abusive exploitation of a dominant position on the Common Market or in a substantial part of it. Now, within this circumscribed area, the Commission's powers are far-reaching. It can not only carry out investigations, it can also order injunctions or, in the case of an infraction, payment of fines or penalties (Articles 81 to 83 of the Amsterdam Treaty and the Council's Regulation 27/62 of February 1962).

The sanctions, which are at least administrative–criminal if not criminal, come with procedural guarantees that were progressively imposed by the Luxembourg Court by application of the unwritten general principle of respect for the right to a defence.[35] However, the ECJ refused to hold that Article 6 of the European Convention on Human Rights, which sets out rules for a fair trial applicable in civil and criminal matters (in the broad sense indicated in Part II), would apply to the repression of Community competition-law violations, considering that the Commission was not a 'tribunal' within the meaning of Article 6.

The question was none the less raised in Strasbourg in 1990, before the European Commission on Human Rights.[36] The petitioner claimed the German government had 'granted *exequatur*' – that is, executed the Commission of the Communities' order to pay a fine (which had been reduced, in fact, following an initial appeal to the Court in Luxembourg) – while the procedure followed by the Commission constituted a violation of Article 6 of the Convention on Human Rights. One can imagine

[35] See J.-L. Bonichot, 'La Répression des pratiques anticoncurrentielles et le respect des droits fondamentaux', *RSC* (1990), p. 160, and the jurisprudence cited.

[36] *M and Co. v. West Germany*, HRC decision of 9 February 1990, see M. Delmas-Marty, 'La Convention européenne des droits de l'homme et le droit pénal des affaires, aspects de droit processuel', *Droit et pratiques du commerce international* 17(3) (1991), pp. 366ff; see also *Cantoni v. France*, ECHR, 15 November 1996.

the German government's surprise at being pursued for a violation of the European Convention on Human Rights when it had respected its commitments with regard to the European Community – as well as the Human Rights Commission's embarrassment, which may explain the caution of its decision. After emphasising that a transfer of powers to an international organisation 'does not necessarily preclude a state's liability in virtue of the Convention when the exercise of the transferred powers is involved', the Commission nevertheless denied the petition, basing its denial on the fact that 'the European Communities' legal system not only recognises fundamental rights, it also controls their respect'. It added that it 'has taken into account the fact that it would be contrary to the very idea of a transfer of powers to an international organisation to hold the member states liable, in each individual case, before giving *exequatur* to a decision of the European Court of Justice, for examining whether Article 6 of the Convention was respected in the proceeding in question'.

The Commission emphasised, however, that 'the antitrust proceeding in question would fall within Article 6 if it had been brought by German, rather than European, judicial authorities'.

In fact, the current tendency in Community law is to develop a new system of sanctions: a mixed system, in the sense that the sanctions are defined by the Commission of the Communities, but sent to the member states' judicial or administrative authorities regarding their implementation. It seems this is the only way for the Commission, in the sensitive areas of agricultural and fishing policy, to fight against frauds committed to the detriment of Community finances.[37] Challenged by the German government, which denied the competency of the Community or the Commission to institute sanctions that are not provided for by the Treaty of Rome (unlike the fines and penalties under competition law), the system was finally accepted by the European Court of Justice in 1992. The Community and the Commission are given competence to institute sanctions (increases and temporary exclusion from subsidies) that, without being true fines, go beyond simple restitution of amounts unduly paid and are applied by the states.[38] This means the question is likely to arise again in Community law on rules for a

[37] See, on the size of these frauds, E. Mennens, 'Fraud on the financial interests of the Community', in M. Delmas-Marty (ed.), *What kind of criminal policy for Europe?* (Kluwer, 1996), pp. 127ff.

[38] ECJ, 27 October 1992, *RSC* (1993), p. 147, Soulard note.

fair trial within the meaning of the European Convention on Human Rights.

Without exhausting the subject, which is undergoing many other developments, especially in the areas of labour law, biotechnology and the environment, these few examples show the complexity that the coexistence of two simultaneously applicable European legal systems takes on. They also give an idea of the pragmatic approach for looking, from one system to another, if not for European unity, at least for harmony.

This pragmatism is born of proven experience that has already supplied some of the keys to European harmony.

Keys to European harmony

Harmonisation does not mean unification. It accepts differences and organises them. This is the meaning of André-Jean Arnaud's appeal – '[l]egal Europe will come to be only if it makes hers the pluralism and complexity that, from the beginning, have been inscribed in her history'[39] – and Edgar Morin's conclusion that '[t]he concept of Europe must be conceived according to a multiple and complete complexity'.[40] Yet it is important to discover the keys to this mysterious process by which plurality and complexity may give birth to singularity.

Edgar Morin suggests 'two principles of intelligibility specific to elucidating complex phenomena of this order: the dialogical principle and the principle of recursion'. But his definition is somewhat redundant: the principle of recursion refers to the process (examined in Part I, above) of tangled hierarchies and strange loops, where 'each moment, component or instance is both product and producer of other moments, components or instances'; whereas the dialogical principle 'signifies that two or more logics are related in one unity in a complex way (complementary, concurrent or antagonistic) without losing the duality in the unity'.[41]

To get past the redundancy and avoid elucidating complexity by reference to a relationship that is itself 'complex', one must no doubt return

[39] Arnaud, *Pour une pensée juridique européenne*, p. 300.
[40] E. Morin, *Penser l'Europe* (Gallimard, 1987), p. 26. [41] *Ibid.*, p. 28.

to the process of determining norms, through the three components (predetermination, co-determination and super-determination) described in Part II. With regard to the predetermination of norms, Europe superposes that of the European Community and the Council of Europe (author of the European Convention on Human Rights and the Additional Protocols) on national legislatures, creating three types of internormative relationships at once: a dual relationship between one of the European systems and the national systems (Europe/states); a triangular relationship between each of the European systems and the national systems (Europe/Europe/states); and finally, a dual, but supranational, relationship of the European systems between each other (Europe/Europe).

As for the co-determination process, which falls within the national or European judge's interpretation, I demonstrated above that it was organised in the Europe/Europe/states relationship according to several logics. Classical logic (identity and conformity) is followed whenever European primacy or national sovereignty are imposed without a margin of appreciation. However, recognising a margin (either a national margin of appreciation or a European margin of control) implies recourse to a logic of gradation (proximity and compatibility). Looking at the two other relationships (Europe/states and Europe/Europe), for this duality of norm co-determination logics – this 'dialogic', in its most precise meaning – in the judge's work of interpretation, a difference seems to form here between practice and scholarship. As described above, the practices indicate the progressive emergence of general principles taken from various national and European systems and reconstituted into common principles. This appears to be a gradation logic technique, and therefore a task of making norms compatible by bringing them together (proximity) rather than by unifying them (identity). Yet some authors do not want the reader to envisage 'normative subordination of the Communities to the Convention',[42] a subordination that could take the legal form of the Community's adherence to the European Convention on Human Rights.[43]

[42] G. Cohen-Jonathan, 'La Cour des communautés européennes et les droits de l'homme', *Revue du marché commun* (1978), pp. 74ff.

[43] G. Cohen-Jonathan, 'La Problématique de l'adhésion des Communautés européennes à la Convention européenne des droits de l'homme', *Mélanges Teitgen* (Pedone, 1984), pp. 81ff.; R. Lecourt, 'Cour européenne des droits de l'homme et Cour de Justice des Communautés

In such a perspective, the relationship Europe/Europe would align with the Europe/states relationship and would absorb the triangular Europe/Europe/states relationship, since the primacy of the European Convention over Community law would progressively reduce its autonomy. Of course, the fifteen member states of the European Union have ratified the European Convention on Human Rights and accepted the right of individual appeal to the Strasbourg courts, but this has not solved all the problems. There are legal problems – firstly, because the fifteen member states ratified the Convention, but with highly diverse reservations and without, for the most part, ratifying all the Additional Protocols. There are practical problems as well, with the danger of multiple appeals that will prolong each suit interminably. Above all, there are political difficulties, because subordinating one system to another would consequently lead to the possibility of judges who represent third-party states that are members of the Council of Europe exercising control over European Union law.

Unless one assumes that all the countries subscribing to the European Convention will one day become part of the Union, the membership formula seems difficult to accept, given the current state of European construction, which would explain the Council's resistance and the European Court of Justice's position, despite insistence of the European Parliament, and even of the Commission, on such adherence.[44] This resistance could also be due to the fact that the Union's adherence, pure and simple, to the European Convention on Human Rights seems to proceed from a certain confusion between the co-determination and super-determination of norms. A study on 'the protection of fundamental rights in the legal order of the European Communities' is informative on this point. The author emphasises that fundamental rights have not only a function of protecting individuals, but also a function related to the political order: they represent the 'common judgments',

européennes' and P. Pescatore, 'La Cour de Justice des Communautés européennes et la Convention européenne des droits de l'homme', both in *Mélanges Wiarda* (2nd edn, N. P. Engel Verlag, 1990), pp. 335ff. and 441ff. respectively.

[44] The first stages are recalled in Cohen-Jonathan's article 'La Cour des communautés': membership was requested by two European Parliament resolutions in 1977 and 1979, then by a memorandum of the Commission of the Communities in 1979, followed by a new resolution of the Parliament in 1982. The idea was revived by the Commission in November 1990 and again sustained by a Parliamentary resolution in July 1991. See the ECJ Opinion of 24 March 1996 on the ratification of the Convention on Human Rights by the European Community.

of order and value, of a society looking for a new, European identity,[45] which means that fundamental rights are linked to the process of super-determination. This is even more clear with regard to rights guaranteed by the European Convention on Human Rights, where one must take into account the fact that their function is not limited to interpreting norms according to the process of co-determination described earlier (namely to the work of making them compatible that would be aided by the adoption of guiding principles that have become truly common to the various national and European systems). As seen above, the Convention also fulfils a function specific to legitimating, based on a set of values that are imposed on both the legislature and the judge and super-determine the norms, and constituting the ultimate reference point. Hence the value of formulae, other than pure and simple adhesion, by which the European Communities (now the Union) indicate their desire to recognise the European Convention on Human Rights as a source of legitimacy of Community law. The Charter of Fundamental Rights of the European Union can be understood in this light.

Common principles on the one hand, judgments of common values on the other, European harmonisation would be subject to a double set of keys: the keys to interpretation that guiding principles supply, and the key to legitimation imposed by the ethical primacy of human rights.

The keys to interpretation: the technique of common principles

Amidst the European systems, there is a nebula of principles with shifting outlines that are still only partially shared. While some come from written law, for the most part contained in the European Convention on Human Rights and the Additional Protocols, and more rarely in the Treaty of Rome (where the principles of free movement and non-discrimination appear, however), many are born of unwritten general principles. These are occasionally taken from the comparative law of the member states (such as the right to a defence and non-retroactivity in Community law, or the democratic spirit in human rights), and sometimes deduced from the very structure of the institutions, such as proportionality, upheld by both the Court of Human Rights and the ECJ,

[45] M.-A. Dauses, 'La Protection des droits fondamentaux dans l'ordre juridique des Communautés européennes', *RAE* 4 (1992), pp. 9ff.

which since 1956 refer to each other to control both the lawfulness of Community measures and the compatibility of domestic law with Community law.

It is not always easy to say just how common a principle is to the two systems. It happens, in fact, that an identical formulation – non-discrimination or right to a defence, for example – in reality hide partially different contents. Thus non-discrimination, within the Community law meaning (Amsterdam Treaty, Article 17), establishes equal rights for aliens and equality between the sexes, but only with regard to Community citizens, while the non-discrimination provided for in the European Convention on Human Rights applies to every person and to any discrimination (based, says Article 14 of the European Convention, 'on the sex, race, colour, language, religion, political or any other opinion, national or social origin, association with a national minority, property, birth or other status'). However, the conditions for implementation of the non-discrimination principle are more restrictive in Strasbourg than in Luxembourg, because, according to the case law of the Court of Human Rights, Article 14 does not exist independently and has value only for the enjoyment of rights and liberties guaranteed by the other normative clauses of the Convention: 'there can be no room for its application unless the facts at issue fall within the ambit of one or more of the said clauses'.[46]

Similarly, the right to a defence contained in Article 6 of the European Convention on Human Rights is considered to be a fundamental principle of the Community legal order.[47] It is applied, at least in part, as soon as a person (individual or company) is subject to an inquiry prior to any pursuit.[48] However, the Court in Luxembourg has not stated clearly whether the presumption of innocence, expressly provided for by the European Convention in criminal matters (in the broad sense indicated earlier), is a right 'granted to companies in the Community order'.[49] Moreover, there are divergences with regard to protection against searches during proceedings. The Court of Justice grants protection to the private homes of physical persons, 'as a principle common

[46] *Abdulaziz, Cabales and Balkandali v. United Kingdom*, ECHR, 28 May 1985.

[47] *Michelin*, ECJ, 9 November 1983, collection p. 3461.

[48] *Hoechst* and *Dow Benelux*, ECJ, 21 September 1989, collection pp. 2859 and 3137, *Dow Chemical Iberica*, ECJ, 17 October 1989, collection p. 3165.

[49] *Dow Chemical Iberica*.

to the laws of the member states', but it considers that the same is not true for companies, as the legal systems of the member states 'present non-negligible differences regarding the nature and extent of protection given commercial premises in the face of interventions by public authorities'.[50] As for the argument taken from the right to respect for the domicile and for privacy by reference to Article 8 of the European Convention, the Luxembourg Court sets this aside as well, considering that 'this article concerns the area of fulfilment of personal liberty and cannot be extended to commercial premises'. The Strasbourg Court thereafter held that the guarantee in Article 8 could apply to the professional domicile, as both professional and private activities can be exercised in the same place.

Conversely, two principles formulated differently can prove, on implementation, to be very comparable to one another. Thus the concept of restrictive measures necessary in a democratic society (within the meaning of Articles 8 to 11 of the European Convention on Human Rights) is interpreted by reference to the legitimate state objective and according to a principle of proportionality reminiscent of the conditions placed by Community law on the limitations states can place on the rule of free movement. Justified 'on grounds of public policy, public security or public health' (Amsterdam Treaty, Articles 30, 39 and 46), these limitations must themselves respect, *per* the Luxembourg case law, the principle of proportionality. This means that in both systems, national public order combines with the guiding European principle of proportionality to create a certain national margin of compatibility.

Based on this nebula, the search for principles fully common to both European legal orders is organised more systematically, first through a set of cross-references – tangled hierarchies and strange loops, as explained in Part II – that indicate the two courts' (and even sometimes the European legislature's) desire for harmony.

The courts' desire for harmony is already expressed invisibly, though highly efficiently, in the concern for reciprocal information and the practice of informational meetings, and even the co-ordinated examination of points of convergence (and possibly divergence from) one body of jurisprudence to the other.

[50] *Hoechst*, ECJ, 21 September 1989.

More visible are the express references from one order to the other, especially in the previously mentioned areas of aliens' rights and the right to hold property. Thus, with regard to the registration of aliens, the ECJ expressly mentioned the principles established in the European Convention on Human Rights[51] when interpreting the EEC Directive of 1964, while the Commission on Human Rights in Strasbourg raised Community law on the same occasion to emphasise, with regard to citizens of the European Union but not of the state in which they are incarcerated, that 'the lawfulness of the incarceration will be affected if the deportation decision was itself contrary to the Treaty of the European Economic Community'.[52]

As for the right to hold property, tied only to the common general principles of law and constitutional traditions in Community law but expressly included, as seen above, in an Additional Protocol to the European Convention on Human Rights, it provides the occasion for the Court of Justice to acknowledge progressively the Convention's influence on Community law. This acknowledgment was first merely hinted at in a decision written at a time when France had not yet ratified the Convention, hence the caution of the statement that 'the international instruments concerning the protection of human rights, to which the member States have co-operated or adhered, can provide the indications that should be taken into account in Community law'.[53] The position of the ECJ was strengthened once, with French ratification, all the member states of the Communities had adhered to the European Convention on Human Rights. But it remained cautious, preferring merely to cite the Convention and look for the legal solution in a comparative analysis of the constitutional rules and practices of the member states.[54]

Harmonisation, from one legal order to another, is most often still left to the discretion of European judges. But the practice of cross-referencing recently appeared in the texts themselves and is therefore imposed on the judge like a sort of injunction to interpret the rule of law by combining the two European systems.

[51] *Rutili*, ECJ, 28 October 1975.

[52] *Caprino v. United Kingdom*, HRC, 17 July 1980 report. See also the report of the Commission in *Bozano v. France*, 7 December 1984, raising the differences from *Caprino* and setting aside the French government's argument drawn from the EEC directive of 1964.

[53] *Nold*, ECJ, 15 May 1974, collection p. 491.

[54] *Hauer*, ECJ, 13 December 1979, collection p. 3727.

Community Directive 89/552 of 3 October 1989, known as the 'Television without Frontiers Directive', is exemplary in this regard. Taken in an area where there are divergences from one legal order to another, it recalls in the Preamble that the 'right as applied to the broadcasting and distribution of television services is also a specific manifestation in Community law of a more general principle, namely the freedom of expression as enshrined in Article 10(1) of the Convention for the Protection of Human Rights and Fundamental Freedoms ratified by all member states'. From this link between the free movement of a service – a Community law principle – and the freedom of expression – a principle established by the European Convention on Human Rights – the writers of the text draw to the judge's attention a rule of interpretation regarding the free exercise of the activity of broadcasting and distributing television programmes. This must be assured, 'subject only to the limits provided for in paragraph 2 of the same article [Article 10 of the European Convention] and in Article 56(1) of the Treaty [EEC Treaty of 1957]'.

There is an analogous inspiration in the recommendations of a group of experts appointed by the Commission of the European Communities to study the harmonisation of national provisions regarding criminal or quasi-criminal sanctions of frauds on the Community budget. In effect, the proposal for aligning national legislation was based both on Community-law requirements, particularly the principle of assimilation of Community finances into national finances, which the ECJ deduced from Article 10 of the Amsterdam Treaty, and on the respect for the principles set out in the European Convention on Human Rights, namely those with regard to the presumption of innocence.

But this does not involve ad hoc applications, which in some cases illustrate only the possibility of guiding principles common to both legal orders, namely principles that, without creating a hierarchy between the principles, participate in bringing the two legal orders together, and thus assist with European harmonisation. But there may also exist situations of greater conflict, where the differences between one order and the other are so strong that they raise the question, not just of the incompatibility of norms, but of their legitimacy. The search for harmonisation therefore moves from the purely legal plane of interpretation (co-determination of norms) to the more political one of legitimating choices (super-determination).

The key to legitimating: the ethic of human rights

Expressed by authors such as the European judge Pierre Pescatore, the idea is that 'the European Convention on Human Rights is the expression of a form of political and legal culture common to the States that created the European Community, a form of life in society that respects democracy, individual rights and liberties, and the principle called the rule of law'.[55] When discussing the 'common legal and political culture', the author expresses well the idea that human rights would have the double function of interpreting norms and legitimating choices, and would therefore be imposed on the European Community because it, 'as an institution common to several States party to the Convention, is necessarily in the same political and legal sphere'. Hence the consequence, known as the doctrine of state succession, that the Community of fifteen member states 'is bound to observe the Convention, as are the states that instituted it and who, therefore, have become its member states'. Thus with regard to the Convention and its organs, the ECJ would become, according to Judge Pescatore, 'domestic jurisdiction', with the consequence that 'if the Court applied the Convention, and if it continues to apply it, it is because it is held to apply it; it is its obligation and not its free choice'.[56] Hence the uselessness of the Community's adherence to the European Convention, despite the insistent demands of the Commission of the Communities and the European Parliament.[57]

The point of departure of the analysis seems unarguable, especially since the concept of human rights as 'legal and political culture' common to the European states is implicit in the resistance expressed several times by the Italian and German constitutional courts during certain crisis periods when the fear was born that with regard to the fundamental rights of the person, 'the process of European integration has not yet reached a sufficiently advanced level', especially when confronted with the fundamental German law or an Italian constitutional order.[58] And while

[55] P. Pescatore, 'La Cour de Justice et la Convention des droits de l'homme'. See also D. Simon, 'Y a-t-il des principes généraux du droit communautaire?', *Droits* (1993), pp. 73ff.

[56] Pescatore, 'La Cour de Justice'.

[57] See above, note 44.

[58] Italian constitutional court, 27 December 1973, *Frontini, Jurisprudencia constituzionale* 1 (1973), p. 2401; German constitutional court, 29 May 1974, '*Solange Beschluss no. 1*', *Revue trimestrielle de droit européen*, (1975), p. 136. See also German constitutional court, 12 May 1989, *Europaïsche Grundrechte Zeitschrift*, (1989), p. 339, and Italian Court, 21 April 1989, *Frogat, Revista di Diritto internazionale* (1989), pp. 103ff.

the idea of the Communities' adhering to the European Convention on Human Rights was manifestly launched in 1977–9, then relaunched in 1990–1 in response to these constitutional court 'rebellions', I would agree with Pescatore that this is certainly not the most appropriate response. However, invoking the doctrine of state succession to show that the Convention is already part of the Community legal order appears to proceed from the same confusion as that that would control the Communities' (now included in the Union) adherence to the European Convention on Human Rights, and therefore would take Europe back to a pyramidal structure where the triangular Europe/Europe/states relationship would be absorbed by a double relationship of subordination, of the Community Europe to that of human rights, and of each state to the thus-unified Europe.

This makes clear the value of other formulae that, without aligning the European Communities (components of the Union) with any state, nor allowing Community law to be absorbed by that of the European Convention on Human Rights, try to indicate the primacy of human rights as a norm super-determination process, imposed equally on legislatures and European judges.

Two roads have been cut, if not completely explored. One consists of reintroducing fundamental rights into the Community legal order, the other of referring to such rights through references to the European Convention on Human Rights. On 12 April 1989, after a long series of solemn declarations begun in 1977, the European Parliament, favouring the first road, adopted a Declaration of Fundamental Rights and Freedoms that reaffirms, for the most part, the rights recognised by the European Convention on Human Rights. But it offers a highly simplified version that, had the European Court of Justice given it legal effect in Community law as the Parliament had wanted, may well have created conflicts of interpretation.

It is thus important to explore the other road, which consists of incorporating by reference the European Convention into the founding treaties of the Community legal order, creating a genuine 'constitutional charter' of Europe.[59]

Absent from the Treaty of Rome, it is true that the European Convention makes only a very shy appearance in the Preamble of the Single

[59] Regarding the 'constitutionalisation' of treaties in Community law, see J.-P. Jacqué, 'Le Droit dans l'intégration européenne', *Philosophie politique* 1 (1991), pp. 119ff.

European Act signed in 1986, where it is associated with the constitutions and laws of the member states and the European Social Charter as a means for the states to 'work together to promote democracy on the basis of . . . fundamental rights'. The phrase indeed places the European Convention in a process of legitimating Community norms, but on a level equal to national laws, without implementing a specific procedure in the case of conflict with a Community norm. By comparison, the Treaty on European Union, decided in Maastricht and signed on 7 February 1992 and modified by the Amsterdam Treaty of 1997 by the member states, goes further. First, it confirms in its Preamble the attachment of member states to the principles of free democracy, respect for human rights and the rule of law; but above all, it incorporates the European Convention into the Community legal order for the first time. It does this in two ways: first, via the 'common provisions', by affirming in Article F that the European Union 'shall respect fundamental rights, as guaranteed by the European Convention for the Protection of Human Rights and Fundamental Freedoms . . . and as they result from the constitutional traditions common to the Member States, as general principles of Community law'; and secondly, the Maastricht Treaty institutes co-operation in the areas of justice and home affairs (Title VI) and in this perspective, sets out a list of issues such as political immigration, the fight against drug addiction and fraud on an international scale, or even diverse types of judicial, customs and police co-operation, considered as 'matters of common interest' (Article K.1). Article K.2 provides that the questions defined as such in Article K.1 'shall be dealt with in compliance with the European Convention on the Protection of Human Rights and Fundamental Freedoms', to which the treaty associates another international text, the 1951 Convention on the Status of Refugees, adding – the only reference to national laws – that 'the protection afforded by Member States to persons persecuted on political grounds' shall also be taken into account.

The usual reservation for public order remains (Article K.2(2)): 'This Title shall not affect the exercise of the responsibilities incumbent upon Member States with regard to the maintenance of law and order and the safeguarding of internal security.' But with the ratification of the Treaty by the fifteen states that have become members of the European Union, the primacy of human rights should be reinforced, in particular for the areas considered as 'questions of common interest', without Community law losing its autonomy in these areas.

However, the European Union was careful to provide for a specific mechanism in the case of conflict between a Community norm and the Convention on Human Rights. One formula could be to give the Court of Luxembourg the ability officially to consult the Strasbourg Court 'every time that a serious question of interpretation arises',[60] and not to authorise individual appeal to Strasbourg for Community acts that appear incompatible with the Convention unless the opinion will not be respected by the ECJ. At the end of the legitimating process, the primacy of human rights will have taken on legal value, but every effort will be made to keep the incorporation of the European Convention on Human Rights from eliminating the specificity of Community law, just as the recourse to margins of appreciation avoid the disappearance of national legal specificities. The Charter of Fundamental Rights of the European Union does, in fact, seem to choose the route of granting autonomy. It is still too early to measure the impact of these ideas, especially since the declaration will probably not have any legal force.[61]

Preserving the pluralism of norms whenever possible, but making it an ordered pluralism through the proper use of the keys: this is the ongoing search that transforms Europe into a sort of laboratory of legal pluralism. Success is not guaranteed. As for failure, it will signal the likely failure of such a pluralism on a worldwide scale for decades to come.

[60] Proposition defended by Cohen-Jonathan in 'La Problématique de l'adhésion'.

[61] See www.europarl.eu.int and http://ue.en.int.

9

The worldwide stakes

At the heart of Europe, war again: not just any war, but one to destroy the very idea of pluralism, through 'ethnic cleansing'. For the UN special rapporteur, this frightful concept is not the consequence of the war in the former Yugoslavia, but its objective: 'Massacres, brutalities, rapes, destruction of homes and threats work together to realise this objective, which is already partially attained.'[1] Hence the cry of observers sent by the CSCE (Conference for Security and Co-operation in Europe): 'The mission saw the concept of European civilisation being torn to shreds.'[2]

The choice of responses is limited, but one can still look to reason and the respect for rights: 'We want the world to rise up once again against injustice, to defend with firmness the respect for the rights and laws on which our civilisation and contemporary society are founded.'[3] And, for the first time, there has been a tentative taking of action. By its Resolution 827 (27 May 1993), the UN Security Council decided 'to establish an international tribunal for the sole purpose of prosecuting persons responsible for serious violations of international humanitarian law committed in the territory of the former Yugoslavia between 1 January 1991 and a date to be determined by the Security Council upon the restoration of peace'. 'For this purpose', it adopted the statute appended to the Secretary-General's report.[4]

Of course, it is not the first international tribunal created to judge crimes committed during a war: the Nuremberg and Tokyo tribunals

[1] M. T. Mazowiecki (special rapporteur from the UN Commission on Human Rights), Second Report, 27 October 1992, *Le Livre noir de l'ex-Yougoslavie* (Arléa, 1993), p. 303. See also 'Rape as an instrument of ethnic cleansing', *Le Livre noir*, pp. 420ff.

[2] CSCE September 1992 Mission Report, *Le Livre noir.*

[3] Report by Save the Humanity and five other organisations, 3 June 1992, *Le Livre noir*, pp. 3ff.

[4] J. Jones, *The practice of the International Criminal Tribunals for the Former Yugoslavia and Rwanda* (2nd edn, Transnational Publishers Inc., 2000).

were set up after the Second World War. The trial did not end the war, 'Hitlerian atrocities were put to an end by arms, not arguments.'[5] Even if the trial of crimes committed in the former Yugoslavia arrives much too late – too late for many victims – it is lawfully imposed by the international community, not, as in Nuremberg and Tokyo, by the victors. Imposed by virtue of Chapter VII of the United Nations Charter, entitled 'Action with respect to threats to the peace, breaches of the peace, and acts of aggression', it is the first time an international tribunal has been created 'to maintain or restore international peace and security'. In prior conflicts, economic, then military sanctions were favoured, with Resolution 678 authorising the states to use armed force against Iraq.[6]

But once the decision to create a tribunal is taken, it must be implemented. Since its inception, some have deplored this latest tribunal's lack of material means, though its budget has increased considerably over the years. Worse is the criticism regarding the legal weaknesses of a tribunal that cannot judge absent parties. This legal weakness is coupled with political weakness when the prime suspects are the leaders with whom the peace treaty was negotiated.

There are, however, a number of advantages to the new tribunal. The first is an extremely complex and precise statute that shows a constant concern for the respect of general principles of criminal law (crimes and punishments must be defined by statute, statutory non-retroactivity, liability based on fault) and procedure (right to an impartial and independent tribunal, avenues of appeal, protection of victims and witnesses), and that reproduces most of the major proposals of several national preparatory reports (those of France, Italy, Canada and the United States). In addition, the text proposed by the Secretary-General,[7] approved and adopted by the UN Security Council in its Resolution of May 1993, recognises the right of the accused to be present at the trial (International Covenant on Civil and Political Rights, Article 14), though this procedural guarantee had been set aside in the French report for

[5] P. Legendre, *The crime of Corporal Lortie* (Fayard, 1989), p. 19.

[6] See B. Stern (ed.), *Guerre du Golfe. Le dossier d'une crise internationale, 1990–1992* (La Documentation française, 1993).

[7] Report of 3 May 1993 established in application of Resolution 808 of the Security Council, UN Doc. S/25704. See also the report established in France under the direction of P. Truche by the Comité de réflexion sur la création d'un tribunal pénal international (February 1993), cf. R. de Gouttes, *Archives de politique criminelle* 16 (1994), pp. 35–50.

reasons of repressive efficiency. None the less, the text authorises the prosecutor to establish the charge even in the accused's absence, and if it is confirmed, a judge can issue a warrant to arrest, detain and bring the accused before the tribunal, and every state must co-operate (this interpretation was confirmed by the tribunal in its communiqué of 11 February 1994).

As for the practical difficulties in locating evidence, they were partially resolved by the work already accomplished by the various investigative commissions set up in the framework of the UN and European institutions, as well as by the major non-governmental organisations for humanitarian action.[8]

Was this a 'major turning point', or a 'sudden as quickly closed' parenthesis[9] in the desire manifested by the international community finally to see international law respected by all the states? I am tempted here to transpose this question, asked by Brigitte Stern regarding the affair known as the Gulf War, but the simple fact of asking it twice in the period between November 1990 (Resolution 678) and May 1993 (Resolution 827) indicates that we are undoubtedly talking about more than a simple parenthesis. As for whether there is a 'major turning point' that will inaugurate a 'new world order, the outline of which is still imprecise and of which the Gulf crisis appears to be a sort of warning',[10] it will be for future historians to decide.

In illustrating the worldwide stakes of certain conflicts, these two examples already offer food for thought regarding the law as a common reference, and, more particularly, the human rights that are at the centre of the Yugoslav conflict and that are, while less visible, none the less present in the Gulf War and its consequences for the Kurds and the Shiite minorities. The first manifestations of this common reference, however, present two faces. Human rights require granting the same rights to everyone – universalisable if not effectively universal. First proclaimed as a 'common ideal' in 1948, the Universal Declaration on Human Rights is slowly moving closer to positive law. In 1993, beyond the 'common language of humanity' evoked by the UN Secretary-General in his opening address, the Universal Declaration constitutes, according to the final document of the World Conference in Vienna, a 'common standard of

[8] See the reports published in *Le Livre noir*. [9] See *Guerre du Golfe*, pp. 11 and 25.
[10] *Ibid.*, p. 11.

achievement for all peoples and all nations'. It is difficult to maintain the charge of Euro-centrism or westernism in Vienna, however, when close to 180 states and numerous non-governmental organisations were represented. While not all the obstacles have been lifted, they are at least discussed, and the debate is open on this 'universal' recognition that is still at high risk: of remaining purely incantatory and of continuing to exclude those cast out of the legal sphere; or of forced assimilation, which, under the pretext of integration, eliminates all differences. Do not use 'them', which can exclude; avoid 'we', which can mean automatically assimilated; perhaps learn to say 'they', as a sign of accepted otherness. In fact, this 'heads' side of human rights is difficult to decipher.

However, that is not all. Do not forget the other side of the coin. Human rights as common reference also means learning limits, this time on the global level. We must once again erect landmarks and give ourselves underlying taboos to establish, in the full meaning of the word, the human of humanity, the 'irreducible human element' invoked by the UN Secretary-General at the opening of the Vienna Conference in June 1993. States are forbidden to derogate from it, and individuals to transgress it: 'inviolable' rights and 'imprescriptable' crimes would be the legal expression of the major taboos that protect, without daring to name, this irreducible human element that is so urgently sought.

Them, us, they

Before giving in to the 'delights of universality', one must try to identify the traps hidden by 'the apparent simplicity of human rights'.[11] The most visible is exclusion in all its forms, individual and collective, civil and political, or social and economic, which has resisted many a proclamation of rights for all. There is also the trap of good intentions, in the name of which a civilisation imposes forced assimilation on others in good conscience, persuaded that it is superior to 'archaic' and 'barbaric' practices against which it fights the good fight. This is sometimes known as 'overhanging' universality, to distinguish it from the other – 'plural', 'reiterative' or even 'lateral' – which, through the use of dialogue, confrontation and even opposition and conflict, tries to co-ordinate the

[11] P.-I. Imbert, 'L'Apparente Simplicité des droits de l'homme, réflexions sur les différents aspects de l'universalité des droits de l'homme', *RUDH* (1989), pp. 19ff.

differences[12] in these 'communities endowed with common sense' that Hannah Arendt evokes to designate 'men in the plural, who are in fact at the centre of our pre-occupations and whose true end is . . . sociability'.[13]

Exclude

Exclusion is what is most targeted in human rights; and yet, the equal recognition of rights does not go without saying, even in France in 1789. In his book on 'the emancipation of the Jews', Robert Badinter reminds readers that this was voted by the Assembly ruling at the last moment, by the decree of 27 September 1791. But the very next day, by the decree of 28 September, they upheld slavery in the colonies: 'Two years after having proclaimed that all men were born free and equal in rights, the Assembly lowered its head before the planters and their metropolitan allies.'[14] The 'Black Code', a result of the Order of 1685, remained in force, with its set of mutilations cleverly graduated from the first escape to the third, which led to being put to death. It was not until the Revolution of 1848 that the definitive elimination of slavery in the French colonies was decreed and written into the Constitution, and it took until the twentieth century for the abolition of slavery to take on international value, first with the League of Nations (Convention of 1926) then the United Nations (Universal Declaration of Human Rights of 1948, Article 4). It was only in the late twentieth century that human civil and political rights came to be fully recognised for women, and for the traditional 'legal incapacity' of married women to be abolished.[15] This latter recognition was limited to only a part of the world, requiring us to wait until 1993 for the World Conference on Human Rights to

[12] See M. Walzer, 'Les Deux Universalismes', *L'Universel au risque de culturalisme* 187 (1992), pp. 114ff.; P. Hassner, 'Vers un universalisme pluriel?', *L'Universal au risque de culturalisme* 187(1992), pp. 102ff.; see also G. Soulier, 'Droit des minorités et pluralisme juridique', *Revue de recherche juridique – Droit prospectif* 2 (1993), 2, pp. 625ff.

[13] H. Arendt, *Juger. Sur la philosophie politique de Kant* (Editions du Seuil, 1991), p. 49.

[14] R. Badinter, *Free and equal . . . The emancipation of the Jews, 1789–1791* (Fayard, 1989), p. 220; C. Courvoisier, 'Minorités et différences dans les cahiers de doléances, quelques exemples', in A. Fenet and G. Soulier (eds.), *Les Minorités et leurs droits depuis 1789* (L'Harmattan, 1989), pp. 13ff. (showing a perception of the problems often dominated by economic pre-occupations, such that the case of black people is sometimes placed in the rubric 'commerce').

[15] For prior periods, see G. Duby and M. Perrot (eds.), *L'Histoire des femmes* (Plon, 1990–1), especially volume IV (edited by G. Fraisse and M. Perrot).

adopt, in its closing document, a provision entitled 'The equal status and human rights of women', by which the Conference 'urges the full and equal enjoyment by women of all human rights, and that this be a priority for governments and for the United Nations'.

In effect, various types of exclusion are still strongly felt in the contemporary era. Admittedly, the twentieth century was marked by the recognition of equality: 'All human beings are born free and equal in dignity and rights', proclaims Article 1 of the Universal Declaration of 1948, every article of which begins with a reminder of this universal concept: 'everyone', 'all', or 'no one'. However, there are still many inequalities and even many exclusions, in principles as well as practices.

I mentioned earlier the efforts to reduce the opposition between civil and political rights and economic and social rights, but there are still huge gaps. On the domestic level, the French Commission consultative des droits de l'homme considers it a 'national priority' to fight against poverty, insisting on the fact that 'material improvements or aids, as indispensable and even vital as they sometimes are, are not sufficient'. In fact, the fundamental demand of the most disadvantaged bears on the right to have a home, to live with one's family, to be respected and to be the subject of rights.[16]

At the international level, the symmetry between the two types of rights is only superficial, as for economic, social and cultural rights 'the mechanisms of control are less rigorous and demanding than those provided for civil and political rights'.[17] While this particularity is in part explained by the fact that it is easier to require and control the recognition of 'rights–liberties' than of 'rights–debts', the explanation remains only partial because there are economic and social 'rights–liberties' (namely the right to strike and union rights), just as there are civil and political 'rights–debts', inasmuch as some require positive state action for their realisation (for example, for the rules for a fair trial to be followed, in the case of non-state regulation by arbitrators or professional authorities). Hence the tendency of the European Court of Human Rights to combine these two categories, as already noted (for example, with regard

[16] See the report of the Commission consultative des droits de l'homme, 'Grande pauvreté et droits de l'homme', *1992: La Lutte contre le racisme et le xénophobie* (La Documentation française), 1993, pp. 457ff. See also, on poverty 'of position' not 'of conditions', the petty poverty of daily life, testimonies presented under the direction of Pierre Bourdieu, *La Misère du monde* (Editions du Seuil, 1993).

[17] Imbert, 'L'Apparente Simplicité des droits de l'homme', p. 19.

to equal access to justice implying free legal aid for the most disadvantaged). Hence, above all, there is a need to remember that personal dignity cannot be divided and that it falls as much within the scope of economic and social rights as civil and political rights. In its closing document, the World Conference on Human Rights affirmed 'that extreme poverty and social exclusion constitute a violation of human dignity'. It also reaffirmed that 'the right to development', as it is established in the corresponding declaration, 'is a universal and inalienable right'.

But economic exclusion is not the only form of exclusion. I mentioned earlier the situation of women and the 1993 World Conference's call to the states, while awaiting the organisation of the 1995 Beijing Conference. In demanding that women have 'full and equal enjoyment of all human rights', the World Conference (like the Convention on the Elimination of all Forms of Discrimination against Women) was referring to both civil and political rights and economic and social rights (the right to equal pay, for example). It also took into consideration certain specific situations, such as sexual harassment, the exploitation of women and the female slave trade, and even 'the elimination of gender bias in the administration of justice' and 'the conflicts which may arise between the rights of women and the harmful effects of certain traditional or customary practices, cultural prejudices and religious extremism'. Finally, violations of women's fundamental rights are addressed in situations of armed conflict, 'including and in particular murder, systematic rape, sexual slavery and forced pregnancy', which require 'particularly efficient measures'.

There are also forms of exclusion that are not of recent appearance, but which have only recently become the subject of indignation, especially when children are concerned. Despite the speedy ratification of the UN Convention on the Rights of the Child, signed in New York in 1990, the World Conference returned insistently to the need for effective application of these rights, encouraging states to adopt 'all the legislative, administrative or other measures necessary and to assign maximum resources for this purpose'. It also recommends 'reinforcing national and international mechanisms and programmes of defence and protection of children, especially young girls, abandoned children, street children, children who are victims of economic and sexual exploitation, namely for purposes of pornography, prostitution, or the sale of organs, children who are victims of illnesses such as AIDs, refugee and displaced children, children in detention, children involved in armed conflicts, and children who are victims of famine, drought or other emergency situations'. This is a painful list that grows with current affairs, and that says more than any other indictment.

In sum, the list is revealing with regard to contemporary practices and the concern for protecting the rights of persons 'belonging to groups which have been rendered vulnerable'. Hence the reference to the rights of refugees 'to seek and find asylum in other countries to escape persecution', as well as 'to return to their own country'; to the rights of migrant workers and their family members (the states are invited to 'envisage the possibility' of signing and ratifying the International Convention); and even the call to apply, without reservation, human rights and fundamental liberties to handicapped persons, and to 'guarantee them the same opportunities' by eliminating obstacles 'such as inhibit them, in whole or in part, from participating fully in the life of the society'.

The underlying idea – to eliminate all forms of discrimination – also leads to naming the discriminations, and thus to name exclusions that are racial and, more broadly, those that are based (to borrow the phrase in the European Convention on Human Rights) on association with a national, ethnic, religious or linguistic minority. The question thus raised is whether the rights of the minority member or the minority itself are recognised – an essential question, because it complicates the analysis considerably. Recognising the rights of a minority member is relatively simple. Instead of excluding because different, we recognise as equal because identical, and thus we assimilate him or her. Logically (in respecting classical logic that is), the choice remains binary: exclude or assimilate. However, everything becomes scrambled if the rights of a minority are recognised as such, because it leads to a so-called 'right to be different', which respects the minority, but at the same time legitimates the exclusion of minority members through apartheid and the creation of ghettos of all kinds. Assimilating the minority member thus appears to be the only way to avoid his or her exclusion.

Assimilate

For the most part, assimilation is the choice of countries such as France, sensitive to the dangers of declarations of group identity that, most of the time, are not based on voluntary membership:

> That the group seeks its unity in an ideology, and the gulag opens for those who refuse it, that this ideology is the superiority of the race, and the right of the Aryan ethnicity to impose its just domination on the world, legitimates Dachau, Auschwitz and Meydenek. Over the rights of groups, the smoke of the cremation ovens projects the greatest of threats, because their recognition risks giving the seal of justice to domination of the strong over the weak.[18]

The French government thus traditionally includes a reservation in international agreements that recognise the rights of minorities as such. For example, the reservation made to Article 30 of the Convention on the Rights of the Child, recognises, if applicable, the right, 'in community with other members of his or her group, to enjoy his or her own culture, to profess and practise his or her own religion, or to use his or her own language'. Similarly, on the domestic level, the Haute Conseil à l'intégration has affirmed since its first report in 1991 'its conviction that the French concept must obey a logic of equality and not a logic of minorities . . . a concept shared by countries such as Germany and Belgium, while the Netherlands and United Kingdom largely leave room for minority politics'.[19]

It was in fact in the name of equality of all citizens before the law, whatever their origin, that the Conseil constitutionnel censured Article 1 of the law concerning the status of Corsica, in so far as it legally established the existence of the 'Corsican people, component of the French people', while the Constitution 'recognises only the French people, composed of all French citizens without distinction of origin, race or religion'.[20]

At the European level, despite the differences from one tradition to another (raised in the report by the High Council on Integration), the European Convention on Human Rights refers only to the rights of minority members (Article 14, cited above). Thus, the ECHR refused to take into consideration the problem of a linguistic minority considered in itself, 'as if it wanted to avoid – beyond the reasons it gave expressly – any reference to minorities having the character of a national minority; however, the Court purposely used the term minority in matters of general scope by referring to the notion of democracy, which leads

[18] J. Rivero, Introduction to *Les Droits de l'homme: droits collectifs ou droits individuels?* (LGDJ, 1980).

[19] Haut Conseil à l'intégration, First Report (La Documentation française, 1991).

[20] CC, 9 May 1991 (Dalloz, 1991), p. 624, Debbasch note.

to an extensive conception of minorities'.[21] Moreover, the Council of Europe decided in 1992 to proceed to drafting a European Convention on Minority Rights.[22]

At the international level, well before the 1990 Convention on the Rights of the Child, the 1966 International Covenant on Civil and Political Rights recognised that 'all peoples have the right to self-determination' (Article 1(1)) and provides that 'in those states where ethnic, religious or linguistic minorities exist, persons belonging to such minorities shall not be denied the right, in community with the other members of their group, to enjoy their own culture, to profess and practise their own religion, or to use their own language' (Article 27). Even if this does not openly recognise the rights of minorities, but of minority members, the evocation of 'group' and the group's life 'in common' leads to a certain collective protection, as is shown by a decision of the UN Committee on Human Rights noting the violation of this text in a case where petroleum-prospecting operations carried out by Canada in the Lake Lubicon region were considered a threat to the way of life and the culture of the Indian minority concerned.[23]

The World Conference in Vienna seems to vacillate between minority members and minorities. On the one hand, it demands the promotion and effective protection of the rights 'of persons' belonging to national or ethnic, religious and linguistic minorities, and not of the minorities themselves; on the other, it borrows the phrase from the 1966 Covenant, missing in 1948, establishing for all peoples 'the right of self-determination' and calls for the drafting of a declaration on the rights of 'autochthone populations'; finally, it introduces a reference to the 'needs of current and future generations in matters of development and ecology'. Hence, there are many examples that indicate the desire to recognise collective, and not merely individual, rights.

The relative caution of the text adopted in Vienna, with regard to minorities, stems no doubt from the fear of ethnic confrontations that even North America, qualified as a 'veritable laboratory of collective

[21] G. Soulier, 'Minorités, état et société', in A. Fenet and G. Soulier (eds.), *Les Minorités et leurs droits depuis 1789* (L'Harmattan, 1989). The author discusses the so-called 'Belgian linguistic case' (the ECHR decisions of 9 February 1967 and 23 July 1968) and the Council of Europe's 1995 Framework Convention for the Protection of National Minorities.

[22] See N. Rouland, legal anthropology chronicle, 'The time of minorities', *Droits*; see also University of Fribourg (ed.), *Les Droits culturels* (1993).

[23] UN Committee on Human Rights, decision of 26 March 1990, *RUDH* (1991), p. 69.

rights',[24] did not know how to avoid. This is a very current danger if we recall that, in the close to 185 states affiliated with the UN, there are between 8,000 and 20,000 ethnic groups, and that the autochthone populations alone are evaluated at close to 300 million persons.

At the legal level, there is the added imprecision of the concept of minority, the expression itself making a late appearance: 'The expression "national minority" made its appearance in the *Larousse* dictionary of 1980, and the expression "ethnic minority" entered the *Larousse du vingtième siècle* [Larousse dictionary of the twentieth century] in 1931; in fact, it was not until after the First World War and the signing of treaties concerning minorities that these expressions really entered legal language.'[25] They entered rather clumsily, evoking a purely statistical notion: hence the value of an expression that, as provocative as it is, better indicates the qualitative idea of groups subject to the rules of a dominant group: 'a subset of humans generally considered as a set of sub-humans'.[26]

It is still the case that between 'hierarchical pluralism', which characterises the notion of minority in Islam,[27] and the plural and democratic societies of which anthropologists dream,[28] the path is narrow for those who wish to co-ordinate the differences while avoiding both assimilation and exclusion.

Co-ordinate

Although the Declaration of 1948 foreshadowed the 1966 Covenants in recognising the place of economic, social and cultural rights alongside civil and political rights, its universal nature fell within that 'apparent simplicity'[29] that had not yet revealed all its snares. In Vienna in 1993, these pitfalls were revealed to such an extent, and the contradictions debated to such an extent, that the world consensus on human rights was almost shattered. Under pressure from Asia and some Islamic countries, the 'dictates of human rights imposed by the West' were denounced. But from the very outset, the Secretary-General, showing wisdom, linked

[24] Rouland, 'Time of minorities'. [25] Soulier, 'Droits des minorités', p. 625. [26] *Ibid.*

[27] M. Rodinson, *L'Islam, politique et croyance* (Fayard, 1993), p. 117.

[28] Rouland, 'Time of minorities'.

[29] Imbert, 'L'Apparente Simplicité des droits de l'homme', p. 19.

human rights and democracy – 'Democracy constitutes the political project in which the guarantee of human rights must be inscribed' – stating forcefully that 'democracy belongs to no one', that it 'may be and must be assimilated by all cultures', and that it is 'susceptible of taking on multiple forms, to be better inscribed in a people's reality'.

This pluralistic language was understood by those attending the Conference, as the constant reference to interdependence in the Conference's closing document proves: 'democracy, development and respect for human rights and fundamental freedoms are interdependent and mutually reinforcing'. There are also constant references to 'historic, cultural and religious' diversity, the importance of which is recognised, like that of 'national and regional particularities', but within limits compatible with development and the respect for human rights. Such limits are drawn several times, particularly by the injunction already cited to eliminate 'contradictions' – this is essentially the idea of incompatibility – 'that may exist between the rights of women and the harmful effects of certain traditional or customary practices, cultural prejudices and religious extremism'.

In comparison to the slightly naive universalism of 1948, the year 1993 marked the passage toward a 'plural universalism'. This expression, used earlier,[30] is politically seductive. But is it legally practicable? This is where the experiments carried out in the 'European laboratory' can help point the way, not as a model to be followed – this would take us back to the 'overhanging' universality so criticised for its latent Euro-centrism – but rather as travel diaries or log books that travellers exchange before heading down a new trail.

The first European experiments show the possibility of harmonising different national and supranational legal systems, as distinguished from unifying them, such that no strict hierarchy, and thus no strict identity of norms, is imposed. It is thus possible to conceive of a normative space made of several sets, some perfectly ordered, others only partially, and still others not yet at all. Classical logic can understand only the first model, and concludes that the rest is disorder. However, if the classical logic is combined with a logic of gradation (that is, combine the proximity–compatibility pair with the identity–conformity pair), we can understand a greater portion of the normative space.

30 See Hassner, 'Vers un universalisme pluriel?', p. 102.

On a worldwide scale, the normative space is still not very orderly. It is therefore valuable to combine conformity and compatibility to try to organise the various systems, without imposing unity, which is impossible because the search for a unified global order may result in a totalitarian order that would impose the hegemony of one culture, state or region on the others. In this respect, superposing the national, regional and world normative sets that already exist, or whose creation is encouraged by the closing document of the Vienna Conference, seems to be an adequate instrument. Such superposition allows for an entire set of cross-references (from one country or region to another, and also from one national, regional or world level to another) that facilitate the development of common principles that are not only declarative, but that control the choice and interpretation of national legal norms.

A quick inventory gives an idea of the complexity of the mechanism in place since 1948 and the possibilities it offers, provided it is actually used – meaning, above all, that it is widely ratified by the states.

The International Covenants on Civil and Political Rights and on Economic, Social and Cultural Rights form an essential, worldwide instrument that, unlike the Universal Declaration, is legally imposed on the states, and therefore on national legislation and jurisprudence. The Covenant on Civil and Political Rights, which includes an Optional Protocol providing for individual petition to the Committee on Human Rights, has been ratified by about 120 states, roughly 50 of whom have approved the right of individuals to petition, and thus the possibility of at least addressing some 'general observations' to a state guilty of violating protected rights, if not imposing sanctions on it. We have yet to gain wider ratification of both Covenants, especially from the UN Security Council permanent members, who are notable by their absence (with the exception of France, which ratified both Covenants in 1981 and the Additional Protocol in 1984). We have also yet to overcome the reticence on the part of African and Islamic countries, which may in part be due to the Covenant's western-culture inspiration.

This is precisely the value of regional instruments that group together states that are close, not only geographically, but also politically and culturally, thus increasing the chances of ratification and enabling the 'compatibility threshold' to be set at a higher level – that is, to adopt common principles of a more elaborate legal construction and to organise a real control mechanism (with, none the less, highly sensitive regional differences).

The oldest instrument, the European Convention of 1950, is also the most demanding, whether it concerns the contents of protected rights or the control mechanism, going as far as allowing the European Court of Human Rights to grant victims of violations 'equitable satisfaction'. Of course, the American Convention of 1969 also provides for control and for the Inter-American Court of Human Rights not only to require reparations for damages caused by human-rights violations, but also to order that the victim be guaranteed 'the enjoyment of his right or freedom that was violated'. But the definitions of rights, and especially the exceptions that are admitted, are sometimes very vague, particularly with regard to the right to freedom and security, which is coupled with a very general exception authorising incarceration 'for the reasons and under the conditions established beforehand by the constitution of the state party concerned or by a law established pursuant thereto'. Provided that judicial appeal is possible, all sorts of administrative, medical or police confinements are legitimated. As for the African Charter on Human and People's Rights, adopted in 1981, it expresses first of all, by its very title, a more communal and less individualistic conception of human rights. Like the American Convention, but in greater detail, it couples rights with duties 'towards [the] family and society, the state and other legally recognised communities and the international community'. However, the right to freedom and security is coupled with an even broader exception than in the American Convention (the only requirement being lawfulness), and the Charter also presents a major weakness with regard to the control mechanism, which is limited to a report established by a Commission – not a court – whose members depend closely on the states, even though the 1998 Protocol establishes that a court will be created once there are fifteen ratifications.

There are thus considerable obstacles to be overcome, and it would be unrealistic to underestimate the insufficiencies of these regional instruments and the risk both of resistance to their ratification – remember that neither the United States nor Canada have ratified the American Convention on Human Rights – and of ratifications serving as screens and alibis to contrary practices, especially since the regions where the problems of enforcing human rights are the most serious (such as vast Asia and the Middle Eastern countries) still have no regional organisation (but see Arab Commission, www.come.to/achr). It is only if all these obstacles are overcome that regional mechanisms can become not alibis or substitutes, but a lever for the worldwide mechanism.

The national authorities for protection of human rights, for which a draft statute was drawn up at their first International Meeting in Paris in 1991, sometimes act as such levers.[31] Transmitted by Resolution of the Economic and Social Council of the UN General Assembly, this statute, entitled 'Principles relative to the status of national institutions', shows the originality of these courts, intended as places for information and exchange between the state and civil society (their composition and the appointment of their members should assure 'the pluralist representation of social forces' and a 'true independence' *vis-à-vis* the state): hence their role of providing counsel to national political organs, informing the public, and of international co-operation with the United Nations, regional institutions and national institutions of other countries.

This inventory, incomplete in that it does not mention the special Conventions and the organs responsible for supervising their execution (Committee on the Elimination of Racial Discrimination, Committee on the Elimination of Discrimination Against Women, Committee Against Torture, Committee on Children's Rights and so on), indicates a danger of proliferation that requires measures of evaluation and co-ordination. But it also reveals what the UN Secretary-General called a 'new legal permeability', which, according to him, would abolish the traditional distinction between the domestic and international orders.[32] This permeability could more broadly facilitate not only vertical exchanges, but also horizontal exchanges, from one state to another or one region to another, and thereby contribute to this 'plural universality' of human rights that would co-ordinate differences without necessarily returning to forms of disguised exclusion. It is without a doubt within such an interactive network that certain collective rights could be inscribed, but only on the condition – and we are confronted here again with the problem of the limits of compatibility, or lines not to cross – that we not strike a blow to the 'irreducible human element' that expresses both the identity of the human community and the singularity of each individual comprising it.

[31] See Commission nationale consultative des droits de l'homme, 1992 Report, Chapter X, 'International actions' (La Documentation française 1993), p. 585.

[32] Opening address of Boutros-Ghali at the Vienna World Conference, 14 June 1993.

The irreducible human element

This concept cannot be reduced to a philosophical definition, and even less to a denomination. Hannah Arendt even said that 'the impossibility of solidifying with words the living essence of the person' is such that, in every area of human affairs, 'it theoretically precludes our ever being able to treat these affairs as we manipulate things the nature of which is in our grasp because we can name them'.[33]

But if human nature is not 'within our grasp', it is not only because we cannot name it, but also because humankind, in its way, protests against or resists nature. In proclaiming that men 'are born free and equal in rights', the great Declarations, from 1789 to 1948, express precisely this nature/culture separation that is specific to legal systems. Similarly, in designating humans as 'mortals', the Greeks contrasted human mortality, caught in the circular movement of biological life, with immortal nature. 'Mortality', said Arendt in her turn, 'is to move in a straight line in a universe where nothing moves other than in a circle.' In this same sense, she stated, slightly provocatively, that birth and death 'are not natural events, properly speaking'.[34] It is true that we are beginning to see behind the call to generalise, even to impose, organ donations founded on the, in effect, circular notion of 'public health', or behind the practices of preserving stem cells or embryos, how birth and death can lose a large part of their meaning and the human species become a species like any other, and how humans are learning to modify and manufacture themselves, just as they already modify and manufacture animal and vegetable species.

However, it is no doubt an oversimplification to oppose nature and culture and reduce human rights to a protest against nature. In their way, neurosciences perhaps revive the debate by showing how certain cognitive faculties, such as 'representing the other to oneself reflexively, like another self, member of the same social species', and that of representing to oneself 'the organisation of the social group', will be 'characteristic of the human species'.[35]

[33] H. Arendt, *Condition de l'homme moderne* (Calmann-Lévy, 1983), p. 238.

[34] *Ibid.*

[35] J.-P. Changeux, in A. Connes and J.-P. Changeux, *Matière à pensée* (Editions du Seuil, 1992), p. 244. See also J.-P. Changeux (ed.), *Fondements naturels de l'éthique* (Odile Jacob, 1993), especially A. Fagot-Largeault, 'Normativité biologique et normativité sociale', pp. 191ff.,

Nevertheless, neurosciences will never be a foundation for human rights, primarily because of the ambivalence of these cognitive faculties: the act of representing the other to oneself can explain not only great altruism, but also the worst perversities – criminality as well as human rights.[36] This is especially true since one must succeed in isolating the 'regularities imposed by the genetic heritage' of humankind.

Now there is – and in fact, this seems to be another characteristic of the human species – very great epigenetic variability. Defined as a 'connectional variability that is freed from the genes' power by the modalities of growth and stabilisation of the synaptic connections',[37] this variability would explain the multiplicity and diversity of particular cultures. The rules specific to each culture are also fixed in the brain during the individual's development. In the end, between the regularities specific to the human species and the rules that characterise each culture, distinction 'remains very difficult, due to the very deep entanglement of these two components during successive stages of development'.[38]

In the absence of being able to isolate the hard and irreducible core of human rights as an expression of the genetic heritage common to humanity, I retain the idea that the neurosciences do not invalidate the existence of a certain universality, albeit coupled, it is true, with this very great epigenetic variability. It is as if biology came to confirm the first intuition of the humanity, both one and multiple, that human rights try to organise around this hard core. It is no doubt not by chance that the irreducible human element, subjected to difficult trials during the Second World War, took the legal form of a two-pronged prohibition: the states are prohibited from derogating from certain rights – this is the appearance of so-called 'inviolable' rights – and people are prohibited from transgressing certain values – this is the appearance, beyond the old underlying taboo that crimes bear, of the new category of so-called

adopting a 'weak naturalist position', and D. Sperber, 'Remarques anthropologiques sur le relativisme moral', pp. 319ff., showing that there are at least 'four possible relativist theses', depending on how metaphysical and anthropological relativism are combined in the cognitive and moral domains.

[36] Biology thus joins sociological observation. See E. Durkheim, *Règles de la méthode sociologique* (18th edn, PUF, 1973), p. 70: 'Crime is therefore necessary; it is related to the fundamental conditions of all social life, and in this itself it is useful; because these conditions with which it has solidarity are themselves indispensable to the normal evolution of morals and law.'

[37] J.-P. Changeux, *L'Homme neuronal* (Feyard, 1983), pp. 301ff.

[38] Changeux, in *Matière à pensée*, p. 248.

'imprescriptible' crimes, precisely because they touch the irreducible human element.

Inviolable rights

The Universal Declaration of 1948 says nothing about inviolable rights. It proclaims human rights as an 'ideal to attain', but not as a model to follow. It was with the European (1950) and American (1969) Conventions, and more broadly the Covenant on Civil and Political Rights (1966), that the subtle set of restrictions, exceptions and derogations already mentioned appeared. At the same time, the principle of intangibility of certain fundamental rights arose.

But the first manifestation of this idea that no circumstance, even an exceptional one such as war, can justify certain violations of fundamental rights goes back to what is generally referred to as international 'humanitarian' law, consisting of an entire set of Conventions (the first dates from 1864) signed at the private initiative of the International Committee of the Red Cross (ICRC) to protect, in wartime, the wounded, ill and shipwrecked of the armed forces, prisoners of war and civilians. The core of this humanitarian law is contained in the four Conventions signed in Geneva in 1949, completed by the additional Protocols of 1977, on the protection of victims of armed conflict, whether in international or civil war. Ratified quasi-unanimously, the Geneva Conventions prohibit attacks on the life, bodily integrity (mutilations, for example) or dignity (humiliating or degrading treatment) of the persons cited.

However, war and armed conflicts are not the only circumstances in which states can be tempted to derogate, or permit derogation, from the respect of fundamental rights – there is another set of 'exceptional situations'. Designating the use of exceptional powers tied to crisis situations (political crises, diverse cataclysmic events or special economic circumstances), the expression makes it obvious that there is a temptation to abuse these powers. Hence the need for a higher bar than the others – impassable, in fact – that indicates, for all these crisis situations, the supreme prohibition. The need for such a prohibition has increased through the banalisation of exceptional situations: a report established by the UN in 1988[39] indicates that between August 1987

[39] Despouy Report, UN Commission on Human Rights, 6 December 1988.

and November 1988, thirty-nine states proclaimed, extended, or simply continued a state of exception, never mind the exceptional situations indicated to the special rapporteur that were not the subject of official declarations, and thus escaped investigation. This is why, as of 1982, the idea was put forward that the principle of inviolability of certain fundamental rights had become, beyond the written law of international or regional Conventions, a general principle constituting for all states – whether they had ratified these Conventions or not – 'an imperative norm of general international law',[40] at least for the 'minimum standard' common to the various texts. The list is short and includes, do not forget, the prohibitions of torture and inhuman or degrading punishment or treatment, of slavery and servitude, and of retroactive criminal statutes. To this common minimum, the UN Covenant – which aims at universal applicability – adds the prohibition that 'No one shall be subjected without his free consent to medical or scientific experimentation' and, the only two rights formulated positively, the right to recognition of one's legal personality and the right to freedom of thought, conscience and religion. If we set aside the non-retroactivity of criminal statutes, a more technical than directly ethical prohibition, this list of common minimum inviolable rights clearly indicates the desire to incorporate this irreducible human element – the term 'inhuman' treatment is particularly significant – into a supreme value that surpasses that of human life.

Of course, the right to life is mentioned in the list of inviolable rights, but an exception for the death penalty is usually admitted, and the Additional Protocols that eliminate it reserve the case of war. This is why the right to life cannot be considered, in the strict sense, an inviolable right, unless we take into account circumstances that combine homicide with inhuman or degrading treatment (the conditions of capital punishment)[41] or – but this falls more within imprescriptible crimes – forced or involuntary disappearance,[42] or even genocide.

40 Questiaux Report, UN Commission on Human Rights, 27 July 1982.

41 *Soering v. United Kingdom*, ECHR, 7 July 1989, Series A, No. 161. Compare, however, the more qualified position of the Conseil d'Etat, CE, 15 October 1993 (Dalloz, 1993), IR 238.

42 The General Assembly of the Organisation of American States declared in November 1983 that the forced disappearance of persons was a crime against humanity, Article 7(1) of the Rome Convention on the ICC now establishes this as a crime against humanity, and on 18 December 1992, the General Assembly adopted the United Nations Declaration on the Protection of All Persons from Enforced Disappearance.

While it is important to insist on the difference between the right to life and this unnamed right that I said (see Part II, above) would protect 'dignity' in its strongest sense, there are many practices that are or will be possible with the development of biotechnology that consist more of manufacturing life or maintaining survival than of causing death. As regards the manufacturing of life, we think of embryonic manipulation, which involves less the rights of some 'potential human' person than, quite simply, the respect for the dignity of all humanity. As for maintaining survival, the question was openly asked by A. Milhaud, in his book *Testaments of life*, pleading in favour of experimentation on patients in a persistent vegetative state or beyond comatose, which has no therapeutic purpose for the patient, but which the author, a doctor, justifies as an 'ethical battle', because its purpose is to 'make death useful'.[43]

This type of experimentation was prohibited by the French Comité consultative national d'ethique and sanctioned by the Order of Doctors (Ordre des médecins), with the approval of the Conseil d'Etat, which considered that 'the fundamental ethical principles relative to the respect for the human person, which are imposed on doctors in their relations with their patients, do not cease to apply at the latters' death'.[44] But this is but one example among many, including gene manipulation or genetic engineering,[45] or the use of embryos or human foetuses for therapeutic, scientific, industrial or commercial purposes. The European Convention on Human Rights and Biomedicine (1997)[46] sets out a fair number of more precise prohibitions, in line with the earlier recommendations of the Parliamentary Assembly of the Council of Europe, and the 1998 Additional Protocol adds reproductive cloning of humans. But the texts do not provide for petitioning the European Court of Human Rights in the case of violation, and the sanctions are left up to the states. Similarly,

[43] A. Milhaud, *Testaments of life* (Barrault, 1988), pp. 146ff. See, however, Cour d'appel of Bordeaux, 18 April 1991 (Dalloz, 1992), p. 15, and A. Fagot-Largeault, 'Reflections on the notion of quality of life', *Archives de philosophie du droit* 36 (1991), pp. 135ff.

[44] CE, Ass., 2 July 1993, *JCP* 2 (1993), 21133, P. Gonod note.

[45] The recommendation adopted in 1982 by the Parliamentary Assembly of the Council of Europe on genetic engineering envisages providing for the express recognition, in the European Convention on Human Rights, of the right to a genetic heritage having received no manipulation, except in application of certain principles received as fully compatible with the respect of human rights.

[46] Convention for the Protection of Human Rights and Dignity of the Human Being with regard to the Application of Biology and Medicine: Convention on Human Rights and Biomedicine (4 April 1997).

the Universal Declaration on the Human Genome and Human Rights,[47] adopted by UNESCO in 1997 and copied by the United Nations General Assembly in 1998, has no restrictive force.[48]

These examples show that it is urgent that a more precise definition is formulated of this irreducible human element, a definition that, in the name of inviolable rights, would in fact protect much more than the life of an individual, because it involves a value both individual (the most precious of each human being) and collective (the very idea of humanity). If the list of inviolable rights gives a glimmer in the right direction, it is only by analysing imprescriptible crimes, especially those called crimes against 'humanity', that we can begin, if not to define, at least to look for, its components.

Imprescriptible crimes

Prescription is not a voluntary act like amnesty or pardon (in legal systems that admit it). It is not the pardon of humans, but the passage of time that guarantees impunity for crimes after a certain period following the acts (so-called 'public prosecutor' prescription, which blocks all pursuit), or following the conviction (prescription of the punishment, which will not be carried out).

Despite its calming virtues, impunity, especially when it blocks all trials, blocks the formation of a memory. As Paul Valéry said, the essential function of memory, 'the future of the past', is not to regurgitate the past, but to nourish the present and prepare the future.[49]

At Nuremberg and Tokyo, when the crimes committed during the Second World War were judged, there was too little distance for the issue of imprescriptibility to be raised. It was in 1964 that a law was unanimously passed in France to 'establish' – which implied it already involved a general principle of international law – the imprescriptibility of crimes against humanity. Now an international principle of written law along with the UN Convention of 1968 and the European Convention of 1947,

[47] Universal Declaration on the Human Genome and Human Rights (11 November 1997) and the Additional Protocol to the Convention for the Protection of Human Rights and Dignity of the Human Being with regard to the Application of Biology and Medicine, on the Prohibition of Cloning Human Beings (12 January 1998).

[48] See H. Atlan, M. Augé, M. Delmas-Marty, R. P. Droit and N. Fresco, *Le Clonage humain* (Seuil, 1999).

[49] 'Mémoire', in *Cahiers de Paul Valéry* (Gallimard, 1993), pp. 1211ff.

which both associate imprescriptibility of crimes against humanity with war crimes, France had very consciously set it aside, primarily because of the colonial wars (and in fact it has not ratified either of the two International Conventions).

So close as to be confused in the Nuremberg judgment, the two categories – war crimes and crimes against humanity – have progressively become distinct. In France, this distinction was necessary in the *Barbie* and *Touvier* cases, because the 1964 law established imprescriptibility for crimes against humanity only; hence the recourse to legal subtleties that would be amusing were their goal not to impose a sort of graduated scale of horror to determine the threshold at which the violence inflicted on those who resist becomes a crime against humanity.[50] The 1992 French *Code pénal* (which entered in force in March 1994) isolates crimes against humanity, which appear at the head of crimes and felonies against persons. Without really innovating as to the definition, directly taken from the international law then in force, the Code none the less specifies the 'massive and systematic' nature of such crimes.

At the international level, the two categories are also separated. The concept of war crimes, defined at Nuremberg by reference to customary international law, was completed by the humanitarian law resulting from the Geneva Conventions. It is, in fact, the violation of these Conventions that appears at the head of the list of crimes referred to in the international tribunal statute adopted in 1993 by the UN Security Council. Added to this are violations of 'the laws or customs of war', genocide and crimes against humanity (but the question of imprescriptibility is evaded, because the tribunal was created to judge crimes committed on the territory of the former Yugoslavia since 1991).

As for the concept of crimes against humanity, it follows its own path. Beyond the general Nuremberg definition referring to 'assassination, extermination, selling into slavery, deportation and any other inhuman act committed against any civilian population', as well as 'persecution for political, racial or religious reasons', committed in relation with a crime within the competence of the tribunal, two UN Conventions added special categories considered as crimes against humanity from the point

[50] Regarding the *Barbie* trial, see Crim., 20 December 1985, *Bull.* 407, *JCP* 2 (1986), 20655, Le Gunehec report and Dontenville conclusions; and C. Lombois, 'Un Crime internationale en droit positif', *Mélanges Vitu* (Cujas, 1989), pp. 367ff. On the *Touvier* case, see Crim., 27 November 1992, *Bull.* 394, *RSC* (1993), Grynfogel commentary, p. 62 and Massé, p. 372.

of view of imprescriptibility: genocide in 1948 and apartheid in 1973, but not the crime of torture (contained in a UN Convention of 1984). More recent debates on the dangers of impunity as 'a stumbling block to democracy', 'check on the law's authority' and an 'encouragement to new violations'[51] have led to declaring that the systematic practice of forced disappearance 'is of the order of a crime against humanity' (UN General Assembly Resolution of December 1992, and Rome Convention on the International Criminal Court of July 1998, Article 7(1)) and must be qualified as a 'continuing crime', which connects it to an imprescriptible crime by tying the point of departure of the prescription period to either the day of the disappeared's reappearance, or of the proof of his or her death.[52] Also, we are beginning to ask whether there should be recognition of an inviolable right of victims of such crimes to have their case heard by a tribunal that would exclude not only prescription, but also amnesty.[53] Finally, the question remains open as to whether certain crimes committed in the ecological and biotechnological fields should also be considered crimes against humanity, in so far as they place our common heritage in danger.

There is a danger, however, in extending the concept, of banalising the meaning. All imprecision need not be eliminated – as emphasised in Part II, a certain subdetermination, even certain misunderstandings, can facilitate communication between systems and cultures that have different histories and structures. But the underlying prohibition, the transgression of which is at the same time the metaphysical destruction of the person, to use Jean Ladrière's expression (see Part II, above), must be declared other than by continually redrafting the list of acts of transgression. In short, the prohibition must be named, not negatively, by inference, but positively, by declaring the value that is to be protected by the prohibition of crimes against 'humanity'.

We thus come up against the multiple meanings of this word, which Pierre Truche emphasised designates a sentiment 'of goodness, sensibility, kindness, compassion' (humane), 'the human genre, people in

[51] See G. Fellous, General Report presented at the International Meetings on Impunity in Geneva in 1992, reproduced in the Commission consultative des droits de l'homme report, 'Grande pauvreté et droits de l'homme'.

[52] See the Guissé and Joinet Interim Report on the question of impunity for the authors of human rights violations, UN Commission on Human Rights, 19 July 1993.

[53] See Joinet in Interim Report, *ibid.* Also the study on amnesty legislation and its role in protecting and promoting human rights, UN Commission on Human Rights, 21 June 1985.

general, the collective name of the group they form' (human) and, finally, 'human nature, the essence of Man, that which makes one human'.[54] Hannah Arendt[55] raised this polysemy in the text already cited. 'We have three very different concepts, or three perspectives according to which we can envisage human affairs: we have the human species and its progress; we have Man as moral being and end in itself; and we have people in the plural, who are, in fact, at the centre of our preoccupations and of whom the true end is sociability.'[56] To go forward along these lines while avoiding any metaphysical or ideological prejudices, the inductive method is, no doubt, the least unsatisfactory.

Returning to the prohibitions set out as crimes against humanity, a first reading raises a feeling of heterogeneity because murder and assassination are placed with slavery, deportation, persecutions or diverse discriminations going as far as apartheid. Torture, however, as already mentioned, does not appear on this list, even though the prohibition against torture is one of the inviolable rights. This is because the basis for inviolable rights remains an individual basis – it concerns 'human' rights, even if here it means dignity of the person, in the strongest sense of the word. With the crime against 'humanity', the idea of a collective basis appears. This is the common point amongst the various prohibitions listed as crimes against humanity. In fact, Article 6(c) of the Nuremberg Statute refers to crimes committed 'against any civilian population'; genocide implies the intention 'to destroy all or part of a national, ethnic, racial or religious group' (Article II of the UN Convention for the Prevention and Repression of Genocide 1948), and apartheid the purpose 'of instituting or maintaining the domination of one racial group of human beings and to systematically oppress it' (UN Declaration on Apartheid 1973). Similarly, the new French *Code pénal* refers either to acts that are collective by nature, such as genocide, deportation or reduction to slavery, or to the 'massive and systematic' practice of an entire series of acts (including torture or inhuman acts), undertaken for political, philosophic, racial or religious reasons, and organised 'by executing a concerted plan against a civilian population group'. Moreover, the Statute of the International Tribunal for the . . . Former Yugoslavia adopted in 1993 and

[54] P. Truche, 'La Notion de crime contre l'humanité', *Esprit* (1992), pp. 67ff.: also his 'Le Crime contre l'humanité', *Droits* (1993), pp. 19ff.

[55] Arendt, *Juger*, p. 49. [56] *Ibid.*

the 1998 Rome Convention refer to crimes perpetrated on the territory of the former Yugoslavia and directed against 'any civilian population whatsoever'.

This all means that the human being, even when deeply inscribed in a familial, cultural or religious group, should never lose its individuality – its 'personality', says the UN Covenant – and find itself reduced merely to an element of this group and, *as such*, rejected in its otherness – that is, in both its singularity of unique being and its equal membership in the human community.

Singularity and equal membership, these would be the components of humanity understood as a plurality of unique beings, which is the same as saying that the expression 'crimes against humanity' designates any deliberate, political, legal, medical or scientific practice comprising the violation of either the principle of singularity (an exclusion that can go as far as the extermination of human groups reduced to a racial, ethnic or genetic category, or, conversely, the manufacture of identical beings and cloning, if it means manufacturing identical beings), or the principle of equal membership in the human community (discriminatory practices such as apartheid, the creation of 'super-humans' by genetic selection, or of 'sub-humans' by species hybridisation).

Via the supreme prohibition of crimes against humanity, we are indeed trying to invent a common law of humanity. The effort must always be renewed, with limits always to be redefined, because 'nothing is more common than good things';[57] discerning them is the issue here – and their very proximity distances them from us and makes them almost invisible.

[57] B. Pascal, *De l'esprit géométrique et de l'art de persuader* (Gallimard, 1969 [1728]), p. 602.

AUTHOR INDEX

Note: Page references in this index occasionally imply a reference to a footnote.

INDEX

The structure and terminology of this index follow closely that of the text with generous use of cross-references to guide the user to less familiar concepts. Every attempt has been made to meet the needs of both the person who has read the book and the newcomer. As much of the text is written by reference to France, except where otherwise indicated, statutes referred to are French.

9 780521 812313